BAKING

BAKING

bay books

CONTENTS

BREADS
AND
MUFFINS

Makes: one 25 cm (10 inch) oval loaf

Preparation time: 2 hours

Cooking time: 40 minutes

2½ teaspoons (7 g) instant dried yeast
1 teaspoon caster (superfine) sugar
450 g (1 lb/3⅔ cups) white bread
  (strong) flour
2 teaspoons salt

SIMPLE WHITE BREAD

1 Sprinkle the yeast and sugar over 150 ml (5 fl oz) warm water in a small bowl. Stir to dissolve the sugar, then leave in a draught-free place for 10 minutes, or until the yeast is foamy.

2 Combine the flour and 2 teaspoons salt in the bowl of an electric mixer with a dough hook attachment and make a well in the centre. Add another 150 ml (5 fl oz) warm water to the yeast mixture, then pour the mixture into the well. With the mixer set to the lowest speed, mix for 2 minutes, or until a dough forms. Increase the speed to medium and knead the dough for another 10 minutes, or until it is smooth and elastic. Alternatively,

mix the dough by hand using a wooden spoon, then turn out onto a floured work surface and knead the dough for 10 minutes, or until smooth and elastic.

3 Grease a large bowl with oil, then transfer the dough to the bowl, turning the dough to coat in the oil. Cover with plastic wrap and leave to rise in a draught-free place for 1–1½ hours, or until the dough has doubled in size.

4 Knock back the dough by punching it gently, then turn out onto a lightly floured work surface. Shape into a rounded oval and transfer to a greased baking tray. Cover loosely with a damp cloth and leave for

30 minutes, or until doubled in size. Meanwhile, preheat the oven to 190°C (375°F/Gas 5).

5 Using a sharp knife, make three diagonal slashes, about 4 cm (1½ inches) apart, on the top of the loaf. Bake the loaf for 40 minutes, or until it sounds hollow when tapped on the base. Transfer to a wire rack to cool completely.

TIP Because home-baked bread has no preservatives, it is best eaten on the day of baking; otherwise, use it to make toast. Bread can also be tightly wrapped and frozen for up to 3 months

Makes: 8

Preparation time: 2 hours 30 minutes

Cooking time: 20 minutes

1½ teaspoons (4½ g) instant dried yeast
a pinch of caster (superfine) sugar
1½ teaspoons sea salt flakes
2½ tablespoons oil from the sun-dried
   tomatoes, or extra virgin olive oil,
   plus extra for brushing
2 teaspoons finely chopped rosemary
150 g (5½ oz) sun-dried tomatoes,
   drained well (oil reserved) and
   patted dry
450 g (1 lb/3⅔ cups) plain (all-purpose)
   flour

DRIED TOMATO AND ROSEMARY FOUGASSE

1 Sprinkle the yeast and sugar over 125 ml (4 fl oz/½ cup) warm water in a small bowl. Stir to dissolve the sugar, then leave in a draught-free place for 10 minutes, or until the yeast is foamy.

2 Transfer the mixture to the bowl of an electric mixer. Add another 185 ml (6 fl oz/¾ cup) warm water, sea salt and remaining ingredients, then, using a low speed, mix for 7 minutes, or until the dough is smooth and elastic (the dough will be quite soft).

Cover the bowl with a damp cloth and leave to rise in a draught-free place for 1½–2 hours, or until the dough has doubled in size.

3 Knock back the dough by punching it gently, then turn out onto a floured work surface and cut into eight even-sized pieces. Using a floured rolling pin, roll out each piece to form an 18 x 9 cm (7 x 3½ inch) oval shape. Place the fougasse on a board and, using a sharp knife, cut angled slits down each half of the oval, cutting

through to the board (do not cut through the edges of the dough). Gently pull the cuts apart to form long gaps. Transfer to two greased baking trays, brush with olive oil, then cover loosely with a damp cloth. Leave for 20–25 minutes, or until slightly risen and puffy. Meanwhile, preheat the oven to 200°C (400°F/Gas 6).

4 Bake for 20 minutes, or until golden and crisp. Transfer to a wire rack to cool.

Makes: 16

Preparation time: 2 hours 20 minutes

Cooking time: 20 minutes

1 tablespoon (12 g) instant dried yeast
115 g (4 oz/½ cup) caster (superfine)
  sugar
200 ml (7 fl oz) evaporated milk
2 eggs, lightly beaten
80 g (2¾ oz/½ cup) wholemeal
  (whole-wheat) flour
500 g (1 lb 2 oz/4 cups) white bread
  (strong) flour
1½ teaspoons ground cardamom
50 g (1¾ oz) unsalted butter, softened

GLAZE
1 egg
60 ml (2 fl oz/¼ cup) milk

FINNISH CARDAMOM RINGS

1 Sprinkle the yeast and 1 teaspoon of the sugar over 125 ml (4 fl oz/½ cup) warm water in a small bowl. Stir to dissolve the sugar, then leave in a draught-free place for 10 minutes, or until the yeast is foamy.

2 Combine the evaporated milk and eggs in a small bowl and stir to mix well. Combine the wholemeal flour, 250 g (9 oz/2 cups) of the white bread flour, the cardamom, remaining sugar and 1½ teaspoons salt in the bowl of an electric mixer with a dough hook attachment and make a well in the centre. Pour in the yeast and evaporated milk mixtures. With the mixer set

Add the remaining flour then, using the dough hook, knead until the dough is smooth and elastic.

Sprinkle the yeast and sugar over the water and leave in a draught-free place until the yeast is foamy.

to the lowest speed, mix for 1 minute, or until a dough forms. Add the butter and mix to combine well. Add the remaining flour, 60 g (2¼ oz/½ cup) at a time, and knead for 10 minutes, or until the dough is smooth and elastic (the dough will be very soft).

3 Grease a large bowl with oil, then transfer the dough to the bowl, turning the dough to coat in the oil. Cover with plastic wrap and leave to rise in a draught-free place for 1–1½ hours, or until the dough has doubled in size.

4 Knock back the dough by punching it gently, then turn out onto a floured work surface. Divide the dough into 16 equal portions. Using your hands, roll each piece of dough to measure 25 cm (10 inches) in length, then join the ends to form a ring. Gently press the joins to seal. Transfer the rings to two lightly greased baking trays. Cover loosely with a damp cloth and leave for 45 minutes, or until doubled in size. Meanwhile, preheat the oven to 180°C (350°F/Gas 4).

5 To make the glaze, whisk together the egg and milk and brush it over the rings. Bake for 18–20 minutes, or until golden.

Makes: 12 lunch rolls or 16 dinner rolls

Preparation time: 2 hours

Cooking time: 35 minutes

90 g (3¼ oz/¼ cup) molasses
30 g (1 oz) butter
1 tablespoon (12 g) instant dried yeast
30 g (1 oz/¼ cup) unsweetened
   cocoa powder
1 tablespoon soft brown sugar
1½ tablespoons caraway seeds
2 teaspoons fennel seeds
300 g (10½ oz/3 cups) rye flour,
   plus extra for dusting
375 g (13 oz/3 cups) white bread
   (strong) flour

PUMPERNICKEL ROLLS

1 Heat 500 ml (17 fl oz/2 cups) water, the molasses and butter in a small saucepan over low heat until the butter has melted.

2 Combine the yeast, cocoa powder, sugar, caraway seeds, fennel seeds, 200 g (7 oz/2 cups) of rye flour and 1 teaspoon salt in the bowl of an electric mixer with a dough hook attachment. Pour in the butter mixture and, with the mixer set to the lowest speed, mix until the ingredients are incorporated, scraping down the bowl as necessary. Add the remaining rye flour and mix for 2 minutes. Add the bread flour, 60 g (2¼ oz/½ cup) at a time, mixing to form a soft dough. Increase the speed to medium and knead for 5 minutes, or until the dough is smooth and elastic. Alternatively, mix the dough by hand using a wooden spoon, then turn out onto a floured work surface and knead for 5 minutes, or until smooth and elastic.

3 Grease a large bowl with oil, then transfer the dough to the bowl, turning the dough to coat in the oil. Cover with plastic wrap and leave to rise in a draught-free place for 45–60 minutes, or until the dough has doubled in size.

4 Knock back the dough by punching it gently, then turn out onto a floured work surface and divide into 12 equal portions (or 16 if making dinner rolls). Shape each piece into a round, then gently roll to form an oval shape. Transfer the rolls to greased baking trays and dust the tops with extra rye flour. Using a sharp, lightly floured knife, make a 1 cm (½ inch) deep cut across the top of each roll. Cover with a damp cloth and leave for 45 minutes, or until doubled in size. Meanwhile, preheat the oven to 180°C (350°F/Gas 4).

5 Bake the rolls for 35 minutes (or 25–30 minutes for the dinner rolls), or until they sound hollow when tapped on the base. Transfer to a wire rack to cool. Serve the rolls with cheese, olives, smoked salmon and dill pickles.

TIP When dividing the dough into portions, weigh each portion so they are all the same size.

Mix the ingredients together until the dough is smooth and elastic.

Use a floured knife to make a cut across the tops of the rolls.

Makes: one 20 cm (8 inch) round loaf

Preparation time: 20 minutes

Cooking time: 40 minutes

250 g (9 oz/2 cups) plain (all-purpose)
   flour
225 g (8 oz/1½ cups) wholemeal
   (whole-wheat) flour
1 tablespoon baking powder
1 teaspoon bicarbonate of soda
   (baking soda)
1 tablespoon soft brown sugar
60 g (2¼ oz/½ cup) walnut pieces,
   chopped
175 g (6 oz/1½ cups) grated mature
   cheddar cheese
40 g (1½ oz) butter, melted and cooled
2 eggs, lightly beaten
250 ml (9 fl oz/1 cup) buttermilk

WALNUT AND CHEDDAR SODA BREAD

1 Preheat the oven to 180°C (350°F/ Gas 4). Line a baking tray with baking paper.

2 Sift the flours, baking powder and bicarbonate of soda into a large bowl (tip any husks from the wholemeal flour left in the sieve back into the mixture). Stir in the sugar, walnuts and cheese. Make a well in the centre. Combine the butter, eggs and buttermilk in a bowl and pour into the well. Stir with a wooden spoon until a soft dough forms, then turn out onto a lightly floured work surface. Using lightly floured hands, knead briefly just until smooth, then shape the dough into a 20 cm (8 inch) round. Transfer to the baking tray.

3 Using a sharp, lightly floured knife, cut a 1 cm (½ inch) deep cross into the top of the loaf. Bake for 30–40 minutes, or until golden.

TIP For a variation, replace the cheddar cheese with 100 g (3½ oz/ ½ cup) chopped dried pear and 1 teaspoon aniseed. Bake as above and serve warm, with cheese.

Makes: 12

Preparation time: 3 hours 20 minutes

Cooking time: 15 minutes

90 g (3¼ oz/¾ cup) raisins
3 teaspoons (9 g) instant dried yeast
80 g (2¾ oz/⅓ cup) caster (superfine)
 sugar
400 g (14 oz/3¼ cups) white bread
 (strong) flour
1 teaspoon almond extract
1 tablespoon olive oil
finely grated zest from 1 orange
40 g (1½ oz/¼ cup) mixed peel
40 g (1½ oz/¼ cup) pine nuts
1 egg, lightly beaten
115 g (4 oz/½ cup) caster (superfine)
 sugar, extra

ITALIAN DRIED FRUIT BUNS

1 Cover the raisins with 250 ml (9 fl oz/1 cup) boiling water in a small bowl and set aside for 20 minutes. Drain, reserving the liquid. Put half the liquid into a bowl, add the yeast, a pinch of the sugar and 30 g (1 oz/¼ cup) of the flour. Stir to combine, then leave in a draught-free place for 10 minutes, or until the yeast is foamy.

2 Sift the remaining flour, sugar and 1 teaspoon salt into the bowl of an electric mixer with a dough hook attachment and make a well in the centre. Combine the remaining raisin water with the almond extract and oil, then pour it, along with the yeast mixture, into the well. Add the raisins, orange zest, mixed peel and pine nuts. With the mixer set to the lowest speed, mix until a dough forms. Increase the speed to medium and knead the dough for 5 minutes, or until it is smooth and elastic; add a little more flour if necessary. Alternatively, mix the dough by hand using a wooden spoon, then turn out onto a floured work surface and knead for 5 minutes, or until smooth and elastic.

3 Grease a large bowl with oil, then transfer the dough to the bowl, turning the dough to coat in the oil. Cover with plastic wrap and leave to rise in a draught-free place for 2 hours, or until the dough has doubled in size.

4 Knock back the dough by punching it gently, then turn out onto a lightly floured work surface. Divide the dough into 12 equal portions and shape each piece into an oval. To glaze the rolls, coat them in egg, then roll them in the extra sugar to coat. Transfer the rolls to a greased baking tray and leave for 30–40 minutes, or until the rolls have risen a little (they won't quite double in size). Meanwhile, preheat the oven to 200°C (400°F/ Gas 6).

5 Bake the rolls for 15 minutes, or until golden, then transfer to a wire rack to cool.

Makes: one 25 cm (10 inch) ring

Preparation time: 2 hours 20 minutes

Cooking time: 40 minutes

110 g (3¾ oz/¾ cup) currants
2 tablespoons dry sherry or rum
60 ml (2 fl oz/¼ cup) milk
¼ teaspoon saffron threads
1 tablespoon (12 g) instant dried yeast
115 g (4 oz/½ cup) caster (superfine)
   sugar
125 g (4½ oz) unsalted butter, softened
3 eggs
25 g (1 oz/¼ cup) ground almonds
grated zest from 1 orange
375 g (13 oz/3 cups) plain (all-purpose)
   flour
icing (confectioners') sugar, for dusting

SAFFRON CURRANT BREAD

1 Combine the currants and sherry in a small bowl and set aside for 30 minutes. Heat the milk in a small saucepan over medium heat until the milk reaches simmering point, then remove from the heat. Add the saffron and set aside for 20 minutes to allow the saffron to infuse.

2 Sprinkle the yeast and a pinch of the sugar over 60 ml (2 fl oz/¼ cup) warm water in a small bowl. Stir to dissolve the sugar, then leave in a draught-free place for 10 minutes, or until the yeast is foamy. Grease a 25 cm (10 inch) ring tin.

3 Cream the butter and remaining sugar in a bowl using an electric mixer until pale and fluffy. Add the eggs one at a time, beating well after each addition. Add

½ teaspoon salt, the milk and yeast mixtures, ground almonds, orange zest and currant mixture and beat gently to combine. Add the flour, 60 g (2¼ oz/½ cup) at a time, and mix until incorporated. Using the lowest speed, beat the mixture for another 5 minutes, or until the dough is shiny and elastic (the dough will be soft).

4 Spoon the dough into the prepared ring tin and cover with plastic wrap. Leave to rise in a draught-free place for 1½–2 hours, or until the dough has doubled in size. Meanwhile, preheat the oven to 180°C (350°F/Gas 4).

5 Bake the bread for 35–40 minutes, or until golden, and a skewer inserted into the centre of the bread comes out clean. Cool in the tin for 10 minutes, then turn out onto a wire rack to cool. Serve dusted with icing sugar.

Makes: two 20 cm (8 inch) loaves

Preparation time: 3 hours

Cooking time: 50 minutes

2½ teaspoons (7 g) instant dried yeast
55 g (2 oz/¼ cup) caster (superfine) sugar
90 g (3¼ oz) dark chocolate, roughly
  chopped
50 g (1¾ oz) unsalted butter
375 g (13 oz/3 cups) white bread
  (strong) flour
30 g (1 oz/¼ cup) unsweetened
  cocoa powder
1 egg, lightly beaten
½ teaspoon natural vanilla extract
90 g (3¼ oz/½ cup) dark chocolate chips

CHOCOLATE BREAD

1 Sprinkle the yeast and a pinch of the sugar over 185 ml (6 fl oz/¾ cup) warm water in a small bowl. Stir to dissolve the sugar, then leave in a draught-free place for 10 minutes, or until the yeast is foamy.

2 Put the chocolate and butter in a heatproof bowl. Sit the bowl over a saucepan of simmering water, stirring frequently until the chocolate and butter have melted. Take care that the base of the bowl doesn't touch the water.

3 Combine the flour, cocoa powder, ¼ teaspoon salt and the remaining sugar in the bowl of an electric mixer with a dough hook attachment. Combine the egg and vanilla with the chocolate and butter, then pour the chocolate and yeast mixtures into the flour mixture. With the mixer set to the lowest speed, mix for 1–2 minutes, or until a dough forms. Increase the speed to medium and knead the dough for another 10 minutes, or until the dough is smooth and elastic. Alternatively, mix the dough by hand using a wooden spoon, then turn out onto a floured work surface and knead for 10 minutes, or until the dough is smooth and elastic.

4 Grease a large bowl with oil, then transfer the dough to the bowl, turning the dough to coat in the oil. Cover with plastic wrap and leave to rise in a draught-free place for 1½–2 hours, or until the dough has doubled in size.

5 Knock back the dough by punching it gently, then turn out onto a floured work surface. Divide the dough in half. Gently press out each half until 1 cm (½ inch) thick, then scatter the chocolate chips over each. Roll up each piece of dough to form a log. Transfer to a greased baking tray. Cover with a damp cloth and leave for 1 hour, or until doubled in size. Meanwhile, preheat the oven to 180°C (350°F/Gas 4).

6 Bake for 45–50 minutes, or until the bread is light brown and sounds hollow when tapped on the base. Transfer to a wire rack to cool. This chocolate bread is not overly sweet, so serve freshly sliced or toasted with sweetened mascarpone.

Melt the chocolate and butter over a saucepan of simmering water.

Scatter the chocolate chips over the dough, then roll it up to form a log.

Makes: one 25 cm (10 inch) round bread

Preparation time: 2 hours

Cooking time: 30 minutes

60 ml (2 fl oz/¼ cup) warm milk
2 teaspoons (6 g) instant dried yeast
115 g (4 oz/½ cup) caster (superfine) sugar
2 eggs, lightly beaten
grated zest from 1 lemon
2 teaspoons finely chopped rosemary
185 g (6½ oz/1½ cups) white bread (strong) flour
150 g (5½ oz) unsalted butter, softened, cut into pieces
10 plums, halved and stoned, or 800 g (1 lb 12 oz) tinned plums, drained
whipped cream or mascarpone, to serve

PLUM AND ROSEMARY FLAT BREAD

1 Grease a 25 cm (10 inch) spring-form cake tin or a loose-based flan tin with butter.

2 Combine the milk and yeast in the bowl of an electric mixer. Stir in 55 g (2 oz/¼ cup) of the sugar, eggs, lemon zest and 1 teaspoon of the rosemary, then add the flour. Using the beater attachment, mix for 1 minute, or until a soft dough forms. Add the butter, then continue mixing for a further minute, or until the dough is smooth, shiny and

thick. Alternatively, mix the dough by hand using a wooden spoon.

3 Spoon into the prepared tin and cover with plastic wrap. Leave in a draught-free place for 1½–2 hours, or until doubled in size.

4 Knock back the dough by punching it gently. Dampen the palms of your hands with water and press the dough into the edges of the tin. Arrange the plums, cut side up, over the top, pressing them gently

into the dough. Leave for 30 minutes. Meanwhile, preheat the oven to 200°C (400°F/Gas 6).

5 Sprinkle the plums with the remaining sugar and scatter over the remaining rosemary. Bake for 10 minutes, then reduce the oven to 180°C (350°F/Gas 4) and bake for a further 20 minutes, or until light golden and slightly spongy when pressed in the centre. Serve warm, cut into wedges, with cream or mascarpone.

Makes: one 25 x 11 cm
(10 x 4¼ inch) loaf

Preparation time: 3 hours 15 minutes

Cooking time: 1 hour 35 minutes

500 g (1 lb 2 oz/2¾ cups) mixed
    dried fruit
185 ml (6 fl oz/¾ cup) strong,
    hot black tea
125 g (4½ oz/⅔ cup) lightly packed
    soft brown sugar
1 egg, lightly beaten
125 g (4½ oz/1 cup) plain (all-purpose)
    flour
¾ teaspoon baking powder
1 teaspoon ground cinnamon
¼ teaspoon ground nutmeg
a large pinch of ground cloves

FRUIT AND TEA LOAF

1 Combine the fruit and hot tea in a large bowl, cover with plastic wrap and leave for 3 hours or overnight.

2 Preheat the oven to 160°C (315°F/ Gas 2–3). Grease a 25 x 11 cm (10 x 4¼ inch) loaf tin and line the base with baking paper. Dust the sides of the tin with a little flour, shaking off any excess.

3 Stir the sugar and egg into the fruit mixture to combine well. Sift the flour, baking powder and spices into a bowl, then add the fruit mixture. Using a large slotted spoon, stir to combine well.

4 Spoon the mixture into the tin and bake for 1 hour 35 minutes, covering the top with foil if it browns too quickly. The loaf is

cooked when a skewer inserted into the centre of the loaf comes out clean. Cool the loaf in the tin, then turn out and serve, sliced and buttered, if desired.

5 The loaf will keep, wrapped in plastic wrap and stored in an airtight container in a cool place, for up to 1 week, or up to 8 weeks in the freezer.

Makes: 6

Preparation time: 2 hours

Cooking time: 12 minutes

1½ teaspoons (4½ g) instant
    dried yeast
½ teaspoon caster (superfine) sugar
450 g (1 lb/3⅔ cups) white bread
    (strong) flour
1 tablespoon olive oil
lemon wedges, to serve
Greek-style yoghurt, to serve

TOPPING
2 tablespoons olive oil
1 small onion, finely chopped
1 garlic clove, finely chopped
250 g (9 oz) minced (ground) lamb
400 g (14 oz) tinned tomatoes,
    drained and chopped
40 g (1½ oz/¼ cup) pine nuts,
    toasted
¼ teaspoon ground allspice
¼ teaspoon ground cinnamon
1 tablespoon lemon juice

*Cook the garlic and lamb until browned,
then add the tomatoes.*

*Spread the topping over the pizza bases,
leaving a border around the edge.*

MIDDLE EASTERN LAMB AND PINE NUT PIZZAS

1 Sprinkle the yeast and sugar over 60 ml (2 fl oz/¼ cup) warm water in a
   small bowl. Stir to dissolve the sugar, then leave in a draught-free place for
   10 minutes, or until the yeast is foamy.

2 Put the flour and 1 teaspoon salt into the bowl of an electric mixer with
   a dough hook attachment and make a well in the centre. Pour the yeast
   mixture into the well, then, with the mixer set to the lowest speed, gradually
   add 250 ml (9 fl oz/1 cup) water and the oil, mixing for 3 minutes, or until
   a dough forms. Increase the speed to medium and knead for another
   10 minutes, or until the dough is smooth and elastic. Alternatively, mix the
   dough by hand using a wooden spoon, then turn out onto a floured work
   surface and knead for 10 minutes, or until the dough is smooth and elastic.

3 Grease a large bowl with oil, then transfer the dough to the bowl, turning
   the dough to coat in the oil. Cover with plastic wrap and leave to rise in a
   draught-free place for 1½–2 hours, or until the dough has doubled in size.

4 Meanwhile, prepare the topping. Heat the oil in a frying pan over medium
   heat. Add the onion and cook for 5 minutes, or until softened, then add the
   garlic and lamb and cook for 5 minutes, stirring, until browned. Add the
   tomatoes, pine nuts, spices and lemon juice and season to taste. Remove
   from the heat and cool.

5 Preheat oven to 220°C (425°F/Gas 7) and grease three baking trays. Knock
   back the dough by punching it gently, then turn out onto a floured work
   surface and divide into six equal portions. Shape each portion into a ball
   and then roll each ball out until 5 mm (¼ inch) thick. Transfer the pizza
   bases to the baking trays. Divide the topping between the pizzas, leaving
   a 1 cm (½ inch) border around the edges.

6 Bake the pizzas, one tray at a time, for 10–12 minutes, or until the edges
   are golden and the base is crisp. Serve immediately with lemon wedges
   and yoghurt.

Makes: 32

Preparation time: 1 hour 30 minutes

Cooking time: 20 minutes

1 teaspoon (3 g) instant dried yeast
a pinch of caster (superfine) sugar
1 tablespoon extra virgin olive oil
250 g (9 oz/2 cups) white bread
  (strong) flour
60 g (2¼ oz/⅔ cup) grated parmesan
  cheese

PARMESAN GRISSINI

1 Sprinkle the yeast and sugar over 170 ml (5½ fl oz/ ⅔ cup) warm water in a small bowl. Stir to dissolve the sugar, then leave in a draught-free place for 10 minutes, or until the yeast is foamy. Stir in the olive oil.

2 Put the flour in a large bowl, add the parmesan and 1 teaspoon salt and stir to combine well. Pour in the yeast mixture and stir until a dough forms. Turn the dough out onto a lightly floured work surface and knead for 5 minutes, or until the dough is smooth and elastic.

3 Grease a large bowl with oil, then transfer the dough to the bowl, turning the dough to coat in the oil. Cover with plastic wrap and leave to rise in a draught-free place for 1 hour, or until the dough has doubled in size.

4 Preheat the oven to 200°C (400°F/Gas 6). Lightly grease two baking trays. Knock back the dough by punching it gently, then turn out onto a floured work surface and cut in half. Roll out one piece of dough to form a 20 x 16 cm (8 x 6¼ inch) rectangle, then cut into sixteen 1 cm (½ inch) wide strips. Using your hands, gently roll each strip to form a 22–24 cm (8½– 9½ inch) long stick, then place on the baking tray. Repeat for the second piece of dough. Bake for 17–20 minutes, or until golden and crisp, swapping the trays halfway through to ensure even cooking. Transfer to a wire rack to cool.

5 Grissini will keep, stored in an airtight container, for up to 7 days. Re-crisp in a 180°C (350°F/Gas 4) oven for 5 minutes if they become soft.

Makes: 10

Preparation time: 2 hours 45 minutes

Cooking time: 15 minutes

1 teaspoon (3 g) instant dried yeast
1 teaspoon caster (superfine) sugar
1 tablespoon olive oil
335 g (11¾ oz/2⅔ cups) white bread
   (strong) flour
90 g (3¼ oz/⅓ cup) tahini
60 g (2¼ oz/⅓ cup) soft brown sugar
2 teaspoons vegetable oil

TAHINI SPIRALS

1 Sprinkle the yeast and sugar over 250 ml (9 fl oz/1 cup) warm water in a large bowl. Stir to dissolve the sugar, then leave in a draught-free place for 10 minutes, or until the yeast is foamy, then stir in the olive oil.

2 Combine the yeast mixture and a third of the flour in the bowl of an electric mixer with a dough hook attachment. With the mixer set to the lowest speed, gradually add the remaining flour, 60 g (2¼ oz/½ cup) at a time, mixing until a dough forms. Increase the speed to medium and knead for 7 minutes, or until the dough is smooth and elastic. Alternatively, mix the dough by hand using a wooden spoon, then turn out onto a floured work surface and knead the dough for 7 minutes, or until smooth and elastic.

3 Grease a large bowl with oil, then transfer the dough to the bowl, turning the dough to coat in the oil. Cover with plastic wrap and leave to rise in a draught-

free place for 2 hours, or until the dough has doubled in size.

4 Preheat the oven to 190°C (375°F/Gas 5). Lightly grease two baking trays. Put the tahini, brown sugar and vegetable oil in a small bowl, stirring to mix well.

5 Knock back the dough by punching it gently, then turn out onto a floured work surface and divide into 10 equal portions. Working with one portion at a time, roll each to form a 20 x 10 cm (8 x 4 inch) rectangle. Spread about 1 tablespoon of tahini mixture over the dough, spreading it to the edges. Starting at the long edge of the rectangle, roll it up to form a long cylinder. Tightly coil the cylinder to form a round, then tuck the end underneath. Transfer the spirals to the prepared baking trays and, using the palm of your hand, flatten slightly. Bake for 12–15 minutes, or until golden. Serve warm or at room temperature.

Makes: about 48 pieces

Preparation time: 5 minutes

Cooking time: 10 minutes

½ cup (125 ml) olive oil
3 garlic cloves, crushed
6 slices lavash bread
2 teaspoons sea salt flakes
2 teaspoons dried mixed Italian herbs

HERBED LAVASH

1 Preheat the oven to 180°C (350°F/Gas 4). Heat the oil and garlic in a small saucepan over low heat until the oil is warm and the garlic is fragrant but not browned.

2 Brush the lavash bread on both sides with the garlic oil. Cut each piece of bread into eight triangular wedges and position side-by-side on baking trays. Sprinkle the upper side with the sea salt and herbs. Bake the lavash for 8–10 minutes, or until crisp.

Makes: 2

Preparation time: 1 hour 5 minutes

Cooking time: 20 minutes

PIZZA BASE

500 g (4 cups) plain (all-purpose) flour
7 g (⅛ oz) sachet dried yeast
1 teaspoon salt
1 teaspoon sugar
1 tablespoon olive oil

8 courgettes (zucchini), cut into
    fine rounds
2 teaspoons grated lemon zest
1 large handful finely chopped parsley
2 teaspoons thyme sprigs
4 garlic cloves, crushed
4 tablespoons olive oil
500 g (1 lb 2 oz) bocconcini (baby
    mozzarella) cheese, finely diced
50 g (½ cup) grated parmesan cheese
1 tablespoon extra virgin olive oil

BOCCONCINI

*Means literally 'small mouthful' and is
used to describe various foods, but
generally refers to small balls of
mozzarella, about the size of walnuts.
True mozzarella is made from buffalo
milk: that made from cow's milk is
called* fior di latte. *The curds (*mozzata*)
are stretched and shaped into balls by
hand (though some balls are now factory
made). Mozzarella should be white,
fresh-smelling and have tiny holes that
weep whey when it is very fresh.*

COURGETTE, THYME AND BOCCONCINI PIZZA

1 Preheat the oven to 220°C (425°F/Gas 7). To make the pizza base, mix
together the flour, yeast, salt and sugar in a large bowl, and make a well in
the centre. Pour the oil and 310 ml (1¼ cups) lukewarm water into the well
and mix until the flour is incorporated and a soft dough forms. Turn onto a
floured bench and knead for 10 minutes, or until the dough is smooth and
elastic. Put the dough in a lightly greased bowl, cover with plastic wrap and
leave in a warm place for about 40 minutes, or until doubled in size. Punch
the dough down, and knead for 1 minute. Divide in half and roll each half
out to 5 mm (¼ inch) thick. Transfer the bases to two pizza trays.

2 Place the courgette rounds, lemon zest, parsley, thyme, garlic and olive
oil in a bowl and mix together. Top each pizza base evenly with half the
bocconcini and half the parmesan, then spoon on the courgette mixture.
Evenly distribute the remaining bocconcini and parmesan over the top,
season well with salt and pepper, and drizzle with the extra virgin olive
oil. Cook for 15–20 minutes, or until the base is crisp, and the topping
is warmed through and golden.

Makes: 24

Preparation time: 1 hour 25 minutes

Cooking time: 15 minutes

2½ teaspoons (7 g) instant dry yeast
1 teaspoon caster (superfine) sugar
500 g (1 lb 2 oz/4 cups) plain (all-
    purpose) flour
60 ml (2 fl oz/¼ cup) olive oil
4 tablespoons chopped fresh basil
50 g (1¾ oz/½ cup) finely grated
    parmesan cheese
2 teaspoons sea-salt flakes

BASIL AND CHEESE GRISSINI

1 Combine the yeast, sugar and 315 ml (10¾ fl oz/1¾ cups) warm water in a bowl and leave in a warm place for 5–10 minutes, or until foamy. Sift the flour and 1 teaspoon salt into a bowl. Stir the yeast and oil into the flour to form a dough, adding a little more water if necessary.

2 Gently gather the dough into a ball and turn out onto a lightly floured surface. Knead for 10 minutes, or until soft and elastic. Add the basil and parmesan, and knead for 1–2 minutes to incorporate evenly.

3 Place the dough in a lightly oiled bowl and cover with plastic wrap. Leave in a warm place for 1 hour, or until doubled in volume. Preheat the oven to 230°C (450°F/Gas 8) and lightly grease two large baking trays.

4 Punch down the dough and knead for 1 minute. Divide into 24 portions, and roll each portion into a 30 cm (12 inch) long stick. Place on the trays and brush with water. Sprinkle with the salt flakes. Bake for 15 minutes, or until crisp and golden.

BASIL
One of the most common herbs used in Italian cuisine, basil (basilico) adds a fresh flavour to cooked dishes and salads. It loses its flavour easily so add it at the end of cooking, tearing rather than chopping the leaves, to prevent the cut edges blackening.

Makes: 6 large muffins

Preparation time: 25 minutes

Cooking time: 25 minutes

60 ml (2 fl oz/¼ cup) oil,
    plus 2 teaspoons
5 French shallots
2 slices bacon, finely chopped
250 g (9 oz/2 cups) plain
    (all-purpose) flour
1 tablespoon baking powder
1 tablespoon caster (superfine) sugar
1 teaspoon dry mustard
140 g (5 oz/scant 1¼ cups) mature
    cheddar cheese shredded
185 ml (6 fl oz/¾ cup) milk
1 egg
sweet paprika to serve

FRENCH SHALLOT, BACON AND CHEDDAR BREAKFAST MUFFINS

Served warm with lashings of butter, these muffins are just the thing for cold weekend mornings. They can be made the day before, stored in an airtight container and reheated when needed. french shallots are preferable, but Asian shallots can be used too.

1 Preheat the oven to 200°C (400°F/ Gas 6). Grease a 6-hole giant muffin tin.

2 Finely slice 1 of the shallots into rings. Finely chop the remaining 4 shallots. Heat 2 teaspoons of the oil in a small non-stick frying pan over low heat. Add the sliced shallot and fry, without browning, for 3 minutes. Remove from the pan and drain on paper towels. Increase the heat to medium–low and add the chopped shallots and bacon to the pan. Fry for about 5 minutes, until the shallots are soft. Drain on paper towels.

3 Sift the flour, baking powder, sugar, mustard and ½ teaspoon salt into a large bowl. Add 90 g (3¼ oz/¾ cup) of the cheddar and the bacon mixture and stir through. Combine the milk, egg and remaining oil in a pitcher. Pour into the bowl and fold gently until combined. Do not beat; the batter should be lumpy.

4 Divide the batter among the muffin holes. Top each with a few of the fried shallot rings and some of the remaining shredded cheddar. Bake for 20–25 minutes, or until the muffins are risen and golden and a fine skewer inserted into the centre of a muffin comes out clean. Cool in the tin for 5 minutes before turning out. Sprinkle a little paprika on top to serve.

Fry the bacon and chopped shallots until the shallots are soft.

Makes: 10 scones

Preparation time: 25 minutes

Cooking time: 12 minutes

250 g (9 oz/2 cups) plain
  (all-purpose) flour
1 tablespoon baking powder
1/8 teaspoon cayenne pepper
30 g (1 oz) unsalted butter,
  chilled and diced
185 ml (6 fl oz/3/4 cup) milk

FILLING
40 g (1½ oz/¼ cup) goat's cheese,
  crumbled
40 g (1½ oz/½ cup) grated parmesan
  cheese
40 g (1½ oz/⅓ cup) grated mature
  cheddar cheese
2 tablespoons chopped flat-leaf (Italian)
  parsley

CHEESE PINWHEEL SCONES

1 Preheat the oven to 220°C (425°F/ Gas 7). Grease or line a baking tray.

2 Sift the flour, baking powder, a pinch of salt and cayenne into a large mixing bowl. Using your fingertips, rub in the butter until the mixture resembles breadcrumbs. Add the milk and, using a flat-bladed knife, mix to form a soft dough. Add a little extra flour if the dough is too sticky.

3 Turn the dough out onto a floured work surface and roll out to form a 20 x 25 cm (8 x 10 inch) rectangle. Sprinkle the goat's cheese over the surface, then sprinkle over the parmesan, cheddar and parsley. Starting from the long side, roll the dough into a cylinder. Cut the cylinder into 10 equal 2 cm (3/4 inch) thick slices. Transfer the slices to a baking tray, spacing them 2 cm (3/4 inch) apart.

4 Bake for 10–12 minutes, or until golden and cooked through. Cool on a wire rack. Serve warm.

Makes: two 20 x 10 cm
(8 x 4 inch) loaves

Preparation time: 2 hours

Cooking time: 30 minutes

375 g (13 oz/3 cups) white bread
   (strong) flour
125 g (4½ oz/1 cup) semolina
1 tablespoon (12 g) instant dried yeast
1 teaspoon caster (superfine) sugar
2 tablespoons olive oil
60 g (2¼ oz/1 bunch) dill,
   finely chopped
grated zest from 1 lemon
200 g (7 oz/1⅓ cups) coarsely
   crumbled feta cheese, well drained

GREEK LEMON, DILL AND FETA BREAD

1 Combine the flour, semolina, yeast, sugar and 1½ teaspoons salt in the bowl of an electric mixer with a dough hook attachment and make a well in the centre. Pour 250 ml (9 fl oz/1 cup) warm water and the oil into the well. With the mixer set to the lowest speed, mix for 3 minutes, or until a dough forms. Increase the speed to medium, add the dill and lemon zest and knead for another 8 minutes, or until the dough is smooth and elastic. Add the feta and knead for 2 minutes, or until the feta is incorporated into the dough.

2 Alternatively, mix the dough by hand using a wooden spoon, then turn out onto a floured work surface, sprinkle over the dill and lemon zest and knead for 8 minutes or until the dill and zest are incorporated and the dough is smooth and elastic. Pat the dough into a rectangle approximately 20 x 10 cm (8 x 4 inches) and sprinkle over the feta. Fold the dough over several times, then knead for 2 minutes, or until the feta is incorporated.

3 Grease a large bowl with oil, then transfer the dough to the bowl, turning the dough to coat in the oil. Cover with plastic wrap and leave to rise in a draught-free place for 1½–2 hours, or until the dough has doubled in size.

4 Knock back the dough by punching it gently, then turn out onto a floured work surface. Divide the dough in half and form each into a loaf shape and place, seam side down, into two greased 20 x 10 cm (8 x 4 inch) loaf tins. Cover with a damp cloth and leave for 30 minutes, or until doubled in size. Meanwhile, preheat the oven to 200°C (400°F/Gas 6). Bake the bread for 10 minutes, then reduce the oven to 180°C (350°F/Gas 4) and bake for a further 20 minutes, or until golden and sounds hollow when tapped on the base. Transfer to a wire rack to cool.

Makes: 12 muffins or 48 mini muffins

Preparation time: 20 minutes

Cooking time: 25 minutes

155 g (5½ oz/1¼ cups) self-raising flour
110 g (3¾ oz/¾ cup) polenta
 (cornmeal)
60 g (2¼ oz/¾ cup) grated pecorino
 cheese
1 egg, lightly beaten
250 ml (9 fl oz/1 cup) milk
80 ml (2½ fl oz/⅓ cup) olive oil
40 g (1½ oz/¼ cup) chopped
semi-dried (sun-blushed) tomatoes
15 g (½ oz/¼ cup) chopped basil

POLENTA, SEMI-DRIED TOMATO, PECORINO AND BASIL MUFFINS

1 Preheat the oven to 180°C (350°F/ Gas 4). Grease a 12-hole standard muffin tin or two 24-hole mini muffin tins, or line the holes with paper cases.

2 Sift the flour into a large bowl, then stir in the polenta and pecorino and season with freshly ground black pepper. Make a well in the centre. Combine the egg, milk and oil in a bowl, then pour into the well. Add the tomatoes and basil and stir quickly until just combined. Do not overmix — the batter will still be slightly lumpy.

3 Divide the mixture evenly between the muffin holes. Bake for 20–25 minutes (or 10–12 minutes for mini muffins), or until the muffins are golden and come away from the sides of the tin. Cool in the tin for 2 minutes before transferring to a wire rack. Serve warm.

TIP Most muffins should be left to cool for a few minutes in the tins once out of the oven. Don't leave them for too long or trapped steam will make the bases soggy.

Makes: 12 scones

Preparation time: 20 minutes

Cooking time: 12 minutes

375 g (13 oz/3 cups) plain (all-purpose) flour
1½ teaspoons bicarbonate of soda (baking soda)
3 teaspoons cream of tartar
1 teaspoon mixed (pumpkin pie) spice
2 teaspoons caster (superfine) sugar, plus extra for sprinkling
50 g (1¾ oz) unsalted butter, chilled and diced
150 ml (5 fl oz) pouring cream
150 ml (5 fl oz) milk, plus extra for brushing
125 g (4½ oz/¾ cup) currants
jam and thick (double/heavy) cream, to serve

CURRANT CREAM SCONES

1 Preheat the oven to 220°C (425°F/Gas 7). Grease a baking tray or line the tray with baking paper.

2 Sift the flour, bicarbonate of soda, cream of tartar, mixed spice and sugar into a large bowl. Using your fingertips, rub in the butter until the mixture resembles breadcrumbs. Add the cream, milk and currants and mix with a flat-bladed knife to form a soft dough, adding a little extra flour if the mixture is too sticky.

3 Using floured hands, gently gather the dough together and lift out onto a lightly floured work surface. Pat into a smooth ball, then press out to a 2 cm (¾ inch)

thickness. Using a 6 cm (2½ inch) pastry cutter, cut the dough into rounds, or use a knife dipped in flour to cut 4 cm (1½ inch) squares.

4 Place the scones on the baking tray, brush the tops lightly with milk and sprinkle with the extra sugar. Bake for 10–12 minutes, or until golden. Transfer to a wire rack lined with a tea towel (dish towel). Serve the scones warm with marmalade or jam and thick cream.

TIP When making scones, handle the mixture with care. Don't be too heavy-handed when mixing the dough or the scones will be tough.

ORANGE AND BLUEBERRY ROLLS

Makes: 20 rolls

Preparation time:
2 hours 15 minutes

Cooking time: 30 minutes

1 tablespoon (12 g) instant dried yeast
75 g (2½ oz/⅓ cup) caster
    (superfine) sugar
250 ml (9 fl oz/1 cup) warm milk
125 g (4½ oz) unsalted butter,
    softened
80 ml (2½ fl oz/⅓ cup) freshly
    squeezed orange juice
2 eggs, lightly beaten
375 g (13 oz/3 cups) white bread
    (strong) flour
icing (confectioners') sugar, for dusting

FILLING

100 g (3½ oz) unsalted butter,
    softened
115 g (4 oz/½ cup) caster (superfine)
    sugar
grated zest from 2 oranges
270 g (9½ oz/1¾ cups) blueberries

1 Sprinkle the yeast and a pinch of the sugar over 100 ml (3½ fl oz) warm milk in a small bowl. Stir to dissolve the sugar, then leave in a draught-free place for 10 minutes, or until the yeast is foamy.

2 Put the remaining milk and sugar, the butter and 1 teaspoon salt in the bowl of an electric mixer. Using the beater attachment, mix until the butter has just melted. Add the orange juice, eggs and yeast mixture and mix to combine. Using the lowest speed, gradually add the flour, 60 g (2¼ oz/½ cup) at a time, mixing until the dough is soft and smooth.

3 Grease a large bowl with oil, then transfer the dough to the bowl, turning the dough to coat in the oil. Cover with plastic wrap and leave to rise in a draught-free place for 1 hour, or until the dough has doubled in size.

4 To make the filling, cream the butter, sugar and orange zest in a small bowl using electric beaters until pale and fluffy. Grease two 20 cm (8 inch) round spring-form cake tins.

5 Turn the dough out onto a lightly floured work surface and divide in half. Roll each piece into a 25 x 15 cm (10 x 6 inch) rectangle. Spread half the filling mixture over one rectangle, then arrange half the blueberries over the top. Repeat with the remaining rectangle of dough, filling and blueberries. Starting from the long side, roll up each rectangle to form a cylinder. Then, using a lightly floured, serrated knife, cut each cylinder into 10 equal rolls. Arrange 10 rolls, cut side up, over the base of each tin. Cover with a damp cloth and leave for 45 minutes, or until the rolls have doubled in size. Meanwhile, preheat the oven to 180°C (350°F/Gas 4).

Scatter the blueberries over the filling and roll up to form a cylinder.

Arrange the rolls, cut side up, over the base of each tin.

6 Bake the rolls for 25–30 minutes, or until the rolls are golden and come away from the sides of the tins. Cool in the tins for 5 minutes, then transfer to a wire rack to cool. Dust with icing sugar to serve.

Makes: 8 muffins

Preparation time: 25 minutes

Cooking time: 30 minutes

20 g (¼ cup) instant espresso coffee
  powder
1 tablespoon boiling water
310 g (2½ cups) self-raising flour
115 g (½ cup) caster (superfine) sugar
2 eggs, lightly beaten
375 ml (1½ cups) buttermilk
1 teaspoon natural vanilla extract
150 g (5½ oz) butter, melted
100 g (3½ oz) white chocolate,
  roughly chopped
30 g (1 oz) butter, extra
3 tablespoons brown sugar

HIGH-TOP CAPPUCCINO AND WHITE-CHOC MUFFINS

1 Preheat the oven to 200°C (400°F/ Gas 6). Cut eight lengths of baking paper and roll into 8 cm (3 in) high cylinders to fit into eight 125 ml (½-cup) capacity ramekins. When in place in the ramekins, secure the cylinders with string and place all the ramekins onto a baking tray.

2 Dissolve the coffee in the boiling water and allow to cool. Sift the flour and sugar into a bowl. Combine the egg, buttermilk, vanilla, melted butter, white chocolate and the coffee mixture and roughly combine with the dry ingredients. Spoon the mixture into each cylinder.

3 Heat the extra butter and the brown sugar and stir until the sugar dissolves. Spoon this mixture onto each muffin and gently swirl into the muffin using a skewer. Bake for 25–30 minutes, or until risen and cooked when tested with a skewer.

Makes: 12 muffins

Preparation time: 20 minutes

Cooking time: 25 minutes

125 g (4½ oz/1 cup) medium oatmeal
375 ml (13 fl oz/1½ cups) milk
250 g (9 oz/2 cups) plain (all-purpose)
   flour
1 tablespoon baking powder
115 g (4 oz/½ cup) soft brown sugar
1 egg, lightly beaten
90 g (3¼ oz/¼ cup) honey
60 g (2¼ oz) unsalted butter, melted
150 g (5½ oz/1¼ cups) raspberries

OATMEAL AND RASPBERRY MUFFINS

1 Preheat the oven to 190°C (375°F/ Gas 5). Grease a 12-hole standard muffin tin, or line the holes with paper cases.

2 Put the oatmeal in a bowl, stir in the milk and set aside for 5 minutes. Sift the flour and baking powder into a large bowl, then stir in the sugar. Make a well in the centre.

3 Combine the egg, honey and butter in a bowl and stir to mix well. Pour the egg mixture and oatmeal mixture into the well, then stir quickly until just combined. Do not overmix — the batter will still be slightly lumpy. Gently fold in the raspberries.

4 Divide the mixture evenly between the muffin holes. Bake for 20–25 minutes, or until the muffins are golden and a skewer inserted into the centre of a muffin comes out clean. Cool for 5 minutes before transferring to a wire rack. Serve warm.

TIP Softer batter mixes, such as muffin batter, should not be overworked or the muffins will be tough and rubbery. Stir the mixture gently with a metal spoon until just combined.

Makes: a 30 cm (12 inch) calzone

Preparation time: 45 minutes

Cooking time: 25 minutes

PASTRY

280 g (10 oz/2¼ cups) plain
(all-purpose) flour
½ teaspoon bicarbonate of soda
(baking soda)
20 g (¾ oz) butter, chilled and cubed
170 ml (5½ fl oz/⅔ cup) buttermilk

FILLING

20 g (¾ oz) butter
2 tablespoons oil
3 large leeks, white part only, sliced
50 g (1¾ oz/⅓ cup) frozen soya
beans, thawed
2 garlic cloves, crushed
2 slices bacon, cut into thin strips
200 g (7 oz) chicken breast fillet,
cut into thick strips
80 g (2¾ oz) fresh mozzarella cheese
(bocconcini), diced
1 small handful basil, roughly torn
1 egg

LEEK AND CHICKEN CALZONE

Buttermilk pastry is a good choice for turnovers and calzone. It is strong enough to support a filling, yet soft and bread-like. If made 24 hours in advance, it develops a sourdough taste, giving the flavour of a yeast dough without the time involved.

1 To make the pastry, put the flour, bicarbonate of soda, ½ teaspoon salt and the butter in a food processor. Process in short bursts, using the pulse button, until the mixture is fine and crumbly. With the motor running, gradually add the buttermilk, stopping after the dough clumps into a ball. Transfer to a clean, dry work surface. The dough will be soft and just a little sticky, but try not to add extra flour. Knead for 1 minute, or until spongy and smooth. Cover with plastic wrap and set aside at room temperature for at least 30 minutes (or chill overnight).

2 To make the filling, heat the butter and half the oil in a large frying pan over medium–low heat and sauté the leek, without browning, for 7–8 minutes. Add the soya beans and garlic and cook for 1 minute. Transfer to a bowl. Add the remaining oil to the pan and sauté the bacon and chicken for 5–6 minutes, or until browned. Season with freshly ground black pepper and add to the leek mixture, along with the mozzarella and basil. Toss to combine.

3 Preheat the oven to 200°C (400°F/ Gas 6) and put a baking sheet on the middle rack. Lightly beat the egg with 1 teaspoon water. Roll and stretch the dough out on a doubled sheet of baking paper to a 30 cm (12 inch) circle. Spread the filling over half the circle, leaving a 2 cm (¾ inch) border. Brush the border with the beaten egg. Using the baking paper for leverage, fold the uncovered dough over the filling to form a half-moon shape. Press the edges together and fold them over and in on themselves, giving a sealed rolled border. Pinch the edge into a pattern. Brush the calzone with beaten egg.

4 Using the baking paper as handles, transfer the calzone to the baking sheet in the oven. Bake for 20–25 minutes, or until golden brown. Remove from the oven and allow to stand for 5 minutes before serving.

Makes: about 50 toasts

Preparation time: 20 minutes

Cooking time: 1 hour

250 g (9 oz/2 cups) self-raising flour
125 g (4½ oz/1 cup) grated cheddar
    cheese
¼ cup (25 g) freshly grated parmesan
    cheese
50 g (1¾ oz/⅓ cup) pine nuts
250 ml (9 oz/1 cup) milk
1 egg, lightly beaten
30 g butter, melted
60 g (2¼ oz/½ cup) pitted black olives,
    chopped
40 g (1½ oz/¼ cup) sun-dried
    tomatoes, finely chopped
40 g (1½ oz/⅓ cup) grated cheddar
    cheese, extra

CHEESE, OLIVE AND SUN-DRIED TOMATO TOASTS

1 Preheat the oven to 200°C (400°F/Gas 6). Lightly grease two 8 x 26 cm (3¼ x 10½ inch) loaf (bar) tins and cover the bases with baking paper. Combine the flour, cheeses and pine nuts in a bowl. Make a well in the centre of the mixture.

2 Pour in the combined milk, egg, butter, olives and sun-dried tomato, and stir to form a slightly sticky dough.

3 Divide the mixture between the tins. Smooth the surface and sprinkle with the extra cheese. Bake for 45 minutes, or until cooked through when tested with a skewer. Leave in the tins for 5 minutes, then turn onto wire racks to cool.

4 Cut into 5 mm (¼ inch) slices and place on baking trays lined with baking paper. Bake for 15–20 minutes, or until the toasts are golden and crisp.

Makes: two 30 cm (12 inch) pizzas

Preparation time: 2 hours

Cooking time: 20 minutes

2 teaspoons (6 g) instant dried yeast
a pinch of caster (superfine) sugar
300 g (10½ oz/2⅓ cups) white
    bread (strong) flour
115 g (4 oz/¾ cup) wholemeal
    (whole-wheat) flour
1½ teaspoons sea salt flakes
2½ tablespoons olive oil

TOPPING
2½ tablespoons extra virgin olive oil
1 large onion, peeled and finely
    chopped
5 garlic cloves, peeled and thinly sliced
1 bunch silverbeet (Swiss chard),
    stems removed and discarded,
    leaves washed, dried and chopped
85 g (3 oz/⅔ cup) raisins,
    roughly chopped
150 g (5½ oz/1½ cups) grated
    parmesan cheese
a large pinch of chilli flakes, or to taste
2 x 100 g (3½ oz) tins sardines in oil,
    drained

SARDINE AND SILVERBEET WHOLEMEAL PIZZA

1 Sprinkle the yeast and sugar over
   60 ml (2 fl oz/¼ cup) warm water
   in a small bowl. Stir to dissolve the
   sugar, then leave in a draught-free
   place for 10 minutes, or until the
   yeast is foamy.

2 Put the white bread and wholemeal
   flours and sea salt into the bowl of
   an electric mixer with a dough hook
   attachment and make a well in the
   centre. Pour the yeast mixture into
   the well, then, with the mixer set
   to the lowest speed, gradually add
   250 ml (9 fl oz/1 cup) warm
   water and the olive oil, mixing for
   3 minutes, or until a soft dough
   forms. Increase the speed to

medium and knead for 7 minutes,
or until the dough is smooth and
elastic (the dough will be very soft).
Alternatively, mix the dough by
hand using a wooden spoon, then
turn out onto a floured work surface
and knead for 7 minutes, or until
the dough is smooth and elastic.

3 Grease a large bowl with oil, then
   transfer the dough to the bowl,
   turning the dough to coat in the
   oil. Cover with plastic wrap and
   leave to rise in a draught-free place
   for 1½ hours, or until the dough
   has doubled in size.

4 Meanwhile, to make the topping,
   heat the oil in a large saucepan.
   Add the onion and garlic and
   stir over medium–high heat for
   3 minutes, or until soft and light
   golden. Add the silverbeet and
   raisins, cover, then cook for
   3 minutes, stirring often, or
   until the silverbeet has wilted.
   Remove from the heat and cool
   slightly, then stir in the parmesan
   and chilli flakes and season with
   salt and pepper.

5 Preheat the oven to 220°C (425°F/
   Gas 7). Lightly grease two 30 cm
   (12 inch) pizza trays. Alternatively,
   the pizzas can be baked directly
   on a pizza stone.

6 Knock back the dough by punching
   it gently, then turn out onto a
   floured work surface. Cut the
   dough in half and roll out each
   half to form a circle, approximately
   30 cm (12 inches) in diameter.
   Transfer to the trays. Divide the
   silverbeet mixture between the
   pizza bases, scattering to cover,
   then top with sardines. Bake for
   15–20 minutes, or until the bases
   are crisp and golden. Serve hot.

*Divide the topping between the two pizzas
and arrange the sardines over the top.*

Serves 6

Preparation time:
2 hours 30 minutes

Cooking time: 20 minutes

BREAD DOUGH
2 teaspoons dried yeast
250 g (9 oz/2 cups) plain
  (all-purpose) flour
1/2 teaspoon salt
3 tablespoons olive oil

40 g (11/2 oz) butter
1 tablespoon olive oil
1.5 kg (3 lb 5 oz), thinly sliced
  onions
2 tablespoons thyme
1 tablespoon olive oil
16, halved lengthways anchovy
  fillets
24 pitted black olives

PISSALADIÈRE

Soft caramelized onions, olives, plenty of anchovies and fresh thyme flavour this delicious tart that originated in Nice. You can serve pissaladière hot or at room temperature as either lunch or casual dinner fare and, as it transports well, it is great to take on a picnic.

1 To make the bread dough, mix the yeast with 120 ml (4 fl oz) of warm water. Leave for 10 minutes in a warm place until the yeast becomes frothy.

2 Sift the flour into a large bowl and add the salt, olive oil and the yeast mixture. Mix until the dough clumps together and forms a ball. Turn out onto a lightly floured work surface. Knead the dough, adding a little more flour or a few drops of warm water if necessary, until you have a soft dough that is not sticky but dry to the touch. Knead for 10 minutes, or until smooth, and the impression made by a finger springs back immediately.

3 Rub the inside of a large bowl with olive oil. Roll the ball of dough around in the bowl to coat it with oil, then cut a shallow cross on the top of the ball with a sharp knife. Leave the dough in the bowl, cover with a tea towel (dish towel) and leave in a draught-free place for 1–11/2 hours, or until the dough has doubled in size.

4 Knock back the dough by punching it with your fist several times to expel the air and then knead it again for a couple of minutes. (At this stage the dough can be stored in the fridge for 4 hours, or frozen. Bring back to room temperature before continuing.) Leave in a warm place to rise until doubled in size.

5 Melt the butter with the olive oil in a saucepan and add the onion and half the thyme. Cover the saucepan and cook over low heat for 45 minutes, stirring, until the onion is softened but not browned. Season and cool. Preheat the oven to 200°C (400°F/Gas 6).

6 Roll out the bread dough to roughly fit a greased 34 x 26 cm (131/2 x 101/2 in) shallow baking tray. Brush with the olive oil, then spread with the onion.

7 Lay the anchovies in a lattice pattern over the onion and arrange the olives in the lattice diamonds. Bake for 20 minutes, or until the dough is cooked and lightly browned. Sprinkle with the remaining thyme leaves and cut into squares. Serve hot or warm.

Makes: 30

Preparation time: 25 minutes

Cooking time: 10 minutes

155 g (5½ oz/1¼ cups) plain (all-purpose) flour
100 g unsalted butter, chilled and chopped
100 g cup (3½ oz/¾ cup) grated gruyère cheese
1 tablespoon finely chopped fresh oregano
1 egg yolk
1 tablespoon sea salt flakes

CHEESE STICKS

1 Line two baking trays with baking paper. Put the flour and butter in a food processor and process in short bursts until the mixture resembles fine breadcrumbs. Add the gruyère and oregano and process for 10 seconds, or until just combined. Add the egg yolk and about 1 tablespoon water, and process until the dough just comes together.

2 Turn the dough out onto a lightly floured surface and gather into a ball. Form 2 teaspoons of dough into a ball, then roll out into a stick about 12 cm (5 inches) long and place on the baking trays. Repeat with the

remaining dough, then cover with plastic wrap and refrigerate for 15–20 minutes. Preheat the oven to moderately hot 200°C (400°F/Gas 6).

3 Lightly brush the sticks with water and sprinkle with the sea salt flakes. Bake for 10 minutes, or until golden. Cool on a wire rack and serve with dips or as part of an antipasto platter.

STORAGE: Cheese sticks will keep for up to 1 week in an airtight container.

Makes: 24

Preparation time: 1 hour 15 minutes

Cooking time: 20 minutes

155 g (5½ oz/1¼ cups) plain
(all-purpose) flour
70 g (2½ oz/¾ cup) soy flour
½ teaspoon garam masala
½ teaspoon paprika
2½ tablespoons olive oil
2½ tablespoons lemon juice

SPICED SOY CRACKERS

1 Place the flours, garam masala, paprika and ½ teaspoon salt in a food processor. Add the oil, lemon juice and 100 ml water and blend until the mixture comes together in a ball. Cover in plastic wrap and place in the refrigerator for 1 hour.

2 Preheat the oven to warm 160°C (315°F/Gas 2–3). Line 3 baking trays with baking paper. Cut the dough into 5 or 6 pieces, then roll each piece into rectangles as thinly as possible — about 2 mm (¹⁄₁₆ inch) thick. Cut each piece into long thin triangles 4 x 10 cm (1½ x 4 inch). Place on the prepared trays.

3 Bake for 20 minutes, or until crisp and lightly coloured. Serve with your favourite dip.

Makes: 16

Preparation time: 25 minutes

Cooking time: 8 minutes

125 g (4½ oz/1 cup) plain (all-purpose)
   flour
2 tablespoons extra virgin olive oil
½ onion, chopped
1 large handful fresh rosemary sprigs
1 large handful flat leaf (Italian) parsley
1 large handful fresh mint leaves
2 teaspoons extra virgin olive oil, extra
sea salt

HERBED PARCHMENT BREAD

1 Preheat the oven to 180°C
(350°F/Gas 4). Process the flour
and oil until the mixture resembles
fine breadcrumbs. Transfer to a
bowl.

2 Process the onion and herbs until
finely chopped. Add 1 tablespoon
of water and the extra oil and
process until well combined. Add
the herb mixture to the flour
mixture and stir with a flat-bladed
knife until it starts to come together.
Add an extra tablespoon of water,
if necessary. Press together and
knead for 30 seconds.

3 Divide into 16 pieces and roll each
piece between two sheets of
baking paper as thinly as possible.

Place on lightly greased baking
trays in a single layer. Lightly
brush with water and sprinkle with
sea salt.

4 Bake each tray of breads for about
8 minutes, or until lightly browned
and crisp to the touch. Transfer to
wire racks to cool.

Makes: 40

Preparation time: 40 minutes

Cooking time: 10 minutes

2 teaspoons oil
185 g (6½ oz/¾ cup) spring onions
   (scallions), thinly sliced
1 garlic clove, crushed
½ teaspoon grated fresh ginger
215 g (7½ oz/1¾ cups) plain (all-
   purpose) flour
1½ tablespoons chopped fresh
   coriander
oil, for shallow-frying

SPRING ONION FLATBREADS

1 Heat the oil in a frying pan, and cook the spring onion, garlic and ginger for 2–3 minutes, or until soft.

2 Combine the flour and 1 teaspoon salt in a bowl. Stir in the spring onion mix and the chopped coriander. Gradually stir in 250 ml (9 fl oz/1 cup) boiling water, stopping when a loose dough forms. Knead the dough for 1½–2 minutes, or until smooth. Cover with plastic wrap and rest for 30 minutes. Break off walnut-sized pieces of dough and roll them out into thin ovals.

3 Fill a large frying pan with 2 cm (¾ inch) oil and heat over medium heat. When shimmering, cook the breads 2–3 at a time for 25–30 seconds each side, or until crisp and golden. Drain on paper towels and serve warm.

Makes: 12 muffins

Preparation time: 25 minutes

Cooking time: 25 minutes

250 g (9 oz/2 cups) self-raising flour, sifted
90 g (3¼ oz/¾ cup) plain (all-purpose) flour, sifted
½ teaspoon baking soda
3 teaspoons ground ginger
1 teaspoon ground cinnamon
1 teaspoon mixed spice
230 g (8 oz/1 cup) firmly packed soft brown sugar
55 g (2 oz/¼ cup) glacé ginger
235 g (8½ oz/⅔ cup) golden syrup
100 g (3½ oz) unsalted butter
250 ml (9 fl oz/1 cup) buttermilk
1 egg, lightly beaten
50 g (1¾ oz) dark chocolate, chopped, melted

GINGER FROSTING
60 g (2¼ oz) unsalted butter, softened
1½ tablespoons golden syrup
125 g (4½ oz/1 cup) icing (confectiner's) sugar
½ teaspoon ground ginger

GINGER

The knobbly rhizome of a tropical plant, ginger is a Southeast Asian native. This spice is available in many forms and has a sharp, sweet taste with a warming effect.

STICKY GINGERBREAD MUFFINS

1 Preheat the oven to 200°C (400°F/Gas 6). Grease 12 standard muffin holes. Put the flours, bicarbonate of soda, ginger, cinnamon and mixed spice into a large bowl and stir in the brown sugar and glacé ginger. Make a well in the centre. Melt the golden syrup and butter in a pan, stirring until well mixed. Cool. Combine the golden syrup mixture, buttermilk and egg in a large bowl, mix together and pour into the well. Fold until just combined — the batter will be lumpy.

2 Divide the mixture among the muffin holes. Bake for 20–25 minutes, or until the muffins come away from the side of the tin. Cool for 5 minutes in the tin, then transfer to a wire rack.

3 To make the ginger frosting, beat the butter, golden syrup, icing sugar and ground ginger together with electric beaters in a bowl until light and fluffy. Spread over the top of the muffins.

4 Spoon the melted chocolate into the corner of a plastic bag. Snip off the corner to create a nozzle. Pipe the chocolate over the icing in crisscrossing lines. Apply even pressure and move at a steady speed to prevent the chocolate from clumping. Allow to set before serving.

Makes: 6 muffins

Preparation time: 30 minutes

Cooking time: 15 minutes

250 g (9 oz/1²/₃ cups) strawberries,
   hulled
125 g (4½ oz/½ cup) caster
   (superfine) sugar
85 g (3 oz/⅓ cup) cream cheese
1 tablespoon strawberry liqueur
175 g (6 oz/1⅓ cups) plain
   (all-purpose) flour
1 tablespoon baking powder
1 tablespoon butter, melted
1 teaspoon finely grated orange zest
1 egg
125 ml (4 fl oz/½ cup) milk
icing (confectioners') sugar, to dust

STRAWBERRY CHEESECAKE MUFFINS

1 Preheat the oven to 180°C (350°F/Gas 4). Lightly grease six 125 ml (½ cup) non-stick giant muffin holes with oil. Set aside six small strawberries.

2 Place half the sugar in a bowl with the cream cheese and mix together well. Place the remaining strawberries in a blender or food processor with the strawberry liqueur and remaining sugar, and blend until smooth. Strain through a fine sieve to remove the strawberry seeds.

3 Sift the flour and baking powder together in a large bowl and stir in the butter, orange zest and ½ teaspoon salt. In a separate bowl, beat the egg and milk together, then add to the dry ingredients and mix well until combined. Do not overmix.

4 Spoon half of the mixture into the base of the muffin holes, then add a strawberry and a teaspoon of the cheese mixture. Top with the remaining muffin mixture and bake for 15 minutes, or until cooked and golden. Remove from the tins and cool slightly. Place a muffin on each serving plate, dust with icing sugar and serve drizzled with the sauce.

STRAWBERRY

This luscious fruit needs little introduction. Native to both Europe and America, the strawberry is grown in temperate regions around the world and is often available year-round. Look out for wild species, too, which can be more flavoursome than the cultivated varieties. The strawberry is unique in that the seeds grow around the outside of the fruit rather than inside it. Versatile and robust, strawberries can be used in everything from smoothies and purées to cakes and preserves. When buying, don't necessarily choose the biggest and brightest; rather, select those that are plump, glossy, unbruised and firm. Store in the refrigerator and only wash just before eating.

Makes: 12 muffins

Preparation time: 20 minutes

Cooking time: 20 minutes

215 g (7½ oz/1¾ cups) self-raising flour
185 g (6½ oz/¾ cup) caster
(superfine) sugar
1 egg
1 egg yolk
170 ml (5½ fl oz/⅔ cup) milk
½ teaspoon natural vanilla extract
90 g (3¼ oz/ oz) unsalted butter,
melted and cooled
200 g (7 oz/⅔ cup) ready-made
lemon curd
2 egg whites
1 teaspoon caster (superfine)
sugar, extra

LEMON MERINGUE MUFFINS

1 Preheat the oven to 200°C (400°F/Gas 6). Grease 12 standard muffin holes. Sift the flour into a large bowl and stir in 60 g (2¼ oz/¼ cup) of the caster sugar. Make a well in the centre. Put a pinch of salt, the egg and egg yolk in a bowl and beat together. Stir in the milk, vanilla and butter. Pour the egg mixture into the well. Fold until just combined — the batter will be lumpy.

2 Divide the muffin mixture among the holes. Bake for 15 minutes — the muffins will only rise a little. (Leave the oven on.) Cool the muffins in the tin for 10 minutes, then loosen with a knife but leave in the tin. Hollow out the centre of each muffin with a melon baller. Fill a piping bag with the lemon curd and fill the centre of each muffin.

3 Whisk the egg whites in a clean, dry bowl until firm peaks form. Add a quarter of the remaining sugar at a time, beating well after each addition until firm peaks form. Put a heaped tablespoon of meringue on top of each muffin and form peaks with the back of a spoon. Sprinkle over a little caster sugar and bake for 5 minutes, or until the meringue is golden and crisp. Cool in the tin for 10 minutes, then carefully transfer to a wire rack. Serve warm or at room temperature.

Makes: 12 muffins

Preparation time: 25 minutes

Cooking time: 25 minutes

155 g (5½ oz/1¼ cups) self-raising flour
150 g (5½ oz/1 cup) wholemeal (whole
    wheat) self-raising flour
¼ teaspoon ground cinnamon
pinch ground cloves
115 g (4 oz/½ cup) firmly packed soft
    brown sugar
185 ml (6 fl oz/¾ cup) milk
2 eggs
125 g (4½ oz) unsalted butter, melted
    and cooled
2 granny smith apples, peeled, cored,
    grated
155 g (5½ oz/1 cup) blueberries

CRUMBLE
5 tablespoons plain (all-purpose) flour
55 g (2 oz/¼ cup) demerara sugar
35 g (1¼ oz/⅓ cup) rolled oats
40 g (1½ oz) unsalted butter, chopped

APPLES
*Delicious raw or cooked, versatile and
amenable to many other flavours, apples
are for many the first choice among fruit.
They have been cultivated for hundreds
of years and exist in many thousands of
varieties. It's easy to forget that these
everyday companions are seasonal, with
most varieties at their peak from autumn
to winter. Good eating apples are sweet
and often only slightly acidic. They are
also perfect for use in pies and tarts as
their high sugar content means they will
hold their shape well.*

APPLE AND BERRY CRUMBLE MUFFINS

1 Preheat the oven to 190°C (375°F/Gas 5). Line 12 regular muffin holes with
   muffin papers. Sift the flours, cinnamon and cloves into a large bowl, add
   the husks and stir in the sugar. Make a well in the centre.

2 Put the milk, eggs and butter in a jug, whisk and pour into the well. Fold
   gently until just combined — the batter should be lumpy. Fold in the fruit.
   Divide among the muffin holes.

3 To make the crumble, put the flour, sugar and oats in a bowl. Rub the
   butter in with your fingertips until most of the lumps are gone. Sprinkle
   2 teaspoons of the crumble over each muffin. Bake for 25 minutes, or until
   golden. Cool for 5 minutes, then transfer to a wire rack.

Makes: 12 muffins

Preparation time: 20 minutes

Cooking time: 20 minutes

375 g (13 oz/3 cups) plain
    (all-purpose) flour
1 tablespoon baking powder
165 g (5¾ oz/¾ cup) firmly packed soft
    brown sugar
125 g (4½ oz) unsalted butter, melted
2 eggs, lightly beaten
250 ml (9 fl oz/1 cup) milk
185 g (6½ oz/1¼ cups) fresh or thawed
    frozen blueberries

BLUEBERRY MUFFINS

1 Preheat the oven to 210°C (415°F/ Gas 6–7). Grease or brush two trays of six 125 ml (½ cup) muffin holes with melted butter or oil. Sift the flour and baking powder into a large bowl. Stir in the sugar and make a well in the centre.

2 Add the combined melted butter, eggs and milk all at once, and fold until just combined. Do not overmix — the batter should look quite lumpy.

3 Fold in the blueberries. Spoon the batter into the prepared tin. Bake for 20 minutes, or until golden brown. Cool on a wire rack.

Makes: 12 muffins

Preparation time: 2 hours

Cooking time: 20 minutes

325 g (1½ oz/1¾ cups) mixed dried fruit (mixed candied citrus peel)
80 ml (2½ fl oz/⅓ cup) rum or brandy
310 g (11 oz/2½ cups) self-raising flour
1 teaspoon mixed (pumpkin pie) spice
1 teaspoon ground cinnamon
½ teaspoon ground nutmeg
155 g (5½ oz/⅔ cup) firmly packed soft brown sugar
125 ml (4 fl oz/½ cup) milk
1 egg, lightly beaten
2 tablespoons apricot jam
½ teaspoon very finely grated lemon zest
½ teaspoon very finely grated orange zest
125 g (4½ oz) unsalted butter, melted and cooled
125 g (4½ oz) soft ready-made icing
icing (confectioners') sugar, to dust
2 tablespoons apricot jam, extra, warmed and sieved
red and green glacé cherries, for decoration

SPICED CHRISTMAS MUFFINS

1 Place the dried fruit and rum in a large bowl and mix together. Cover and marinate, stirring often, for 1–2 hours.

2 Preheat the oven to 200°C (400°F/Gas 6). Line 12 muffin holes with muffin papers. Sift the flour, mixed spice, cinnamon and nutmeg into a large bowl and stir in the brown sugar. Make a well in the centre.

3 Put the milk, egg, apricot jam, lemon and orange zest and melted butter in a large bowl, mix together and pour into the well. Stir in the dried fruit mixture. Fold gently until just combined — the batter should be lumpy.

4 Divide the mixture evenly among the muffin holes. Bake for 20 minutes, or until a skewer inserted in the middle of the muffins comes out clean. Cool in the tins for 5 minutes, then transfer to a wire rack to cool completely.

5 Place the ready-made icing on a work surface dusted with a little icing sugar. Roll out to 2 mm (¹⁄₁₆ inch) thick and, using a 7 cm (2¾ inch) fluted round cutter, cut out 12 rounds. Brush the muffin tops with the extra apricot jam and top each with a round of icing. Decorate with whole or halved red glacé cherries and small 'leaves' of green glacé cherries.

MIXED (PUMPKIN PIE) SPICE
A combination of spices used in sweet cookery, usually in classic recipes for cakes, puddings and biscuits (cookies).

Makes: 16 buns

Preparation time:
2 hours 30 minutes

Cooking time: 20 minutes

1 tablespoon (12 g) instant dried yeast
80 g (2¾ oz/⅓ cup) caster
 (superfine) sugar
625 g (1 lb 6 oz/5 cups) white bread
 (strong) flour
1½ teaspoons mixed (pumpkin pie)
 spice
1 teaspoon ground cinnamon
1 teaspoon ground nutmeg
250 ml (9 fl oz/1 cup) warm milk
100 g (3½ oz) unsalted butter, melted
2 eggs, lightly beaten
200 g (7 oz/1⅓ cups) currants
70 g (2½ oz/⅓ cup) mixed peel

GLAZE
2 tablespoons caster (superfine) sugar

CROSS DOUGH
60 g (2¼ oz/½ cup) plain
 (all-purpose) flour

HOT CROSS BUNS

1 Sprinkle the yeast and a pinch
 of the sugar over 125 ml (4 fl oz/
 ½ cup) warm water in a small
 bowl. Stir to dissolve the sugar,
 then leave in a draught-free place
 for 10 minutes, or until the yeast
 is foamy.

2 Combine the flour, spices and
 ½ teaspoon salt in a bowl and
 set aside.

3 Combine the milk, butter, remaining
 sugar, eggs and 125 g (4½ oz/
 1 cup) of the flour mixture in the
 bowl of an electric mixer with a
 dough hook attachment. Mix for
 1 minute, or until smooth. Add the
 yeast mixture, currants and mixed
 peel and stir to combine. Add the
 flour, 125 g (4½ oz/1 cup) at a

time, stirring to mix well after each
addition. As the dough becomes
sticky and more difficult to mix,
use the lowest speed and knead for
5 minutes. Alternatively, mix the
dough by hand using a wooden
spoon, then turn out onto a lightly
floured work surface and knead for
5 minutes, or until the dough is
smooth and elastic.

4 Grease a large bowl with oil, then
 transfer the dough to the bowl,
 turning the dough to coat in the
 oil. Cover with plastic wrap and
 leave to rise in a draught-free place
 for 1½–2 hours, or until the dough
 has doubled in size.

5 Knock back the dough by punching
 it gently, then turn out onto a
 floured work surface. Divide the
 dough into 16 equal portions. Roll
 each portion into a ball, then place
 on greased baking trays, spacing
 the rolls about 4 cm (1½ inches)

apart. Cover with a damp cloth and
leave for 30 minutes, or until
doubled in size.

6 Preheat the oven to 180°C (350°F/
 Gas 4). To make the glaze, combine
 the sugar with 2 tablespoons water
 in a small saucepan. Bring slowly to
 the boil over high heat, then remove
 from the heat and set aside.

7 To prepare the cross dough, put the
 flour in a small bowl and gradually
 add 60 ml (2 fl oz/¼ cup) water,
 stirring to form a dough. Roll out the
 dough on a floured work surface to a
 2 mm (1/16 inch) thickness. Cut into
 5 mm (¼ inch) wide strips, about 12
 cm (4½ inches) long. Brush the
 strips with water and
 place two strips over each bun
 to form a cross. Bake the buns
 for 15–20 minutes, or until golden
 brown. Brush the hot buns with
 the glaze and transfer to a wire
 rack to cool.

SWEET YOGHURT PLAIT

Makes: 2 loaves

Preparation time:
2 hours 30 minutes

Cooking time: 30 minutes

650 g (1 lb 7 oz/5¼ cups) white
  bread (strong) flour
1 tablespoon ground cinnamon
3 teaspoons (9 g) instant dried yeast
2 eggs, lightly beaten
250 g (9 oz/1 cup) Greek-style yoghurt
125 ml (4 fl oz/½ cup) lukewarm milk
90 g (3¼ oz/¼ cup) honey
60 g (2¼ oz) butter, chopped
100 g (3½ oz/½ cup) chopped
  dried figs

GLAZE
1 egg
2 tablespoons milk

ICING
375 g (13 oz/3 cups) icing
  (confectioners') sugar, sifted
80 ml (2½ fl oz/⅓ cup) lemon juice

1 Combine 600 g (1 lb 5 oz/4¾ cups) of the flour, cinnamon, yeast and 1 teaspoon salt in the bowl of an electric mixer with a dough hook attachment and make a well in the centre. Combine the eggs, yoghurt, milk and honey in a bowl, then pour into the well. With the mixer set to the lowest speed, mix for 3 minutes to combine well. Increase the speed to medium and add the butter and figs and knead for 10 minutes, or until the dough is smooth and elastic; add the remaining flour if the mixture is still sticky. Alternatively, mix the dough by

Add the butter and figs and mix for another 10 minutes.

hand, using a wooden spoon, then turn out onto a lightly floured work surface and knead for 10 minutes, or until smooth and elastic.

2 Grease a large bowl with oil, then transfer the dough to the bowl, turning the dough to coat in the oil. Cover with plastic wrap and leave to rise in a draught-free place for 1½ hours, or until the dough has doubled in size.

3 Knock back the dough by punching it gently, then turn out onto a floured work surface. Cut the dough into six equal portions, then roll each into 30 cm (12 inch) lengths. Plait three lengths of dough together, tucking the ends underneath for a neat finish. Repeat with the remaining dough lengths to make a second loaf.

4 Transfer to a large, lightly greased baking tray. Cover the tray with a damp cloth and leave for 30 minutes, or until the dough has doubled in

size. Meanwhile, preheat the oven to 220°C (425°F/Gas 7).

5 To make the glaze, mix together the egg and milk and brush over the tops of the loaves. Bake for 10 minutes, then reduce the oven to 180°C (350°F/Gas 4) and bake for a further 20 minutes, or until the bread is golden and sounds hollow when tapped on the base. If the loaves start to brown too quickly, cover them with foil. Transfer to a wire rack to cool.

6 To make the icing, combine the icing sugar, lemon juice and 2 tablespoons boiling water in a bowl and, using a fork, stir until smooth. Drizzle over the cooled loaves. Set aside until the icing has set.

Makes: 12 muffins

Preparation time: 20 minutes

Cooking time: 25 minutes

140 g (5 oz/¾ cup) dried apricots,
  roughly chopped
grated zest from 1 orange
125 ml (4 fl oz/½ cup) freshly squeezed
  orange juice
250 g (9 oz/2 cups) self-raising flour
175 g (6 oz/½ cup) honey
30 g (1 oz) unsalted butter, melted
185 ml (6 fl oz/¾ cup) skim milk
1 egg, lightly beaten

LOW-FAT APRICOT AND ORANGE MUFFINS

1 Preheat the oven to 180°C (350°F/Gas 4). Grease a
12-hole standard muffin tin, or line the holes with
paper cases.

2 Combine the apricots, orange zest and juice in a small
saucepan and cook over medium heat until just
warmed through. Remove from the heat and cool.

3 Sift the flour into a large bowl and make a well in the
centre. Combine the honey, butter, milk and egg in a
bowl, stirring to mix well. Pour into the well, then add
the apricot mixture and stir quickly until just combined.
Do not overmix — the batter will still be slightly lumpy.

4 Divide the mixture evenly between the muffin holes.
Bake for 20–25 minutes, or until golden and a skewer
inserted into the centre of a muffin comes out clean.
Cool in the tin for 2 minutes before transferring to a
wire rack.

TIP When making muffins, always sift the flour. This will
aerate the flour and ensure a light muffin.

Makes: 12 muffins

Preparation time: 20 minutes

Cooking time: 25 minutes

70 g (2½ oz/1 cup) unprocessed bran
375 ml (13 fl oz/1½ cups) buttermilk
185 ml (6 fl oz/¾ cup) maple syrup
1 egg, lightly beaten
60 ml (2 fl oz/¼ cup) vegetable oil
1 cooking apple (such as granny smith),
    peeled, cored and chopped
70 g (2½ oz/½ cup) hazelnuts, toasted,
    peeled (see tip, below) and chopped
250 g (9 oz/2 cups) self-raising flour
1 teaspoon ground cinnamon

APPLE, BUTTERMILK, MAPLE SYRUP AND BRAN MUFFINS

1 Preheat the oven to 180°C (350°F/ Gas 4). Grease a 12-hole standard muffin tin, or line the holes with paper cases.

2 Combine the bran and buttermilk in a bowl, stirring to mix well, then set aside for 5 minutes. Add the maple syrup, egg, oil, apple and hazelnuts and stir to combine well. Sift the flour and cinnamon over the mixture, then gently fold in

until just combined. Do not overmix — the batter will still be slightly lumpy.

3 Divide the mixture evenly between the muffin holes. Bake for 20–25 minutes, or until golden and a skewer inserted into the centre of a muffin comes out clean. Cool in the tin for 2 minutes before transferring to a wire rack.

TIP To toast the hazelnuts, put them in a single layer on a large baking tray. Toast either in the oven at 180°C (350°F/Gas 4) or under a preheated grill (broiler) for about 2 minutes (turn them after 1 minute and watch carefully, as nuts burn quickly). Tip into a tea towel (dish towel) and rub the skins off. Not all the skins will come off entirely; don't worry about those that don't.

PASTRY

Makes: 380 g (13½ oz)

Preparation time: 40 minutes

200 g (7 oz/1⅔ cups) plain (all-purpose) flour, sifted

120 g (4¼ oz) chilled unsalted butter, chopped

SHORTCRUST PASTRY

1 If making pastry using a food processor, put the flour, butter and ¼ teaspoon salt in the food processor. Using the pulse button, process until the mixture resembles coarse breadcrumbs.

2 Add 60 ml (2 fl oz/¼ cup) chilled water, adding the water gradually, and pulse just until a dough forms, being careful not to overprocess. If the dough is dry and not coming together, add a little more water, 1 teaspoon at a time. As soon as the mixture comes together, turn out onto a lightly floured work surface and press into a flat, round disc. Cover with plastic wrap and refrigerate for 30 minutes.

3 If making the pastry by hand, sift the flour and salt into a large bowl and add the butter. Using your fingertips, rub the butter into the flour until the mixture resembles coarse breadcrumbs. Make a well in the centre.

4 Pour 60 ml (2 fl oz/¼ cup) chilled water into the well, then stir with a flat-bladed knife to incorporate the water. When the mixture starts to come together in small beads of dough, gently gather the dough together and lift it out onto a lightly floured work surface. Gently press the dough together into a ball, kneading it lightly if necessary until the dough comes together. Press into a flat, round disc, cover with plastic wrap and refrigerate for 30 minutes. The dough is now ready to use. Roll out the dough and proceed as directed in the recipe.

Serves 8–10

Preparation time: 1 hour

Cooking time: 1 hour

300 g (10½ oz) all-purpose potatoes
  (such as pontiacs), unpeeled
8 garlic cloves
2 teaspoons rosemary leaves, chopped
2 tablespoons extra virgin olive oil
80 g (2¾ oz) feta cheese, crumbled
½ teaspoon grated lemon zest
sea salt
2 quantities shortcrust pastry (page 52)
1 egg yolk
1 tablespoon milk

POTATO, FETA AND ROAST GARLIC PASTIES

1 Preheat the oven to 180°C (350°F/ Gas 4). Lightly grease a baking tray.

2 Boil the potatoes in their skins for 15 minutes, or until just cooked. Drain, allow to cool, then peel and cut into 1 cm (½ inch) pieces.

3 Put the garlic, rosemary and 1 tablespoon of the oil onto a piece of foil, then twist the edges together to make a secure package. Place on the baking tray and roast for 30 minutes. Allow to cool, then squeeze the garlic from its skin and roughly chop.

4 Add the garlic to the potato, along with the rosemary and any oil left in the foil package. Add the remaining oil, the feta and lemon zest. Gently toss together to combine well. Season well with freshly ground black pepper and a little sea salt.

5 Divide the pastry in half. Roll out each half to a 3 mm (⅛ inch) thickness, then cut into a total of eight 15 cm (6 inch) rounds. Put 2 tablespoons of filling on one half of a pastry round. Combine the egg yolk and milk in a small bowl and

lightly brush the unfilled half of the pastry with the egg mix. Fold over the pastry to enclose the filling, pressing gently to seal well. Crimp the edge with your fingers, or gently press with the tines of a fork. Repeat with the remaining filling and pastry rounds.

6 Place the pasties onto the tray, brush the tops with the remaining egg mix, then put the tray in the refrigerator for at least 30 minutes. Remove and bake for 30 minutes, or until golden. Allow the pasties to cool a little before serving, as the filling will be steaming hot.

Serves 4

Preparation time: 20 minutes

Cooking time: 40 minutes

450 g (1 lb) packet frozen spinach,
  thawed
1 large sheet ready-rolled shortcrust
  pastry, thawed
3 garlic cloves, finely chopped
150 g (5½ oz) haloumi cheese, grated
120 g (4½ oz) feta cheese, crumbled
1 tablespoon oregano sprigs
2 eggs
60 ml (2 fl oz/¼ cup) cream
lemon wedges, to serve

OREGANO

*A popular herb, especially in the south
of Italy, oregano (origano) is used both
fresh and dried, but is much more
commonly seen dried. It goes well
with tomato sauces and other stronger-
tasting vegetables and is often used
when roasting meats.*

RUSTIC GREEK PIE

1 Preheat the oven to 210°C (415°F/ Gas 6–7). Squeeze the excess liquid from
the spinach. Place the pastry on a baking tray and spread the spinach in the
middle, leaving a 3 cm (1¼ inch) border around the edge. Sprinkle the
garlic over the spinach and pile the haloumi and feta on top. Sprinkle with
oregano and season well. Cut a short slit into each corner of the pastry, then
tuck each side of pastry over to form a border around the filling.

2 Lightly beat the eggs with the cream and carefully pour the egg mixture over
the spinach filling. Bake for 30–40 minutes, or until the pastry is golden and
the filling is set. Serve with the lemon wedges.

Serves 8

Preparation time: 45 minutes

Cooking time: 45 minutes

TART PASTRY
220 g (7¾ oz) plain (all-purpose)
    flour
pinch of salt
150 g (5½ oz) unsalted butter,
    chilled and diced
1 egg yolk

25 g (1 oz) butter
300 g (10½ oz) streaky bacon, diced
250 ml (9 fl oz/1 cup) thick
    (double/heavy) cream
3 eggs
nutmeg grated

QUICHE LORRAINE

This dish has been much bastardized over the decades—the original though, is a triumph of simplicity. Native to Nancy in the region of Lorraine, quiche Lorraine is defined by its tender pastry base and the shallow slick of soft, baked, savoury custard. This, traditionally, is flavoured with bacon, a hint of nutmeg and no cheese whatsoever.

1 To make the tart pastry, sift the flour and salt into a large bowl, add the butter and rub in with your fingertips until the mixture resembles breadcrumbs. Add the egg yolk and a little cold water (about 2–3 teaspoons) and mix with the blade of a palette knife until the dough just starts to come together. Bring the dough together with your hands and shape into a ball. Wrap in plastic wrap and put in the fridge to rest for at least 30 minutes. You can also make the dough in a food processor, using the pulse button.

Run a knife around the edge of the pastry to trim it

Using a jug makes pouring the filling in the pastry case easier.

2 Roll out the pastry into a circle on a lightly floured surface and use to line a flan (tart) tin. Trim the edge and pinch up the pastry edge to make an even border raised slightly above the rim of the tin. Slide onto a baking tray and rest in the fridge for 10 minutes.

3 Preheat the oven to 200°C (400°F/Gas 6). Line a 25 cm (10 inch) fluted loose-based flan (tart) tin with the pastry. Line the pastry shell with a crumpled piece of baking paper and baking beads (use dried beans or rice if you don't have beads). Blind bake the pastry for 10 minutes, remove the paper and beads and bake for a further 3–5 minutes, or until the pastry is just cooked but still very pale. Reduce the oven to 180°C (350°F/Gas 4).

4 Melt the butter in a small frying pan and cook the bacon until golden. Drain on paper towels.

5 Mix together the cream and eggs and season with salt, pepper and nutmeg. Scatter the bacon into the pastry shell and then pour in the egg mixture. Bake for 30 minutes, or until the filling is set. Leave in the tin for 5 minutes before serving.

Serves 6

Preparation time: 40 minutes

Cooking time: 1 hour 10 minutes

1 quantity shortcrust pastry (page 52)
2 tablespoons olive oil
3 onions, peeled and thinly sliced
60 g (2¼ oz) goat's cheese
3 roma (plum) tomatoes, cut into
    5 mm (¼ inch) thick slices
½ teaspoon thyme
6 egg yolks
2 eggs, lightly beaten
250 ml (9 fl oz/1 cup) pouring cream

TOMATO, GOAT'S CHEESE AND CARAMELIZED ONION FLAN

Crumble the goat's cheese over the onions, then arrange the tomato on top.

Pour the egg and cream mixture over the filling.

1 Lightly grease a 25 cm (10 inch) loose-based round flan (tart) tin.

2 Roll out the pastry on a lightly floured work surface until 3 mm (⅛ inch) thick, to fit the base and side of the tin. Roll the pastry around the rolling pin, then lift and ease it into the tin, gently pressing to fit the side. Trim the edges, cover with plastic wrap and refrigerate for 30 minutes. Preheat the oven to 200°C (400°F/Gas 6).

3 Line the pastry shell with a crumpled piece of baking paper and cover the base with baking beads or uncooked rice. Bake the pastry for 20 minutes, then remove the paper and beads and bake for a further 10 minutes, or until the pastry is golden. Remove the pastry

from the oven, then reduce the oven to 160°C (315°F/Gas 2–3).

4 Heat the olive oil in a large, heavy-based frying pan and add the onions. Cover and cook over low heat for 30 minutes, stirring often. The onions should be reduced in volume and golden in colour.

5 Spread the onions evenly over the pastry shell, crumble the goat's cheese over the onions, top with the tomato slices and sprinkle with the thyme. Whisk the egg yolks, eggs and cream in a bowl until smooth, season with salt and pepper, then pour over the tomato filling. Bake for 30–40 minutes, or until the filling has just set. Allow to cool slightly before serving, either warm or at room temperature.

Serves 8

Preparation time: 50 minutes

Cooking time: 1 hour 15 minutes

2 quantities shortcrust pastry (page 52)
1 tablespoon olive oil
100 g (3½ oz) Italian-style pork
    sausage, skin removed
1 garlic clove, chopped
¼ teaspoon chilli flakes

3 eggs, lightly beaten
500 g (1 lb 2 oz) fresh ricotta cheese
50 g (1¾ oz) provolone cheese, grated
30 g (1 oz) parmesan cheese,
    finely grated
80 g (2¾ oz) mozzarella cheese, grated
100 g (3½ oz) prosciutto, thinly sliced
100 g (3½ oz) mortadella, thinly sliced
2 tablespoons finely chopped flat-leaf
    (Italian) parsley
1 egg yolk
1 tablespoon milk

ITALIAN EASTER PIE

1 Preheat the oven to 180°C (350°F/ Gas 4). Lightly grease a 24 cm (9½ inch) round spring-form cake tin.

2 Using two-thirds of the pastry, roll it out on a lightly floured work surface until 3 mm (⅛ inch) thick, to fit the base and side of the tin. Roll the pastry around the rolling pin, then lift and ease it into the tin, gently pressing to fit the side. Cover with plastic wrap and refrigerate for 30 minutes. Roll out the remaining pastry until 3 mm (⅛ inch) thick, to fit the top of the tin. Put the pastry on a large

plate, cover with plastic wrap and chill for 20 minutes.

3 Line the pastry shell with a crumpled piece of baking paper and cover the base with baking beads or uncooked rice. Bake the pastry for 10 minutes, then remove the paper and beads and bake for a further 20 minutes, or until the pastry is golden.

4 Heat the olive oil in a small frying pan over medium heat, add the sausage meat, garlic and chilli flakes and cook for 5 minutes, stirring to break up the meat. Set aside to

cool. Combine the cooled sausage mixture, eggs, ricotta, provolone, parmesan, mozzarella, prosciutto, mortadella and parsley in a bowl. Spoon into the pastry shell.

5 Combine the egg yolk with the milk and lightly brush the mixture over the edge of the pastry. Cover with the pastry round and gently press the edges to seal. Cut a small hole in the centre to allow steam to escape and brush the top with remaining egg mixture. Bake for 45 minutes, or until the pastry is golden. Cool before serving.

Serves 6

Preparation time: 20 minutes

Cooking time: 1 hour

700 g (1 lb 9 oz) butternut pumpkin
   (squash), cut into 2 cm (¾ inch)
   pieces
4 garlic cloves, unpeeled
5 tablespoons olive oil
2 small red onions, halved and sliced
1 tablespoon balsamic vinegar
1 tablespoon soft brown sugar
100 g (3½ oz) good-quality feta cheese,
   broken into small pieces
1 tablespoon chopped rosemary
1 large sheet ready-rolled shortcrust
   pastry

ONIONS

*Cutting an onion releases a compound
that irritates the eyes. The more cut
surfaces that are exposed to air, the
more volatile the compound becomes.
Try one of these steps to overcome the
discomfort:*
— *Soak the onions in water for
   30 minutes before peeling*
— *Peel under an open window
   or exhaust fan*
— *Chill the onions beforehand*
— *Breathe with your mouth open*

PUMPKIN AND FETA PIE

1 Preheat the oven to 200°C (400°F/ Gas 6). Place the pumpkin and garlic
   cloves on a baking tray, drizzle with 2 tablespoons olive oil and bake for
   25–30 minutes, or until the pumpkin is tender. Transfer the pumpkin to
   a large bowl and the garlic to a plate. Leave the pumpkin to cool.

2 Meanwhile, heat 2 tablespoons oil in a pan, add the onion and cook over
   medium heat, stirring occasionally, for 10 minutes. Add the vinegar and
   sugar and cook for 15 minutes, or until the onion is caramelized. Remove
   from the heat and add to the pumpkin. Cool completely.

3 Add the feta and rosemary to the pumpkin. Squeeze out the garlic flesh and
   mix it through the vegetables. Season with salt and ground pepper.

4 Roll out the pastry between two sheets of baking paper to a 35 cm (14 inch)
   circle. Remove the top sheet of paper and place the bottom paper with the
   pastry on a tray. Arrange the pumpkin and feta mixture on top, leaving a
   4 cm (1½ inch) border. Fold over the edges, pleating as you fold, and bake
   for 30 minutes, or until crisp and golden.

Serves 6

Preparation time: 20 minutes

Cooking time: 30 minutes

800 g (1 lb 12 oz) fresh asparagus
20 g (¾ oz) butter
½ teaspoon chopped thyme
1 French shallot, chopped
1 large sheet ready-rolled shortcrust
  pastry
80 ml (2½ fl oz/⅓ cup) cream
2 tablespoons grated parmesan cheese
1 egg
pinch ground nutmeg
1 egg, extra, lightly beaten

ASPARAGUS PIE

1 Trim the asparagus spears to 10 cm (4 inches) and cut thick spears in half lengthways. Heat the butter in a large frying pan over medium heat and add the asparagus, thyme and shallot. Add a tablespoon of water and season with salt and pepper. Cook, stirring, for 3 minutes, or until the asparagus is tender.

2 Preheat the oven to 200°C (400°F/ Gas 6) and grease a 21 cm (8½ inch) fluted, loose-based flan (tart) tin. Roll the pastry out to a 2 mm (⅛ inch) thick circle with a diameter of about 30 cm (12 inches). Line the tin and trim the pastry using kitchen scissors, leaving about 8 cm (3 inches) above the top of the tin. Arrange half the asparagus in one direction across the bottom of the dish. Cover with the remaining asparagus, running in the opposite direction.

3 Combine the cream, parmesan, egg and nutmeg and season. Pour over the asparagus. Fold the pastry over the filling, forming loose pleats. Brush with beaten egg and bake in the centre of the oven for 25 minutes, or until golden.

ASPARAGUS

Asparagus (asparago) is available in green, white and purple varieties. It is best eaten in season and should be prepared with the minimum of fuss. The best way to cook it is by steaming or gentle grilling. It also features in primavera sauces for pasta and risottos. Choose asparagus that has undamaged tips and firm stalks. Unless your asparagus is particularly young and tender, you will need to snap off the tough woody end of the stalk before use.

Serves 6

Preparation time: 50 minutes

Cooking time: 55 minutes

TART PASTRY
220 g (7¾ oz) plain (all-purpose)
    flour
pinch of salt
150 g (5½ oz) unsalted butter,
    chilled and diced
1 egg yolk

500 g (1 lb 2 oz) leek, white part
    only, finely sliced
50 g (1¾ oz) butter
180 g (6½ oz) Maroilles (soft
    cheese), chopped (you can
    also use Livarot or Port-Salut)
1 egg
1 egg yolk
60 ml (2 fl oz) thick (double/heavy)
    cream
1 egg, lightly beaten

FLAMICHE

Leeks are one of those underrated vegetables that generally play a supporting role in stews, stocks, soups and sauces. However, the French have long appreciated the sweet mildness of well-cooked leeks and here they star in this delicious pie, which is true regional fare from Picardy. Serve Flamiche warm or at room temperature and, like all pastry-based goods, do try to eat it on the day it is made (cooked pastry tastes not so good once refrigerated).

1 To make the tart pastry, sift the flour and salt into a large bowl, add the butter and rub in with your fingertips until the mixture resembles breadcrumbs. Add the egg yolk and a little cold water (about 2–3 teaspoons) and mix with the blade of a palette knife until the dough just starts to come together. Bring the dough together with your hands and shape into a ball. Wrap in plastic wrap and put in the fridge to rest for at least 30 minutes. You can also make the dough in a food processor, using the pulse button.

Rub the butter into the flour mixture using your fingertips.

Roll the remaining pastry out to cover the tart then trim the edges.

2 Roll out the pastry into a circle on a lightly floured surface and use to line a flan (tart) tin, as directed in the recipe. Trim the edge and pinch up the pastry edge to make an even border raised slightly above the rim of the tin. Slide onto a baking tray and rest in the fridge for 10 minutes.

3 Preheat the oven to 180°C (350°F/Gas 4) and put a baking tray on the top shelf. Use three-quarters of the pastry to line a 23 cm (9 inch) fluted flan (tart) tin.

4 Cook the leek for 10 minutes in boiling salted water, then drain. Heat the butter in a frying pan, add the leek and cook, stirring, for 5 minutes. Stir in the cheese. Tip into a bowl and add the egg, egg yolk and cream. Season and mix well.

5 Pour the filling into the pastry shell and smooth. Roll out the remaining pastry to cover the pie. Pinch the edges together and trim. Cut a hole in the centre and brush egg over the top. Bake for 35–40 minutes on the baking tray until browned. Leave in the tin for 5 minutes before serving.

RUSSIAN FISH PIES with mushrooms and sour cream

Serves 4

Preparation time: 50 minutes

Cooking time: 1 hour

PASTRY
300 g (10½ oz/2⅓ cups) plain
   (all-purpose) flour
a pinch salt
175 g (6 oz) butter, chilled and cubed
3 large egg yolks
iced water as needed

FILLING
50 g (1¾ oz) long-grain white rice
450 g (1 lb) firm white fish fillet,
   skinned
50 g (1¾ oz) butter
200 g (7 oz) mushrooms, sliced
200 ml (7 fl oz) sour cream
1 tablespoon lemon juice
3 tablespoons flat-leaf (Italian)
   parsley, chopped

Pies known as *pirogi* are very popular in Russia. They are usually large and rectangular, but this recipe makes individual crescent-shaped pies. The fillings may be savoury or sweet. Fish *pirogi* are traditionally made with sturgeon, but any firm white fish may be used.

1 To make the pastry, sieve the flour with a generous pinch of salt into a large bowl. Rub the butter into the flour until fine crumbs form. Lightly beat 2 of the egg yolks and stir into the flour mixture with a little iced water. Mix together, adding more water if necessary to bring the dough together. Wrap the dough in plastic wrap and refrigerate for at least 30 minutes.

2 To make the filling, put the rice in a small saucepan with 100 ml (3½ fl oz) boiling water and a pinch of salt. Bring to the boil, then reduce the heat to medium-low and cook, covered with a tight-fitting lid, for 15 minutes. Add a further 1–2 tablespoons boiling water if the rice begins to dry out. Allow to cool.

3 Chop the fish coarsely. Melt the butter in a large frying pan and when hot, add the mushrooms. Cook for 4–5 minutes, or until soft. Add the fish and cook, stirring occasionally, for 4–5 minutes, or until the fish is opaque. Remove the pan from the heat and stir in the

cooked rice, sour cream, lemon juice and parsley. Season with salt and freshly ground black pepper and set aside until cold. Preheat the oven to 190°C (375°F/Gas 5).

4 Roll the pastry out on a floured work surface to a thickness of 3 mm (⅛ inch). Cut out 8 or 10 circles, each 12 cm (4½ inches) in diameter. Put a tablespoon of filling on each circle, leaving a border around the edges, and fold the pastry in half to form a crescent shape. Press the edges together to seal. Cut two slits in the top of each pie to allow steam to escape. Transfer the pies to a large oiled and floured baking tray.

5 Mix the remaining egg yolk with a teaspoon of water and use to brush the edges of the pastry. Fold the pastry in half, seal the parcel and brush the outside with the egg yolk. Make two small cuts in the top for steam holes. Bake in the preheated oven for 30–35 minutes, or until the pastry is golden.

Makes: 24

Preparation time: 20 minutes

Cooking time: 35 minutes

80 ml (1/3 cup) olive oil
2 onions, finely chopped
2 garlic cloves, chopped
150 g (5 1/2 oz) small button mushrooms,
    roughly chopped
200 g (7 oz) English spinach, chopped
1/2 teaspoon chopped thyme
100 g (3 1/2 oz) feta cheese, crumbled
750 g (1 lb 10 oz) home-made or
    bought shortcrust pastry
milk, to glaze

MINI SPINACH PIES

1 Heat 2 tablespoons of oil in a frying pan over medium heat and cook the onion and garlic for 5 minutes, or until soft and lightly coloured. Add the mushrooms and cook for 4 minutes, or until softened. Transfer to a bowl.

2 Heat 1 tablespoon of oil in the same pan over medium heat, add half the spinach and cook, stirring well, for 2–3 minutes, or until the spinach has softened. Add to the bowl with the onion. Repeat with the remaining oil and spinach. Add the thyme and feta to the bowl and mix. Season with salt and pepper and set aside to cool.

3 Preheat the oven to 200°C (400°F/ Gas 6) and grease two 12-hole round-based patty tins. Roll out half the pastry between two sheets of baking paper and cut out 24 rounds using a 7.5 cm (2 3/4 inch) cutter. Use these to line the patty tins, then divide the spinach mixture among the holes. Roll out the remaining pastry between the baking paper and cut out 24 rounds using a 7 cm (2 3/4 inch) cutter to top the pies. Cover the pies with the lids and press the edges with a fork to seal. Prick the tops once with a fork, brush with milk and bake for 15–20 minutes, or until golden.

Serves 4–6

Preparation time: 1 hour 30 minutes

Cooking time: 2 hours

PASTRY
250 g (9 oz/2 cups) plain
    (all-purpose) flour
125 g (4½ oz) butter, chilled
    and diced
3–4 tablespoons chilled water

FILLING
600 g (1 lb 5 oz) roma (plum)
    tomatoes, peeled, seeded
    and cored
1 large, halved and seeded
    red pepper (capsicum)
1 tablespoon olive oil
1 small onion, finely chopped
2 garlic cloves, crushed
1 oregano sprig
1 tablespoon tomato paste
    (concentrated purée)
1 bay leaf
1 teaspoon dark brown sugar
80 ml (2½ fl oz/⅓ cup) dry
    white wine
125 ml (4 fl oz/½ cup) chicken stock

CUSTARD
1 scant teaspoon saffron threads
350 ml (12 fl oz) cream (whipping)
2 eggs
4 egg yolks

TOMATO, RED PEPPER AND SAFFRON TART

1 To make the pastry, put the flour and butter in a food processor with a large pinch of salt. Process in short bursts, using the pulse button, until the mixture is fine and crumbly. Add most of the water and again, process in short bursts until the mixture just comes together in small balls. Turn the mixture out onto a lightly floured surface and press together to form a clump. Cover with plastic wrap and chill for 30 minutes.

2 Coarsely chop the flesh of the tomatoes. Finely chop half the red pepper. Heat the olive oil in a large frying pan over low heat. Fry the onion, garlic and oregano for 5 minutes. Stir in the tomato, chopped pepper, tomato paste, bay leaf, sugar and wine and cook for 15 minutes. Add the stock and simmer for 15 minutes, or until the sauce is thick and all the liquid has evaporated.

3 To make the custard, soak the saffron in 1 tablespoon hot water for 15 minutes. Put the saffron and water in a small saucepan with the cream and slowly heat to body temperature. Turn off the heat. Beat the eggs and yolks together in a bowl. Add the saffron cream and mix well. Season with salt and pepper, to taste.

4 Preheat the oven to 200°C (400°F/ Gas 6). Grease a 28 x 20 cm (11¼ x 8 inch) rectangular flan (tart) tin. Roll out the pastry on a lightly floured surface to a rectangle large enough to line the base and side of the tin. Fit the pastry into the tin, neatening the edges. Line the pastry with crumpled baking paper, fill with baking beads, dried beans or uncooked rice and bake blind for 18 minutes. Remove the beads and paper and bake for a further 18 minutes. Set aside to cool for 10 minutes. Reduce the oven temperature to 180°C (350°F/Gas 4) and put a baking sheet on the middle shelf.

5 Discard the bay leaf and oregano sprig from the filling. Spread the filling over the base of the pastry shell. Gently pour the custard over the top. Cut the remaining red pepper into 7–8 strips and arrange over the custard in a parallel row from one corner to its diagonal opposite. Put the tart on the baking sheet and bake for 30–40 minutes, or until set and golden.

Makes: 400 g (14 oz)

Preparation time: 40 minutes

200 g (7 oz/1⅔ cups) plain (all-purpose) flour, sifted

85 g (3 oz/⅔ cup) icing (confectioners') sugar, sifted

100 g (3½ oz) chilled unsalted butter, chopped

1 egg yolk

SWEET SHORTCRUST PASTRY

1 If making pastry using a food processor, put the flour, icing (confectioners') sugar, butter and a pinch of salt in the food processor. Using the pulse button, process until the mixture resembles coarse breadcrumbs.

2 Combine the egg yolk with 1 table-spoon chilled water in a small bowl. Add to the flour mixture and, using the pulse button, process until a dough forms, being careful not to overprocess. If the dough is dry and not coming together, add a little more water, 1 teaspoon at a time. Turn out onto a lightly floured work surface and press the dough into a flat, round disc. Cover with plastic wrap and refrigerate for 30 minutes.

3 If making the pastry by hand, sift the flour, icing (confectioners') sugar and a pinch of salt into a large bowl, then add the butter. Using your fingertips, rub the butter into the flour until the mixture resembles coarse bread-crumbs. Make a well in the centre.

4 Combine the egg yolk with 1 table-spoon chilled water in a small bowl. Pour it into the well, then stir with a flat-bladed knife. When the mixture starts to come together in small beads of dough, gently gather the dough together and lift it out onto a lightly floured work surface. Gently press the dough together into a ball, then press into a flat, round disc. Cover with plastic wrap and refrigerate for 30 minutes. The dough is now ready to use. Roll out the dough and proceed as directed in the recipe.

Makes: 12

Preparation time: 50 minutes

Cooking time: 30 minutes

2 quantities sweet shortcrust pastry
 (page 64)
600 g (1 lb 5 oz) peaches, stoned
 and thinly sliced
20 g (3/4 oz) butter, melted
1 tablespoon honey
1 tablespoon caster (superfine) sugar
1/4 teaspoon ground nutmeg
1 egg yolk
1 tablespoon milk
3 tablespoons apricot jam
25 g (1 oz/1/4 cup) flaked almonds,
 toasted

PEACH GALETTES

1 Lightly grease a baking tray or line it with baking paper.

2 Roll out the pastry on a lightly floured work surface to 3 mm (1/8 inch) thick. Cut out twelve 12 cm (41/2 inch) rounds. Gently toss together the peach slices, butter, honey, sugar and nutmeg in a bowl. Divide the peach mixture between the pastry rounds, leaving a 1 cm (1/2 inch) border around the edge. Fold the pastry over the filling, leaving the centre uncovered, pleating the pastry at 1 cm (1/2 inch) intervals to fit. Place the galettes on the tray and refrigerate for 30 minutes. Meanwhile, preheat the oven to 200°C (400°F/Gas 6).

3 Combine the egg yolk and milk in a small bowl to make a glaze. Brush the glaze over the edges of the pastry. Bake for 30 minutes, or until golden.

4 Combine the apricot jam and 1 tablespoon water in a small saucepan and stir over low heat until smooth. Brush the jam mixture over the hot galettes, then sprinkle with almonds. Cool before serving.

Serves 3–6

Preparation time: 40 minutes

Cooking time: 30 minutes

PASTRY
185 g (1½ cups) plain
  (all-prupose) flour
100 g (3½ oz) unsalted butter,
  chilled and cubed
2 teaspoons grated orange zest
1 tablespoon caster (superfine) sugar
2–3 tablespoons iced water

40 g (½ oz/⅓ cup) crushed amaretti
  biscuits or almond bread
60 g (2¼ oz/½ cup) plain
  (all-prupose) flour
1 teaspoon ground cinnamon
90 g (3¼ oz/⅓ cup) caster (superfine)
  sugar
500 g (1 lb 2 oz/3¼ cups) fresh
  blueberries
milk, for brushing
2 tablespoons blueberry jam
icing (confectioners') sugar, to dust

FREEFORM BLUEBERRY PIE

1 Sift the flour into a large bowl and rub in the butter with your fingertips until the mixture resembles breadcrumbs. Stir in the orange zest and sugar. Make a well, add almost all the water and mix with a flat-bladed knife, using a cutting action, until the mixture comes together in beads. Add a little more water if necessary to bring the dough together. Gather together and lift out onto a lightly floured surface. Press together into a ball and flatten it slightly into a disc. Cover in plastic wrap and refrigerate for 20 minutes.

2 Preheat the oven to 200°C (400°F/Gas 6). Combine the crushed biscuits, flour, cinnamon and 1½ tablespoons of the sugar. Roll the pastry out to a 36 cm (14¼ inch) circle and sprinkle with the biscuit mixture, leaving a 4 cm (1½ inch) border. Arrange the blueberries over the crushed biscuits, then bring up the edges to form a freeform crust.

3 Brush the sides of the pie with the milk. Sprinkle with the remaining sugar and bake for 30 minutes, or until the sides are crisp and brown.

4 Warm the jam in a saucepan over low heat and brush over the berries. Cool to room temperature, then dust the pastry crust with sifted icing (confectioners') sugar.

Serves 6

Preparation time: 50 minutes

Cooking time: 50 minutes

PASTRY

250 g (9 oz/2 cups) plain (all-purpose)
   flour
30 g (1oz) unsalted butter, chilled and
   cubed
70 g (2½ oz) white vegetable
   shortening
2 tablespoons icing
   (confectioners') sugar
160 ml (5¼ fl oz/⅔ cup) iced water

1.5 kg (3 lb 5 oz) rhubarb, trimmed and
   cut into 2 cm (3¼ inch) pieces
250 g (1 cup) caster (superfine) sugar
½ teaspoon ground cinnamon
2½ tablespoons cornflour (cornstarch)
   mixed with 60 ml (2 fl oz) ¼ cup) water
30 g (1 oz) unsalted butter, cubed
1 egg, lightly beaten
icing (confectioners') sugar, to dust

RHUBARB PIE

1 Grease a 25 x 20 x 4 cm (10 x 8 x 1½ inch) ceramic pie dish. Sift the flour
and ½ teaspoon salt into a bowl and rub in the butter and vegetable
shortening until the mixture looks like breadcrumbs. Stir in the icing sugar.
Make a well, add most of the water and mix with a flat-bladed knife, using a
cutting action, until it comes together in beads. Add more water if needed.
Gather the dough together and put on a floured surface. Press into a ball,
flatten a little and cover in plastic wrap. Refrigerate for 30 minutes.

2 Put the rhubarb, sugar, cinnamon and 2 tablespoons water in a pan and stir
over low heat until the sugar dissolves. Simmer, covered, for 5–8 minutes,
or until the rhubarb is tender. Add the cornflour (cornstarch) (cornstarch)
and water mixture. Bring to the boil, stirring until thickened. Cool. Preheat
the oven to 180°C (350°F/ Gas 4) and heat a baking tray.

3 Roll out two-thirds of the dough to a 30 cm (12 inch) circle and put into the
pie dish. Spoon in rhubarb and dot with butter. Roll out the extra pastry for
a lid. Brush the pie rim with egg and press the top in place. Trim the edges
and make a slit in the top. Decorate with pastry scraps and brush with egg.
Bake for 35 minutes, or until golden. Dust with icing (confectioners') sugar.

*Cut the trimmed rhubarb stalks
into short lengths.*

Serves 6

Preparation time: 1 hour 30 minutes

Cooking time: 55 minutes

SWEET PASTRY makes 700 g (1 lb 9 oz)
350 g (12 oz) plain (all-purpose) flour
small pinch of salt
150 g (5½ oz) unsalted butter
100 g (3½ oz) icing (confectioners')
  sugar
2 eggs, beaten

FILLING
4 eggs
2 egg yolks
275 g (9¾ oz) caster (superfine) sugar
190 ml (6½ fl oz) double (thick/heavy)
  cream
275 ml (9½ fl oz) lemon juice
zest of 3 lemons, finely grated

TARTE AU CITRON

1 Sift the flour and salt onto a work surface and make a well in the centre. Put the butter into the well and work, using a pecking action with your fingertips and thumb, until it is very soft. Add the sugar to the butter and mix together. Add the eggs to the butter and mix together.

2 Gradually incorporate the flour, flicking it onto the mixture and then chopping through it until you have a rough dough. Bring together with your hands and then knead a few times to make a smooth dough. Roll into a ball, wrap in plastic wrap and put in the fridge for at least 1 hour. Roll out the pastry into a circle on a lightly floured surface and use to line a 23cm (9 inch) flan (tart) tin. Trim the edge and pinch up the pastry edge to make an even border raised slightly above the rim of the tin. Slide onto a baking tray and rest in the fridge for 10 minutes.

3 Preheat the oven to 190°C (375°F/ Gas 5). To make the filling, whisk together the eggs, egg yolks and sugar. Add the cream, whisking all the time, and then the lemon juice and zest.

4 Line the pastry shell with a crumpled piece of baking paper and baking beads or uncooked rice if you don't have beads). Blind bake the pastry for 10 minutes, remove the paper and beads and bake for a further 3–5 minutes, or until the pastry is just cooked but still very pale. Remove from the oven and reduce the temperature to 150°C (300°F/Gas 2).

5 Put the tin on a baking tray and carefully pour the filling into the pastry case. Return to the oven for 35–40 minutes, or until the filling has set. Leave to cool completely before serving.

Serves 6

Preparation time: 25 minutes

Cooking time: 1 hour 5 minutes

PASTRY
150 g (5½ oz/1¼ cups) plain
  (all-purpose) flour
35 g (1¼ oz/⅓ cup) ground almonds
1 tablespoon caster (superfine) sugar
85 g (3 oz) unsalted butter, chilled
  and cubed
1 egg yolk, at room temperature

FILLING
300 g (10½ oz/2½ cups) mixed
  berries, such as raspberries,
  strawberries and blueberries
1 egg, at room temperature
60 g (2¼ oz/¼ cup) caster
  (superfine) sugar
1 tablespoon lemon juice
150 g (5½ oz/scant ⅔ cup)
  smooth ricotta cheese

icing (confectioners') sugar for
  dusting

RICOTTA AND BERRY TARTLETS

Ricotta is a fresh cheese that proves surprisingly adaptable in the kitchen.
In sweet dishes it goes well with chocolate, dried fruit, nuts and berries.
It makes a nice alternative to a frangipane-style filling in these tartlets and
also protects the fruit during cooking, ensuring a moist filling.

1 To make the pastry, put the flour, ground almonds, sugar, butter and a pinch
   of salt in a food processor. Process until the mixture resembles breadcrumbs.
   Add the egg yolk and 1 tablespoon of cold water. Process until the mixture
   just forms a ball, adding a little extra water if the pastry is too dry. Turn the
   pastry out onto a work surface. Flatten it into a disc, cover with plastic wrap
   and refrigerate for 30 minutes.

2 Lightly grease six 9 x 2 cm (3½ x ¾ inch) deep tartlet tins. Roll
   out the pastry on a lightly floured surface to a thickness of 3 mm (⅛ inch).
   Cut out six 13 cm (5 inch) circles and place in the tins. Prick the base
   of the pastry with a fork and refrigerate for 10 minutes. Preheat the oven
   to 200°C (400°F/Gas 6).

3 To make the filling, hull any strawberries and chop any larger berries. Put
   the egg, caster (superfine) sugar and lemon juice in a heatproof bowl and
   place over
   a saucepan of simmering water, making sure the base of the bowl doesn't
   touch the water. Whisk with an electric whisk for 5–6 minutes, or until light
   and creamy. Stir in the ricotta. Divide the berries among the tartlet cases and
   spoon over the ricotta mixture. Bake for 20–22 minutes, or until the edges
   of the pastry are golden brown. Serve warm or at room temperature, dusted

*Make sure the base of the bowl
doesn't touch the water.*

Serves 8

Preparation time: 30 minutes

Cooking time: 1 hour

375 g (13 oz) ready-made or home-made sweet shortcrust pastry (see page 64)
200 g (7 oz/1¼ cups) dried apricots
100 ml (3½ fl oz) brandy or grappa
icing (confectioners') sugar, to dust
crème fraîche or cream, to serve

ALMOND FILLING
180 g (6 oz) unsalted butter, softened
180 g (6 oz/¾ cup) caster (superfine) sugar
180 g (6 oz/2 cups) flaked blanched almonds
2 eggs
1 teaspoon natural vanilla extract
1 heaped teaspoon plain (all-purpose) flour

When the tart cooks, the filling will puff up and cover the apricots, so make sure you don't push the apricots too far into the mixture if you want the pattern to stand out.

APRICOT AND ALMOND TART

1 Grease a 25 cm (10 inch) loose-bottomed metal flan (tart) tin. Dust work surface with flour and roll out pastry to fit the tin. Line the tin and trim the edges. Refrigerate for 15 minutes. Preheat the oven to 200°C (400°F/Gas 6).

2 Line the pastry shell with crumpled baking paper and baking beads or uncooked rice and bake for 12 minutes, then remove the paper and beads — if the pastry still looks wet, dry it out in the oven for 5 minutes. Cool for a few minutes. Reduce the oven to 180°C (350°F/Gas 4).

3 Put the dried apricots and brandy in a saucepan and cook over low heat for about 5 minutes, or until most of the liquid has evaporated. Leave to cool.

4 To make the almond filling, use a food processor to cream the butter and sugar until light and pale. Add the almonds, eggs, vanilla and flour and briefly blend. If you overbeat it, the mixture may separate. Spoon the filling into the pastry shell, then place the apricots in the shell, arranging them in two circles, one inside the other. Bake for 30–40 minutes, or until the filling is set. Cool and sprinkle with icing (confectioners') sugar just before serving. Serve with crème fraîche or cream.

Serves 6

Preparation time: 30 minutes

Cooking time: 40 minutes

500 g (1 lb 2 oz) ready-made or home-
    made sweet shortcrust pastry (see
    page 64)
500 g (1 lb 2 oz/4 cups) blackberries
160 g (5½ oz/⅔ cup) caster
    (superfine) sugar
2 tablespoons cornflour (cornstarch)
milk, to brush
1 egg, lightly beaten
caster (superfine) sugar, extra, to
    sprinkle

BLACKBERRY PIE

1 Preheat the oven to 200°C (400°F/Gas 6). Grease a
26 cm x 20.5 cm x 4.5 cm (10½ x 8 x 1¾ inch)
ceramic pie dish. Roll out two-thirds of the pastry
between two sheets of baking paper until large enough
to line the base and side of the pie dish. Remove the
top paper, invert the pastry into the dish and press into
place, leaving the excess overhanging the edges.

2 Toss the blackberries (if frozen, thaw and drain well),
sugar and cornflour (cornstarch) together in a bowl until
well mixed, then transfer to the pie dish. Roll out the

remaining pastry between two sheets of baking paper
until large enough to cover the pie. Moisten the rim of
the pie base with milk and press the pastry lid firmly into
place. Trim and crimp the edges. Brush with egg and
sprinkle with the extra sugar. Pierce the top of the pie
with a knife.

3 Bake on the bottom shelf of the oven for 10 minutes.
Reduce the oven to 180°C (350°F/Gas 4) and move the
pie to the centre shelf. Bake for another 30 minutes, or
until golden on top. Cool before serving with cream or

Serves 8

Preparation time: 50 minutes
+ 2 hours refrigeration

Cooking time: 1 hour 10 minutes

155 g (5½ oz/1¼ cups) plain
   (all-purpose) flour
90 g (3¼ oz) unsalted butter, chilled
   and chopped
60 g (3½ oz/¼ cup) caster
   (superfine) sugar
2 egg yolks

FILLING

165 g (5¾ oz) unsalted butter, softened
160 g (5½ oz/⅔ cup) caster (superfine)
   sugar
3 eggs
230 g (8½ oz/2¼ cups) ground
   almonds
1½ tablespoons plain (all-purpose) flour
2 ripe pears, peeled, halved lengthways
   with cores removed

PEARS

*Pears reached their zenith of popularity
in seventeenth-century France where
they were considered the most regal
of fruits. King Louis XIV had much to
do with this; he adored pears and many
a noble found favour at his court by
developing some new variety for his
enjoyment. Indeed, the French are
responsible for some of the varieties we
know and most love today. The perfect
pear for this recipe is the Beurre Bosc.*

PEAR AND ALMOND FLAN

1 Grease a shallow 24 cm (9½ inch) round loose-based flan (tart) tin. Put the
flour, butter and caster (superfine) sugar in a food processor and process
until the mixture resembles breadcrumbs. Add the egg yolks and about 1
tablespoon of water until the mixture just comes together. Turn out onto a
floured surface and gather into a ball. Cover in plastic wrap and refrigerate
for 30 minutes. Preheat the oven to 180°C (350°F/Gas 4).

2 Roll the pastry between baking paper dusted with flour and line the tin with
the pastry. Trim off any excess. Prick the base a few times. Line the pastry
shell with crumpled baking paper and baking beads or uncooked rice and
blind bake the pastry for 10 minutes. Remove the paper and beads and bake
for a further 10 minutes.

3 To make the filling, mix the butter and sugar with electric beaters for
30 seconds only. Add the eggs one at a time, beating after each addition.
Fold in the ground almonds and flour and spread the filling over the cooled
base. Cut the pears crossways into 3 mm (⅛ inch) slices, separate them
slightly, then place on top of the tart to form a cross. Bake for 50 minutes, or
until the filling has set (the middle **may still** be a little soft). Cool in the tin,
then refrigerate for 2 hours before **serving.**

Serves 4–6

Preparation time: 35 minutes

Cooking time: 50 minutes

375 g (13 oz) ready-made or home-made sweet shortcrust pastry (see page 64)

FILLING
30 g (1 oz/¼ cup) plain (all-purpose) flour
30 g (1 oz/¼ cup) cornflour (cornstarch)
250 g (9 oz/1 cup) caster (superfine) sugar
185 ml (6 fl oz/¾ cup) lemon juice
1 tablespoon grated lemon zest
50 g (1¾ oz) unsalted butter, chopped
6 egg yolks

MERINGUE
6 egg whites
1 pinch cream of tartar
340 g (1½ cups) caster sugar

LEMON MERINGUE PIE

1 Grease a 25 cm x 18 cm x 3 cm (10 x 7 x 1¼ inch) pie dish. Roll the pastry out between two sheets of baking paper into a 30 cm circle. Invert the pastry into the plate. Trim the edges. Re-roll the pastry trimmings and cut into three 10 x 2 cm (4 x ¾ inch) strips. Brush the pie rim with water, place the pastry strips around the top and use your fingers to make a decorative edge. Prick over the base with a fork. Cover and refrigerate for 20 minutes. Preheat the oven to 180°C (350°F/Gas 4).

2 To make the meringue, beat egg whites and cream of tartar in a clean, dry bowl with electric beaters until soft peaks form. Gradually pour in caster sugar, beating until the meringue is thick and glossy.

3 Blind bake the pastry for 15 minutes. Remove the beads and bake for 15–20 minutes. Cool. Increase the oven to 200°C (400°F/Gas 6). Put the flours, sugar, lemon juice and zest in a pan. Gradually add 315 ml (10¾ fl oz/1¼ cups) water and whisk over medium heat until smooth. Cook, stirring, for 2 minutes, or until thick. Remove from the heat and vigorously whisk in the butter and egg yolks. Return to low heat and stir constantly, for 2 minutes, or until very thick.

4 Spread the lemon filling into the pastry base, then cover with the meringue, piling high in the centre and making peaks with a knife. Bake for 8–10 minutes, or until lightly browned.

Serves 6–8

Preparation time: 1 hour

Cooking time: 1 hour 20 minutes

PASTRY

210 g (7½ oz/1⅔ cups) plain
(all-purpose) flour
60 g (2¼ oz/¼ cup) caster
(superfine) sugar
25 g (1 oz/¼ cup) ground almonds
150 g (5½ oz) unsalted butter,
chilled and cubed
2 egg yolks, at room temperature
1–2 tablespoons iced water

FILLING

185 g (6½ oz) unsalted butter,
softened
185 g (6½ oz/heaped ¾ cup)
caster (superfine) sugar
2 eggs, at room temperature
70 g (2½ oz/⅔ cup) ground almonds
60 g (2¼ oz/½ cup) plain
(all-purpose) flour
90 g (3¼ oz/1 cup) desiccated
coconut
2 tablespoons coconut cream
1 tablespoon coconut liqueur
1 mango
30 g (1 oz/½ cup) flaked coconut
vanilla ice cream or whipped cream
to serve

COCONUT, MANGO AND ALMOND TART

When you have a lovely, ripe mango to hand it's hard not to just eat it right there and then and hang the dessert. But mango and almonds in buttery pastry is a classic combination, and worth the temporary effort of self-restraint. The almond pastry should be chilled well before using.

1 To make the pastry, put the flour, sugar, ground almonds and butter in a food processor. Process until the mixture resembles fine crumbs. Add the egg yolks and process until smooth. Add the water, ½ teaspoon at a time, until the dough clumps together in a ball. Flatten the dough to a rough rectangle, cover with plastic wrap and refrigerate for 30 minutes.

2 Preheat the oven to 190°C (375°F/Gas 5). Grease a 19 x 27 cm (7½ x 10¾ inch) loose-based flan (tart) tin.

3 To make the filling, cream the butter and sugar with electric beaters for about 3 minutes. Add the eggs, one at a time, beating well after each addition. Fold in the ground almonds, flour and desiccated coconut. Lightly stir in the coconut cream and coconut liqueur.

4 Roll out the pastry on a sheet of baking paper to cover the base and side of the tin. Place the pastry in the tin and trim any excess. Line the pastry with a sheet of crumpled baking paper and pour in some baking beads or uncooked rice. Bake for 10 minutes, remove the paper and beads and bake for another 5 minutes. Reduce the oven to 170°C (325°F/Gas 3).

5 Cut the cheeks from the mango, peel them and cut each into 3 mm (⅛ inch) thick slices. Spread the filling in the pastry case and arrange the mango slices in two rows down the length of the filling. Scatter the flaked coconut over the top and press it into the exposed filling with your fingertips, giving an uneven surface. Bake for 30 minutes, or until the coconut begins to brown, then cover loosely with foil. Bake for another 35 minutes, or until the filling is set and the top is golden brown. Serve warm with vanilla ice cream or serve cold with lightly whipped cream.

Arrange the mango slices in two rows over the filling.

BERRY AND VANILLA BRÛLÉE TART

Serves 6–8

Preparation time: 50 minutes

Cooking time: 1 hour 15 minutes

SWEET SHORTCRUST PASTRY
250 g (9 oz/2 cups) plain
    (all-purpose) flour
125 g (4½ oz) unsalted butter,
    cut into cubes
2 tablespoons caster (superfine) sugar

BERRY CUSTARD FILLING
2 egg yolks
250 ml (9 fl oz/1 cup) cream
    (whipping)
125 ml (4 fl oz/½ cup) milk
1 vanilla bean, split lengthways
55 g (2 oz/¼ cup) caster (superfine)
    sugar
60 g (2¼ oz/½ cup) fresh raspberries
80 g (2¾ oz/½ cup) fresh blueberries
55 g (2 oz/¼ cup) caster (superfine)
    sugar, for sprinkling

1 To make the sweet shortcrust
pastry, put the flour and butter in
a food processor. Process in short
spurts until the mixture resembles
fine breadcrumbs. Briefly pulse in
the sugar. With the motor running,
add 2 tablespoons of iced water,
adding a little more water, if
necessary, until the dough comes
roughly together. Turn out and
press into a ball. Wrap in plastic
wrap and refrigerate for at least
30 minutes.

2 Preheat the oven to 200°C (400°F/
Gas 6). Heat a baking tray. Roll the
pastry between two sheets of baking
paper. Fit into a 23 cm (9 inch)
loose-based flan (tart) tin. Line the
pastry with a sheet of baking paper
and weigh down with rice and/or
baking beads. Bake for 15 minutes
on the preheated hot tray until
lightly golden. Remove the paper

and rice and/or baking beads and
cook for a further 10 minutes.
Reduce the oven temperature
to 170°C (325°F/Gas 3). Cool the
pastry case.

3 To make the brûlée filling, lightly
beat together the egg yolks and
cream in a bowl. Put the milk,
vanilla bean and sugar in a saucepan and stir over low heat until the
sugar has dissolved. Increase the
heat and bring to the boil. Remove
the vanilla bean and scrape the
seeds with a knife. Whisk into the
hot milk, together with the
combined eggs and cream.

4 Scatter the berries over the base
of the pastry. Carefully pour the
custard over the berries. Place on a
hot baking tray and bake for 35–40
minutes, or until the custard has
set. Cool then refrigerate to firm.

5 Preheat the grill (broiler). Sprinkle
the pie evenly with the sugar. Place
under the hot grill for 7–8 minutes,
or until the sugar has melted and
caramelized. Cool and cut into
wedges to serve.

Scatter the berries over the pastry base.

Serves 8

Preparation time: 1 hour

Cooking time: 55 minutes

PASTRY

250 g (9 oz/2 cups) self-raising flour

85 g (3 oz/⅔ cup) cornflour (cornstarch)

180 g (6 oz) unsalted butter, chilled
    and cubed

90 g (3¼ oz/⅓ cup) caster (superfine)
    sugar

1 egg, lightly beaten

40 g (1½ oz) unsalted butter

6 green apples, peeled, cored
    and thinly sliced

1 tablespoon lemon juice

140 g (5 oz/¾ cup) soft brown sugar

1 teaspoon ground nutmeg

2 tablespoons plain (all-purpose) flour
    mixed with 60 ml (2 fl oz/¼ cup)
    water

25 g (1 oz/¼ cup) ground almonds

milk, to brush

sugar, to sprinkle

OLD-FASHIONED APPLE PIE

1 Lightly grease a 20 cm (8 inch) metal pie dish. Sift the flours into a large bowl and rub in the butter with your fingers until the mixture resembles fine breadcrumbs. Stir in the sugar and a pinch of salt. Make a well, add the egg and mix with a knife, using a cutting action, until the mixture comes together in beads. Put the dough on a floured surface and press into a smooth disc, cover with plastic wrap and refrigerate for 20 minutes.

2 Use two-thirds of the dough to line the base and side of the dish. Roll out the remaining dough to make a lid. Cover and refrigerate for 20 minutes. Preheat the oven to 200°C (400°F/Gas 6) and heat a baking tray.

3 Melt the butter in a large frying pan, add the apple and toss. Stir in the lemon juice, sugar and nutmeg and cook for 10 minutes, or until tender. Add the flour and water mixture, then the almonds. Bring to the boil and cook, stirring, for 2–3 minutes. Pour into a bowl and cool. Put the apple in the pastry case. Cover with the pastry lid and press lightly onto the rim. Trim the edges and pinch together to seal. Prick over the top, brush with milk and sprinkle with sugar. Bake on the hot tray for 40 minutes, or until golden.

Serves 6

Preparation time: 1 hour 5 minutes

Cooking time: 1 hour 5 minutes

PASTRY

155 g (5½ oz/1¼ cups) plain
   (all-purpose) flour
2 tablespoons unsweetened
   cocoa powder
2 tablespoons soft brown sugar
100 g (3½ oz) unsalted butter, chilled
   and cubed
2–3 tablespoons iced water

200 g (7 oz/2 cups) pecan nuts, roughly
   chopped
100 g (3½ oz) dark chocolate, chopped
95 g (3¼ oz/½ cup) soft brown sugar
170 ml (5½ fl oz/⅔ cup) light or dark
   corn syrup
3 eggs, lightly beaten
2 teaspoons natural vanilla extract

CHOCOLATE FUDGE PECAN PIE

1 Grease a 23 x 18 x 3 cm (9 x 7 x 1¼ inch) pie dish. Sift the flour, cocoa and sugar into a bowl and rub in the butter with your fingertips until the mixture resembles fine breadcrumbs. Make a well, add almost all the water and mix with a knife, adding more water if necessary.

2 Gather the dough together and lift onto a sheet of baking paper. Press the dough into a disc and refrigerate for 20 minutes. Roll out the pastry between two sheets of baking paper to fit the dish. Line the dish and trim the edges. Refrigerate for 20 minutes.

3 Preheat the oven to 180°C (350°F/Gas 4). Cover the pastry with crumpled baking paper and fill with baking beads or uncooked rice. Bake for 15 minutes, then remove the paper and beads and bake for 15–20 minutes, or until the base is dry. Cool completely.

4 Place the pie dish on a flat baking tray to catch any drips. Spread the pecans and chocolate over the pastry base. Combine the sugar, corn syrup, eggs and vanilla in a bowl and whisk together with a fork. Pour into the pastry shell, and bake for 45 minutes (the filling will still be a bit wobbly, but will set on cooling). Cool before cutting to serve.

Serves 8–10

Preparation time: 50 minutes

Cooking time: 1 hour 25 minutes

PASTRY

185 g (6½ oz/1½ cups) plain
  (all-purpose) flour
125 g (4½ oz) unsalted butter,
  chilled and cubed
3 teaspoons sugar
1 teaspoon finely grated orange zest
1 egg yolk

700 g (1 lb 9 oz) jap (kent) pumpkin
  (squash), peeled, seeded and cubed
80 ml (2½ fl oz/⅓ cup) pouring cream
1 teaspoon ground cinnamon
½ teaspoon ground ginger
½ teaspoon mixed (pumpkin pie) spice
1–2 tablespoons maple syrup
2 tablespoons soft brown sugar
2 eggs
thick (double/heavy) cream, to serve
mixed (pumpkin pie) spice, to serve

SWEET PUMPKIN PIE

1 To make the pastry, put the flour, butter, sugar and orange zest in a small processor fitted with the plastic blade. Whizz in 5-second bursts until the mixture resembles breadcrumbs. Add the egg yolk and 2 tablespoons of cold water and process until the dough comes together into a ball. Add more water if needed, 1 teaspoon at a time. Remove from the processor, shape into a disc and cover with plastic wrap. Chill for 30 minutes.

2 Put the pumpkin in a saucepan and cover with water. Bring to the boil, then simmer for 15–20 minutes, or until tender. Drain thoroughly and set aside to cool. You will need 400 g (14 oz/2 cups) of cooked pumpkin. Put the pumpkin in the cleaned processor or a blender and add the cream, cinnamon, ginger, mixed spice, maple syrup, sugar and eggs. Whizz for 30–40 seconds, or until finely puréed.

3 Preheat the oven to 200°C (400°F/ Gas 6). Grease a 23 cm (9 inch) loose-based flan (tart) tin. Roll out the pastry between two sheets of baking paper to a circle large enough to fit the prepared tin. Use the pastry to line the tin. Line the pastry with a piece of crumpled baking paper and pour in some baking beads or uncooked rice. Bake for 10 minutes, then remove the paper and beads and return to the oven for another 10 minutes, or until golden. Set aside to cool for 5 minutes. Reduce the oven to 180°C (350°F/Gas 4) and place a baking tray on the centre rack.

4 Pour the filling into the pastry shell. Put the pie on the baking tray in the oven and bake for 40–45 minutes, or until set. Serve warm or at room temperature, with thick (double/heavy) cream, sprinkled with mixed spice.

Serves 6–8

Preparation time: 55 minutes

Cooking time: 1 hour 10 minutes

PASTRY
100 g (3½ oz) unsalted butter
55 g (2 oz/¼ cup) caster (superfine)
   sugar
200 g (7 oz/1⅔ cups) plain
   (all-purpose) flour
1 egg, lightly beaten

FILLING
100 ml (3½ fl oz) milk
125 ml (4 fl oz/½ cup) pouring cream
1 teaspoon natural vanilla extract
2 x 5 cm (¾ x 2 inch) piece lemon
   zest, white pith removed
6 egg yolks
55 g (2 oz/¼ cup) caster (superfine)
   sugar
2 teaspoons plain (all-purpose) flour
300 g (10½ oz) rhubarb, cut into
   2 cm (¾ inch) lengths
250 g (9 oz/1⅔ cups) small
   strawberries, hulled

STRAWBERRY AND RHUBARB TART

1 To make the pastry, put the butter and sugar in a small processor fitted with the metal blade. Whizz for 30 seconds, or until combined. Add the flour and a pinch of salt and whizz until just combined. Add the egg and whizz for 10 seconds. With the motor running, add 1 teaspoon of cold water at a time until the dough clumps together. Turn out onto a floured surface and knead until smooth. Form into a ball, flatten slightly, cover with plastic wrap and chill for 30 minutes.

2 Preheat the oven to 200°C (400°F/ Gas 6). Grease a 30 cm (12 inch) loose-based flan (tart) tin. Roll out the pastry between two sheets of baking paper until it is 4 mm (⅛ inch) thick and use it to line the prepared tin. Trim the excess pastry, leaving 5 mm (¼ inch) above the tin. Prick the base with a fork, line with a piece of crumpled baking paper and pour in some baking beads or uncooked rice. Bake for 15 minutes, then remove the paper and beads and return to the oven for another 8 minutes, or until lightly golden. Reduce the oven to 180°C (350°F/Gas 4). Place a baking tray on the centre rack.

3 To make the filling, put the milk, cream, vanilla and lemon zest in a heavy-based saucepan. Gently heat over low heat for 8 minutes, or until just below boiling point. Remove and set aside to infuse for 10 minutes. Discard the lemon zest.

4 Put the egg yolks, sugar and flour in the cleaned processor. With the motor running, gradually add the infused milk and whizz until the custard is smooth. Pour into the prepared pastry case and arrange the rhubarb and strawberries over the top.

5 Put the tart on the baking tray in the oven and bake for 35–40 minutes, or until set. Check the tart after 20 minutes and place a sheet of foil over the top if it is browning too quickly. Serve warm or at room temperature.

Add 1 teaspoon of cold water at a time and whizz until the dough clumps together.

Prick the base of the pastry with a fork before baking.

Serves 4

Preparation time: 20 minutes

Cooking time: 30 minutes

CRUST

200 g (7 oz/2 cups) golden walnuts
3 teaspoons plain (all-purpose) flour
2 tablespoons raw or golden caster
    (superfine) sugar
40 g (1½ oz) butter, melted

FILLING

300 g (10½ oz/1¼ cups) ricotta
    cheese
125 g (4½ oz/½ cup) raw or golden
    caster (superfine) sugar
120 g (4¼ oz/½ cup) crème fraîche
2 eggs
30 g (1 oz/¼ cup) plain (all-purpose)
    flour
1 teaspoon natural vanilla extract
2 teaspoons lemon juice

*Toss the walnut mixture around the
insides of the tins to coat them.*

*Cover the top of each tart with strips of
paper and dust parallel lines of the
walnut mixture over the surface.*

SWEET RICOTTA TARTS
with walnut crust

1 Preheat the oven to 170°C (325°F/Gas 3). Grease four 10.5 x 2.5 cm
   (4 x 1 inch) deep loose-based flan (tart) tins and line the bases with
   baking paper.

2 To make the crust, put the walnuts, flour and sugar in a small processor fitted
   with the metal blade. Whizz in 5-second bursts for 25 seconds, or until fine
   (whizzing may bring out the oil in the walnuts, causing them to clump).
   Remove 3 tablespoons of the walnut mixture. Toss half around the insides
   of the prepared tins, coating them lightly. Reserve the remainder.

3 Add the butter to the processor and whizz for 10 seconds, or until
   combined with the walnut mixture. Divide the crust among the prepared
   tins and press firmly over the bases. Put on a baking tray and bake for
   10 minutes. Set aside to cool.

4 Meanwhile, to make the filling, add the ricotta and sugar to the cleaned
   processor and whizz for 15 seconds, or until smooth. Add the crème
   fraîche or sour cream, eggs, flour, vanilla and lemon juice and whizz
   until just combined. Divide the filling among the tins, levelling the surface.
   Put the tins on the baking tray and bake for 15–18 minutes, or until set.

5 Cool the tarts in the tins before turning out. Cover the top of each tart with
   two strips of paper and, using the reserved walnut mixture, dust two parallel
   lines over the surface.

PINK GRAPEFRUIT MERINGUE TARTLETS

Serves 8

Preparation time: 1 hour 20 minutes

Cooking time: 25 minutes

2 quantities sweet shortcrust pastry (page 64)

GRAPEFRUIT CURD
100 g (3½ oz) butter, chopped
6 eggs, lightly beaten
250 ml (9 fl oz/1 cup) ruby grapefruit juice
1 tablespoon finely grated ruby grapefruit zest
170 g (6 oz/¾ cup) caster (superfine) sugar

MERINGUE
4 egg whites, at room temperature
115 g (4 oz/½ cup) caster (superfine) sugar
1 tablespoon cornflour (cornstarch)

1 Preheat the oven to 180°C (350°F/ Gas 4). Lightly grease eight loose-based tartlet tins, 10 cm x 3 cm (4 x 1¼ inch).

2 Roll out the pastry on a lightly floured work surface to 3 mm (⅛ inch) thick. Cut the pastry into rounds to fit the base and sides of the tins. Gently press the sides to fit, trim the edges, then wrap the tins in plastic wrap and refrigerate for 30 minutes.

3 Line each of the pastry shells with a crumpled piece of baking paper and fill with baking beads or uncooked rice. Blind bake the pastry for 10 minutes, then remove the paper and beads and bake for a further 5 minutes, or until the pastry is golden. Allow to cool.

4 To make the grapefruit curd, combine the butter, eggs, grapefruit juice, zest and sugar in a heatproof bowl. Place over a saucepan of simmering water and whisk constantly for 10–15 minutes, or until the mixture thickens. Set aside to cool. Spoon the curd into the tart shells, smoothing the top. Place in the refrigerator for 30 minutes, or until completely cold.

5 To make the meringue, whisk the egg whites in a clean, dry bowl until soft peaks form. Add the sugar, 1 tablespoon at a time, whisking well after each addition. Whisk until the mixture is stiff and glossy and the sugar has dissolved. Add the cornflour (cornstarch), whisking to mix well.

6 Place the mixture in a piping bag fitted with a 2 cm (¾ inch) plain nozzle. Remove the tartlets from the refrigerator and pipe the meringue over the curd. Bake for 10 minutes, or until the meringue is golden.

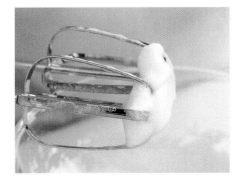

Whisk the egg whites until soft peaks form. You can use either electric beaters or a balloon whisk to do this.

Use a piping bag to pipe the meringue over the top of the grapefruit curd.

Serves 6–8

Preparation time: 40 minutes

Cooking time: 1 hour 10 minutes

PASTRY
215 g (7½ oz/1¾ cups) plain
    (all-purpose) flour
pinch of salt
60 g (5¾ oz) chilled, chopped butter
1 egg yolk

FILLING
60 g (2¼ oz) unsalted butter
170 g (6 oz/¾ cup) caster (superfine)
    sugar
1.3 kg (3 lb) of eating apples, peeled,
    cored and quartered
whipped cream, to serve

THE PERFECT TARTE TATIN

We have the sisters Tatin to thank for popularising this dessert — they were cooks near the town of Orleans at the beginning of the 19th century. This dish is nothing short of genius; cooking the apples in butter, sugar and their own juices, then baking the whole with the pastry on top, ensures caramel-sweet fruit and a golden crust.

1 First make the pastry: sift flour and salt into a large bowl, then rub butter in until mixture resembles breadcrumbs. Add the egg yolk and 3 teaspoons of ice-cold water, using a flat-bladed knife, mix until dough just starts to come together. Turn out onto a work surface and push dough together with your hands, form into a disc then wrap in plastic wrap and refrigerate for 30 minutes.

2 Combine unsalted butter and caster sugar in a deep, 25 cm (10 in) oven-proof frying pan. Heat until the butter is melted and sugar has dissolved. Arrange the apples over the base of the pan, placing them in rings and making sure there are no gaps. Cook over low heat for 35–40 minutes, basting often with pan juices, or until apples

are soft and pan juices are very reduced and are light caramel. Remove from heat. Preheat the oven to 190°C (375°F/Gas 5).

3 Roll out the pastry on a lightly floured board to form a 3 mm (⅛ in) thick circle slightly larger than the frying pan. Lay the pastry over the apples, pressing gently around the edge of the pan to enclose the apples. Trim the edge of pastry, then fold the trimmed edge back on itself to form a neat edge. Bake for 25–30 minutes, or until pastry is golden and cooked through. Remove from the oven, then stand for 5 minutes before inverting the tart onto a plate. Serve the tart warm or at room temperature, with whipped cream.

Makes: 12

Preparation time: 25 minutes

Cooking time: 40 minutes

155 g (5½ oz/1¼ cups) plain
   (all-purpose) flour
25 g (1 oz) vegetable shortening,
   chopped and softened
30 g (1 oz) unsalted butter, chopped
   and softened
250 g (9 oz/1 cup) sugar
500 ml (17 fl oz/2 cups) milk
3 tablespoons cornflour (cornstarch)
1 tablespoon custard powder
4 egg yolks
1 teaspoon natural vanilla extract

PORTUGUESE CUSTARD TARTS

1 Sift the flour into a bowl. Add 185 ml (6 fl oz/¾ cup) water, or enough to form a soft dough. Gather into a ball, then roll out on baking paper to form a 24 x 30 cm rectangle. Spread the vegetable shortening over the surface. Roll up from the short edge to form a log.

2 Roll the dough out into a rectangle again, and spread with the butter. Roll into a log and slice into 12 pieces. Working from the centre outwards, use your fingertips to press each round out to a circle large enough to cover the base and sides of twelve standard muffin holes. Press into the tin and refrigerate.

3 Put the sugar and 80 ml (2½ fl oz/⅓ cup) water into a pan, and stir over low heat until the sugar dissolves. Mix a little milk with the cornflour (cornstarch) and custard powder to form a smooth paste, and add to the pan with the remaining milk, egg yolks and vanilla. Stir over low heat until thickened. Put in a bowl, cover and cool.

4 Preheat the oven to 220°C (425°F/Gas 7). Divide the filling among the pastry bases. Bake for 30 minutes, or until the custard is set and the tops have browned. Cool in the tins, then transfer to a wire rack.

Makes: 8

Preparation time: 25 minutes

Cooking time: 25 minutes

50 g (1¾ oz/½ cup) flaked almonds
125 g (4½ oz) unsalted butter, softened
125 g (4½ oz/1 cup) icing
   (confectioners') sugar
125 g (4½ oz/1¼ cups) ground
   almonds
30 g (1 oz/¼ cup) plain (all-purpose)
   flour
2 eggs
1 tablespoon rum or brandy
1 teaspoon natural almond extract
½ teaspoon natural vanilla extract
4 sheets frozen ready-made puff
   pastry, thawed
1 egg, lightly beaten
sugar, to sprinkle
icing (confectioners') sugar, to dust

ALMOND PIES

1 Preheat the oven to 200°C (400°F/ Gas 6). Bake the flaked almonds on a baking tray for 2–3 minutes, or until just golden. Remove and return the tray to the oven to keep it hot.

2 Beat together the butter, icing (confectioners') sugar, ground almonds, flour, eggs, rum, almond extract and vanilla extract with electric beaters for 2–3 minutes, or until smooth and combined. Fold in the flaked almonds.

3 Cut out eight 10 cm (4 inch) rounds and eight 11 cm (4¼ inch) rounds from the puff pastry. Spread the smaller rounds with equal amounts of filling, leaving a 1 cm (½ inch) border. Brush the borders with beaten egg and cover with the tops. Seal the edges with a fork and, if you wish, decorate the tops with shapes cut from pastry scraps.

4 Pierce with a fork to allow steam to escape. Brush with egg and sprinkle with sugar. Bake on the hot tray for 15–20 minutes, or until the pastry is puffed and golden. Dust with icing (confectioners') sugar before serving.

Serves 6

Preparation time: 15 minutes

Cooking time: 40 minutes

1 sheet frozen puff pastry, thawed
80 g (2¾ oz/¼ cup) apricot jam
1 granny smith apple
2 teaspoons raw (demerara) sugar

APPLE GALETTE

1 Preheat the oven to 210°C (415°F/ Gas 6–7). Place a baking tray in the oven to heat. Trim the corners from the pastry to make a neat circle (use a large plate as a guide if you like).

2 Place the jam in a small saucepan and stir over low heat to warm through and thin. Strain through a sieve to remove any chunks of fruit and brush over the puff pastry, leaving a 1.5 cm (½ inch) border.

3 Peel, halve and core the apple, and cut into 2 mm (¹⁄₁₆ inch)thick slices. Arrange over the pastry in an overlapping circular pattern, leaving a 1.5 cm (½ inch) border around the edge. Sprinkle evenly with the sugar.

4 Carefully place the galette on a lightly greased tray and bake for 35 minutes, or until the edge of the pastry is well browned and puffed.

Makes: 8

Preparation time: 15 minutes

Cooking time: 15 minutes

2 sheets frozen butter puff pastry, thawed
50 g (1¾ oz) unsalted butter, softened
55 g (2 oz/½ cup) ground almonds
½ teaspoon natural vanilla extract
5 large nectarines
55 g (2 oz/¼ cup) caster (superfine)
  sugar
110 g (3¾ oz/⅓ cup) apricot or peach
  jam, warmed and sieved

NECTARINE FEUILLETÉES

When nectarines are in full flight in summer, it's nice to be able to grab a handful and make a fabulous dessert without having to think about it too much. This is just such a dessert. The name of this recipe comes from the french 'pâté feuilletée', meaning puff pastry.

1 Preheat the oven to 200°C (400°F/Gas 6). Line two large baking trays with baking paper.

2 Cut the pastry sheets into eight 12 cm (4½ inch) rounds and place on the prepared trays. Combine the butter, ground almonds and vanilla in a small bowl to form a paste. Divide the paste among the pastry rounds and spread evenly, leaving a 1.5 cm (⅝ inch) border around the edge.

3 Halve the nectarines, removing the stones, and cut them into 5 mm (¼ inch) slices. Arrange the nectarine slices over the pastry rounds, overlapping the slices and leaving a thin border. Sprinkle the sugar over the nectarines.

4 Bake for 15 minutes, or until the pastries are puffed and golden. Brush the nectarines and pastry with the warm jam while the pastries are hot. Serve hot or at room temperature.

Serves 10

Preparation time: 25 minutes

Cooking time: 45 minutes

120 g (4¼ oz) butter, softened
145 g (5½ oz/⅔ cup) caster (superfine) sugar
2 egg yolks
200 g (7 oz/1⅓ cups) pistachios, lightly toasted, then finely ground
½ teaspoon natural vanilla extract
30 g (1 oz/¼ cup) plain (all-purpose) flour
2 sheets frozen butter puff pastry, thawed
1 egg yolk, extra
1 tablespoon milk
2 tablespoons apricot jam
1 tablespoon chopped toasted pistachios

PISTACHIO PITHIVIERS

1 Preheat the oven to 180°C (350°F/Gas 4). Line a baking tray with baking paper.

2 Cream the butter and sugar in a bowl using electric beaters until pale and fluffy, then add the yolks one at a time, beating well after each addition. Stir in the ground pistachios, vanilla and flour.

3 Cut the puff pastry into two 24 cm (9½ inch) rounds. Place one round onto the prepared baking tray. Spoon the pistachio mixture into the middle of the pastry, smoothing the surface, leaving a 4 cm (1½ inch) border around the edge. Combine the extra egg yolk and milk in a small bowl. Lightly brush around the border with the egg mixture, then top with the remaining pastry round to cover. Press the edges together to seal, then use your fingertips to crimp the edge at 2 cm (¾ inch) intervals. Using the back of a small knife, score the pastry into wedges, starting from the centre and working out towards the edge (be careful not to cut all the way through the pastry). Brush the surface with the remaining egg mixture. Bake on the bottom shelf of the oven for 45 minutes, or until golden and puffed.

4 Heat the jam in a small saucepan with 1 tablespoon water. As soon as the pithiviers comes out of the oven, brush liberally with the apricot glaze, then sprinkle with the chopped pistachios. Allow to cool, then serve. The pithiviers is best eaten the day it is made.

Spoon the pistachio mixture into the middle of one puff pastry round.

Top with the second round and use your fingers to seal the edges.

Serves 4

Preparation time: 20 minutes

Cooking time: 2 hours 40 minutes

750 g (1lb 10 oz) boned lamb
    shoulder, cubed
90 g (¾ cup) plain (all-purpose)
    flour, seasoned
2 tablespoons olive oil
200 g (7 oz) bacon, finely chopped
2 garlic cloves, chopped
4 large leeks, sliced
1 large carrot, chopped
2 large potatoes, cut into 1 cm
    (½ inch) cubes
315 ml (1¼ cups) beef stock
1 bay leaf
2 teaspoons chopped flat-leaf
    (Italian) parsley
375 g (13 oz) puff pastry
1 egg, lightly beaten

WELSH LAMB PIE

1 Toss the meat in the seasoned
flour and shake off the excess.
Heat the oil in a large frying pan
over medium heat. Cook the meat
in batches for 4–5 minutes, or until
well browned, then remove from
the pan. Add the bacon and cook
for 3 minutes. Add the garlic and
leek and cook for about 5 minutes,
or until the leek is soft.

2 Put the meat in a large saucepan,
add the leek and bacon, carrot,
potato, stock and bay leaf and
bring to the boil, then reduce
the heat, cover and simmer for
30 minutes. Uncover and simmer
for 1 hour, or until the meat is
cooked and the liquid has
thickened. Season. Remove the
bay leaf, stir in the parsley and set
aside to cool.

3 Preheat the oven to 200°C (400°F/
Gas 6). Divide the filling among
four 375 ml (1½ cups) pie dishes.

Divide the pastry into four and roll
each piece out between two sheets
of baking paper until large enough
to cover the pie. Remove the top
sheet of paper and invert the pastry
over the filling. Trim the edges and
pinch to seal.

4 Cut two slits in the top for steam
to escape. Brush with egg and bake
for 45 minutes, or until the pastry
is crisp and golden.

Serves 4

Preparation time: 25 minutes

Cooking time: 3 hours 30 minutes

12 roma (plum) tomatoes
4 tablespoons olive oil
3 red onions, finely sliced
2 garlic cloves, finely sliced
1 tablespoon balsamic vinegar
1 teaspoon soft brown sugar
15 g (½ oz/¼ cup) finely shredded
    basil
60 g (2¼ oz) goat's cheese
1 sheet butter puff pastry

TOMATO TARTE TATIN

1 Preheat the oven to 150°C (300°F/ Gas 2). Cut a cross in the base of the tomatoes. Cover with boiling water for 30 seconds, then plunge into cold water. Peel the skin away, then cut the tomatoes in half lengthways, and season well. Place the tomatoes cut-side up on a rack on a baking tray. Cook in the oven for 3 hours.

2 Heat 2 tablespoons of oil in a heavy-based saucepan, add onions and cook over very low heat, stirring often, for 1 hour or until caramelized.

3 When the tomatoes are ready, remove from the oven, and increase the oven temperature to 200°C (400°F/Gas 6).

4 In a 20 cm (8 inch) ovenproof frying pan, heat the remaining olive oil over medium heat. Add the garlic, vinegar, sugar and 1 tablespoon of water, and heat until the sugar dissolves. Remove from the heat. Arrange the tomatoes in concentric circles cut-side up in one layer. Top with the onions, basil and crumbled goat's cheese. Cover with the puff pastry, trim the edges, and tuck the pastry down the side of the pan around the tomatoes. Bake for 25–30 minutes, or until the pastry is golden. Invert the tart onto a plate, cool to room temperature and serve.

Serves 4

Preparation time: 1 hour 5 minutes

Cooking time: 30 minutes

800 g (1 lb 12 oz) jap (Kent) pumpkin,
    skin removed and cut into 1 cm (½
    inch) thick slices
2 tablespoons olive oil
3 garlic cloves, crushed
4 sheets butter puff pastry, cut into
    15 cm (6 inch) squares
100 g (3½ oz) marinated feta cheese
3 tablespoons oregano leaves, roughly
    chopped
2 tablespoons pine nuts, toasted
1 egg yolk
1 tablespoon milk
1 tablespoon sesame seeds
sea salt, to sprinkle

ROAST PUMPKIN, FETA AND PINE NUT PASTIE

1 Preheat the oven to 220°C (425°F/ Gas 7). Place the pumpkin on a baking tray and toss with the olive oil, garlic and salt and pepper. Roast in the oven for 40 minutes, or until cooked and golden. Remove and allow to cool.

2 Evenly divide the pumpkin among the four pastry squares, placing it in the centre. Top with the feta, oregano and pine nuts. Drizzle with a little of the feta marinating oil. Bring two of the diagonally opposite corners together and pinch in the centre above the filling. Bring the other two diagonally opposite corners together, and pinch to seal along the edges. The base will be square, the top will form a pyramid. Twist the top to seal where all four corners meet.

3 Place the egg yolk and milk in a small bowl, and whisk with a fork to make an eggwash for the pastry.

4 Place the pasties on a greased baking tray and brush with the eggwash. Sprinkle with sesame seeds and sea salt and bake for 15 minutes, or until golden brown.

Serves 4

Preparation time: 15 minutes

Cooking time: 50 minutes

5 tablespoons olive oil
1 leek, sliced
1 garlic clove, crushed
1 kg (2 lb 4 oz) large field mushrooms,
  roughly chopped
1 teaspoon chopped thyme
300 ml (10½ fl oz) cream
1 sheet ready-rolled puff pastry, thawed
1 egg yolk, beaten, to glaze

MUSHROOM POT PIES

1 Preheat the oven to 180°C (350°F/Gas 4). Heat 1 tablespoon of the oil in a frying pan over medium heat. Cook the leek and garlic for 5 minutes, or until the leek is soft and translucent. Transfer to a large saucepan.

2 Heat the remaining oil in the frying pan over high heat and cook the mushrooms in two batches, stirring frequently, for 5–7 minutes per batch, or until the mushrooms have released their juices and are soft and slightly coloured. Transfer to the saucepan, then add the thyme.

3 Place the saucepan over high heat and stir in the cream. Cook, stirring occasionally, for 7–8 minutes, or until the cream has reduced to a thick sauce. Remove from the heat and season well with salt and pepper.

4 Divide the filling among four 315 ml (1¼ cup) ramekins or ovenproof bowls. Cut the pastry into rounds slightly larger than each dish. Brush the rim of the ramekins with a little of the egg yolk, place the pastry on top and press down to seal. Brush the top with the remaining egg yolk. Place the ramekins on a metal tray. Bake for 20–25 minutes, or until the pastry has risen and is golden brown.

MUSHROOMS
Large field mushrooms are wonderful baked. Look for those with white unblemished skin, and pale gills that haven't darkened or sweated. These days mushrooms come to us in a very clean state. If they are a little dirty, they should be wiped clean with a dampened cloth, never washed.

Makes: 32 pies

Preparation time: 30 minutes

Cooking time: 35 minutes

60 g (2¼ oz) butter
2 tablespoons olive oil
1 onion, finely chopped
3 leeks, finely sliced
1 garlic clove, chopped
1 tablespoon plain (all-purpose) flour
2 tablespoons sour cream
100 g (1 cup) grated parmesan cheese
1 teaspoon chopped thyme
4 sheets frozen puff pastry, thawed
1 egg, lightly beaten

MINI LEEK PIES

1 Heat the butter and oil in a large frying pan over medium heat. Add the onion and cook, stirring occasionally, for 2 minutes. Add the leek and garlic and cook for 5 minutes, or until the leek is softened and lightly coloured. Add the flour and stir into the mixture for 1 minute. Add the sour cream and stir until slightly thickened. Transfer to a bowl and add the parmesan and thyme. Season with salt and cracked black pepper and allow to cool.

2 Preheat the oven to 200°C (400°F/ Gas 6). Place a lightly greased baking tray in the oven to heat. Using a 6 cm (2½ inch) cutter, cut the pastry into 64 circles. Place 2 heaped teaspoons of filling on half the pastry circles, leaving a small border. Lightly brush the edges with egg, then place a pastry circle on top of each. Seal the edges well with a fork. Lightly brush the tops with egg.

3 Place the pies on the heated tray and bake for 25 minutes, or until the pies are puffed and golden.

Serves 6

Preparation time: 30 minutes

Cooking time: 3 hours 10 minutes

60 g (2¼ oz/½ cup) plain (all-purpose)
  flour, seasoned
1.5 kg (3 lb 5 oz) chuck steak, cut into
  2 cm (¾ inch) cubes
1 ox kidney (500 g/1 lb 2 oz), cut into
  2 cm (¾ inch) cubes
2 tablespoons olive oil
2 onions, chopped
125 g (4½ oz) button mushrooms,
  quartered
40 g (1½ oz) butter
250 ml (9 fl oz/1 cup) beef or veal stock
185 ml (6 fl oz/¾ cup) stout
2 tablespoons Worcestershire sauce
1 tablespoon anchovy extract
1 tablespoon chopped flat-leaf (Italian)
  parsley
600 g (1 lb 5 oz) puff pastry
1 egg, lightly beaten

STEAK AND KIDNEY PIE

1 Place the flour in a bowl. Toss the steak and kidney pieces through the flour and shake off any excess. Heat the oil in a large pan over medium heat, add the onion and cook for 5 minutes. Add the mushrooms and cook for 5 minutes. Remove from the pan.

2 Melt a third of the butter in the pan, add a third of the beef and kidney and cook over medium heat, turning occasionally, for 5 minutes, or until brown. Remove and repeat twice with the remaining butter, beef and kidney. Return all the meat to the saucepan, add the stock and stout, stir and bring slowly to boil. Reduce the heat and

simmer for 2 hours. Remove from the heat, leave to cool, then add the onion and mushrooms, Worcestershire sauce, anchovy extract and parsley.

3 Preheat the oven to 180°C (350°F/Gas 4). Place the filling into a 20 x 4 cm (8 x 1½ inch) ceramic pie dish . Roll out the pastry between two sheets of baking paper to fit the top of the pie dish. Moisten the rim of the dish with milk and place the pastry over the filling. Press firmly into place and brush with egg. Decorate with pastry scraps, brush with egg and bake for 40–45 minutes until golden.

Serves 6

Preparation time: 1 hour

Cooking time: 1 hour

60 g (2¼ oz/⅓ cup) basmati rice
2 eggs, hard-boiled, chopped
2 tablespoons dill, chopped
2 tablespoons chopped flat-leaf
    (Italian) parsley
60 ml (2 fl oz/¼ cup) thick
    (double/heavy) cream
60 g (2¼ oz) butter
1 onion, finely chopped
200 g (7 oz), sliced button mushrooms
2 tablespoons lemon juice
500 g (1 lb 2 oz) salmon fillet,
    centre-cut piece, skinned
500 g (1 lb 2 oz) frozen puff pastry
    block, thawed
1 egg, lightly beaten

FISH SUBSTITUTION
ocean trout, trout

SALMON COULIBIAC

Traditionally, this Russian pie would use a yeast dough rather than a flaky pastry dough. The filling almost always contains fish along with hard-boiled eggs, dill and parsley; this version adds mushrooms. Try to buy salmon fillets cut from the centre rather than the tail end of the fish.

1 Cook the rice in boiling salted water until just *al dente*, then drain and transfer to a bowl. When cooled slightly, add the chopped hard-boiled egg, dill and parsley, season with salt and freshly ground black pepper and stir in the cream.

2 Melt half the butter in a frying pan and add the onion. Cook for 5 minutes, or until soft but not brown. Add the mushrooms and cook for 5 minutes, or until soft. Add the lemon juice to the pan and stir to combine. Transfer the mixture to a bowl.

3 Melt the remaining butter in the same frying pan, add the salmon fillet and cook for 2 minutes on each side to brown it. Transfer to a plate and allow to cool slightly.

4 Lightly grease a baking tray. Roll out half the pastry to a rectangle measuring 30 x 40 cm (12 x 16 inch) and place on the baking tray. Spread the rice mixture onto the pastry, leaving a 3 cm (1¼ inch) border all the way around. Top with the piece of salmon and then add the mushroom mixture. Mould the layers to fit the shape of the salmon fillet.

5 Roll out the remaining pastry to approximately 33 x 43 cm (13 x 17 inch) and carefully place over the filling. Press the edges of the pastry together, trim the edges to a neat rectangle and crimp to seal. Decorate with shapes made from offcuts of pastry, if desired, then refrigerate for 30 minutes. Meanwhile, preheat the oven to 210°C (415°F/Gas 6–7). Brush the pastry with the lightly beaten egg and make four slits in the top to allow the steam to escape. Bake for 15 minutes, then reduce the heat to 180°C (350°F/ Gas 4) and bake for a further 15–20 minutes, or until the top is golden brown.

Roll out half the pastry to a 30 x 40 cm (12 x 16 inch) rectangle.

Top the pastry with the rice mixture and the fish fillet.

Serves 4

Preparation time: 25 minutes

Cooking time: 55 minutes

60 g (2¼ oz) butter
1 leek, white part only, thinly sliced
1 garlic clove, finely chopped
1 kg (2 lb 4 oz) raw prawns (shrimp),
    peeled and deveined, tails intact
1 tablespoon plain (all-purpose) flour
185 ml (6 fl oz/¾ cup) chicken or
    fish stock
125 ml (4 fl oz/½ cup) dry white wine
500 ml (17 fl oz/2 cups) cream
2 tablespoons lemon juice
1 tablespoon dill, chopped
1 tablespoon flat-leaf (Italian) parsley,
    chopped
1 teaspoon dijon mustard
1 sheet frozen, just thawed puff pastry
1 egg, lightly beaten
salad and bread, to serve (optional)

PRAWN POT PIES

Raw prawns (shrimp) should smell pleasantly of the sea. Reject any that smell off or fishy, or that have black heads or oozing black juices. Fresh raw prawns are the best choice, but frozen raw prawns may be used. Thaw them on a plate in the refrigerator, and cook without delay.

1 Preheat the oven to 220°C (425°F/Gas 7). Melt the butter in a saucepan over low heat. Cook the leek and garlic for 2 minutes, then add the prawns and cook for 1– 2 minutes, or until just pink.

2 Remove the prawns with a slotted spoon and set aside. Stir the flour into the pan and cook for 1 minute. Add the stock and wine, bring to the boil and cook for 10 minutes, or until most of the liquid has evaporated. Stir in the cream, bring to the boil, then reduce the heat and simmer for 20 minutes, or until the liquid reduces by half. Stir in the lemon juice, herbs and mustard.

3 Using half of the sauce, pour an even amount into each of four 250 ml (9 fl oz/1 cup) ramekins. Divide the prawns among the ramekins, then top with the remaining sauce. Cut the pastry into four rounds, slightly larger than the rim of the ramekins. Put the pastry rounds over the

prawn mixture and press around the edges. Prick the pastry with a fork and brush with beaten egg. Bake for 20 minutes, or until the pastry is crisp and golden. Serve with a salad and bread, if desired.

Thinly slice the white part of the leek.

Cook the leek and garlic in the melted butter for 2 minutes.

Makes: about 40 choux puffs
and 16 éclairs

Preparation time: 15 minutes

Cooking time: 45 minutes

100 g (3½ oz) unsalted butter
1 teaspoon caster (superfine) sugar
140 g (5 oz) plain (all-purpose) flour
3 eggs

CHOUX PASTRY

1 Preheat the oven to 200°C (400°F/
Gas 6). Lightly grease or line a
baking tray with baking paper.

2 Put 250 ml (9 fl oz/1 cup) water,
the butter and sugar in a small
saucepan and heat until the butter
has melted and the mixture has
just come to the boil. Add the flour
and, using a wooden spoon, stir
over medium heat until the mixture
comes away from the side of the
saucepan, forming a ball.

3 Place the mixture into the bowl of
an electric mixer fitted with a whisk
attachment and allow to cool slightly.
Add the eggs one at a time, beating
well after each addition and waiting

until each egg is incorporated before
adding the next. (Alternatively, you
can use a hand mixer or wooden
spoon to mix the ingredients.)
The mixture should be thick and
glossy. The pastry is now ready to
use and may be piped, spooned or
shaped according to the recipe you
are using.

4 To make choux puffs, place
teaspoonfuls of the mixture on
baking trays, spacing them 4 cm
(1½ inches) apart. Bake for 20
minutes, then reduce the heat to
160°C (315°F/Gas 2–3) and bake
for a further 20 minutes, or until
puffed, golden and dry (pull one
puff apart to see if it is dry inside).

Turn off the oven, open the door
slightly, and leave the pastries in
the oven until cool.

5 To make éclairs, put the choux
pastry into a piping bag fitted with
a 2 cm (¾ inch) plain nozzle. Pipe
10 cm (4 inch) lengths of choux
onto the baking tray, spacing them
4 cm (1½ inches) apart. Bake as
for choux puffs.

Pastries will keep, if stored in an
airtight container, for up to 3 days.
To refresh them, if necessary, place
on a baking tray and heat in a
preheated 180°C (350°F/Gas 4)
oven for 5–10 minutes, or until
the pastry is dry and crisp.

Makes: 24 eclairs

Preparation time: 30 minutes

Cooking time: 23 minutes

60 g (2¼ oz) unsalted butter, chopped
125 g (4½ oz/1 cup) plain (all-purpose)
    flour, sifted
4 eggs, beaten
300 ml (10½ fl oz/1¼ cups) whipping
    cream
1 tablespoon icing (confectioners')
    sugar, sifted
½ teaspoon natural vanilla extract
50 g (1¾ oz) dark chocolate, melted

MINI ÉCLAIRS

1 Preheat the oven to 200°C (400°F/ Gas 6) and line two baking trays with baking paper. Put the butter in a pan with 250 ml (9 fl oz/1 cup) water. Stir over low heat until melted. Bring to the boil, then remove from the heat and add all the flour. Beat with a wooden spoon until smooth. Return to the heat and beat for 2 minutes, or until the mixture forms a ball and leaves the side of the pan. Remove from the heat and transfer to a bowl. Cool for 5 minutes. Add the egg, a little at a time, beating well between each addition, until thick and glossy — a wooden spoon should stand upright.

2 Spoon the mixture into a piping bag with a 1.2 cm (⅝ inch) plain nozzle. Pipe 6 cm (2½ inch) lengths of batter on the trays. Bake for 10 minutes, then reduce the heat to 180°C (350°F/ Gas 4) and cook for 10 minutes, or until golden and puffed. Poke a hole into one side of each éclair and remove the soft dough from inside with a teaspoon. Return to the oven for 2–3 minutes. Cool on a rack.

3 Whip the cream, icing (confectioners') sugar and vanilla until thick. Pipe the cream into the side of each éclair. Dip each éclair into the melted chocolate, face-side-down, then return to the wire rack for the chocolate to set.

Makes: 16 eclairs

Preparation time: 1 hour

Cooking time: 40 minutes

1 quantity choux pastry (page 96)
1 x 5 g (⅛ oz) gelatine sheet, or
   1½ teaspoons gelatine powder
200 ml (7 fl oz) puréed mango flesh
1 teaspoon lemon juice
125 ml (4 fl oz/½ cup) thick
   (double/heavy) cream
30 g (1 oz/¼ cup) icing (confectioners')
   sugar

GINGER ICING
60 g (2¼ oz/½ cup) icing
   (confectioners') sugar
10 g (¼ oz) unsalted butter
½ teaspoon ground ginger
½ teaspoon lemon juice

GINGER AND MANGO ÉCLAIRS

1 Preheat the oven to 200°C (400°F/Gas 6). Line two baking trays with baking paper.

2 Put the choux pastry into a piping bag fitted with a 2 cm (¾ inch) plain nozzle. Pipe 10 cm (4 inch) lengths of choux onto the baking tray, spacing them 4 cm (1½ inches) apart. Bake for 20 minutes, then reduce the heat to 160°C (315°F/Gas 2–3) and bake for another 20 minutes, or until puffed, golden and dry. Turn off the oven, open the door slightly and leave the choux in the oven until cool.

3 If using the gelatine sheet, soak it in cold water for 5 minutes, or until softened, then squeeze out the excess moisture. If using gelatine powder, sprinkle the gelatine over 3 tablespoons water in a bowl. Leave the gelatine to sponge — it will swell. Combine the mango purée and lemon juice in a small heatproof bowl over simmering water. Add the softened gelatine sheet or sponged gelatine powder to the warm liquid, whisking to dissolve the gelatine. Remove from the heat, then refrigerate until the mixture is cool and beginning to thicken. Whisk the cream and icing (confectioners') sugar in a bowl until thick, then fold in the cooled mango mixture.

4 To make the ginger icing, combine the icing (confectioners') sugar, butter, ginger and lemon juice in a small bowl. Pour over 2 teaspoons boiling water and whisk until a smooth, thin icing forms, adding a few more drops of water if necessary. Without cutting all the way through, split the éclairs horizontally. Spoon about 1 tablespoon of filling into each, then drizzle the tops with ginger icing. Refrigerate until the icing sets.

5 Eclairs are best served on the day they are made.

Makes: 40 puffs

Preparation time: 45 minutes

Cooking time: 1 hour

1 quantity choux pastry (page 96),
    made into 40 choux puffs, cooled
700 g (1 lb 9 oz/3 cups) caster
    (superfine) sugar

COFFEE CREAM FILLING
1½ tablespoons instant coffee granules
400 g (14 oz) mascarpone
60 g (2¼ oz/½ cup) icing
    (confectioners') sugar
2 tablespoons pouring cream

CROQUEMBOUCHE
with coffee cream filling

1 To make the coffee cream filling, dissolve the coffee in 1 tablespoon boiling water. Put the mascarpone, icing (confectioners') sugar, cream and coffee mixture in a bowl. Using electric beaters, combine well.

2 Place the filling in a piping bag fitted with a nozzle less than 1 cm (½ inch) in diameter. Using the end of a teaspoon, make a small hole in the base of each choux puff, then pipe the filling into the puffs.

3 To make a caramel, put the sugar and 250 ml (9 fl oz/1 cup) water in a heavy-based saucepan and slowly bring to a simmer over medium heat. Cook, without stirring, for 20 minutes, or until the mixture turns a deep caramel colour. Remove from the heat and immediately put the saucepan into a large bowl of cold water to stop the caramel cooking further.

4 To assemble, dip the base of three puffs into the caramel and place them together on a serving plate to form a triangular shape. Dip the base of a fourth puff into the caramel and place on top of the triangle, in the centre, to form a small pyramid. Repeat to make 10 individual pyramids in total.

5 Dip two forks into the remaining caramel, then rub the backs of the forks together until the caramel begins to stick. Gently pull the forks apart to check whether the caramel is cool enough to spin. If it drips, it probably needs longer to cool. When the caramel forms fine threads of toffee, spin it around each croquembouche until they are covered with fine threads of toffee. Serve immediately.

Make a small hole in the choux puffs and pipe the coffee cream filling into the puffs.

Rub the forks together until the caramel is tacky, then gently pull apart.

Makes: 40 gougères

Preparation time: 30 minutes

Cooking time: 45 minutes

100 g (3½ oz) butter
140 g (5 oz) plain (all-purpose) flour
½ teaspoon cumin seeds, lightly
  crushed
3 eggs
150 g (5½ oz) aged gouda cheese,
  finely grated

CUMIN AND GOUDA GOUGÈRES

1 Preheat the oven to 200°C (400°F/Gas 6). Line a baking tray with baking paper.

2 Heat 250 ml (9 fl oz/1 cup) water, the butter and ¼ teaspoon salt in a small saucepan over medium heat until the butter has melted and the mixture has just come to the boil. Add the flour and cumin and stir until the mixture comes away from the side of the saucepan. Transfer to the bowl of an electric mixer and allow to cool a little (alternatively use a hand mixer or wooden spoon). Beating continuously, add the eggs one at a time, beating well after each addition. Stir in the cheese.

3 Put teaspoonfuls of the mixture onto the prepared baking tray, spacing them about 4 cm (1½ inches) apart. Bake for 20 minutes, then reduce the heat to 160°C (315°F/Gas 2–3) and cook for a further 20 minutes, or until the gougères are puffed, golden and dry. Turn off the oven, open the door slightly and leave the gougères to cool a little. Serve warm or at room temperature, with drinks.

TIP Gougères originated in Burgundy, traditionally as an accompaniment to the local wines. They can also be split and filled with savoury fillings, such as chicken or fish.

Serves 4

Preparation time: 25 minutes

Cooking time: 1 hour

75 g (2½ oz) butter
120 g (4¼ oz) plain (all-purpose)
    flour, sifted twice
¼ teaspoon paprika
3 large eggs, beaten
100 g (3½ oz) gruyére cheese, grated

FILLING
400 g (14 oz) smoked trout
100 g (3½ oz) watercress, trimmed
30 g (1 oz) butter
20 g (¾ oz) plain (all-purpose) flour
300 ml (10½ fl oz) milk

SMOKED TROUT GOUGÈRE

Choux pastry isn't difficult to make but is one of those culinary basics that requires a little practice and patience to master; once you have though, you'll be able to whip up a batch in no time at all. Based on choux pastry, and baked with a smoked trout filling, this dish makes a wonderful casual lunch or dinner — just serve it with a vinaigrette-dressed leafy salad.

1 Preheat the oven to 200°C (400°F/ Gas 6) and put a baking tray on the top shelf to heat up.

2 Melt the butter with 185 ml (6 fl oz/ ¾ cup) water in a saucepan, then bring it to a rolling boil. Remove from the heat and sift in all the flour and the paprika. Return to the heat and beat continuously with a wooden spoon to make a smooth shiny paste that comes away from the side of the pan. Cool for a few minutes. Beat in the eggs one at a time, until shiny and smooth — the mixture should drop off the spoon but not be too runny. Stir in two-thirds of the cheese.

3 Spoon the dough round the edge of a shallow, lightly greased baking dish. Put this in the oven on the hot tray and cook for 45–50 minutes, or until the choux is well risen and browned.

4 Meanwhile, to make the filling, peel the skin off the trout and lift off the top fillet. Pull out the bone. Break the trout into large flakes. Wash the watercress and put in a large saucepan with just the water clinging to the leaves. Cover the pan and steam the watercress for 2 minutes, or until just wilted. Drain, cool and squeeze with your hands to get rid of the excess liquid. Roughly chop the watercress.

5 Melt the butter in a saucepan, stir in the flour to make a roux and cook, stirring, for 3 minutes over very low heat without allowing the roux to brown. Remove from the heat and add the milk gradually, stirring after each addition until smooth. Return to the heat and simmer for 3 minutes. Stir in the smoked trout and watercress and season well.

6 Spoon the trout filling into the centre of the cooked choux pastry and return to the oven for 10 minutes, then serve immediately.

Makes: 24 slices

Preparation time: 30 minutes

Cooking time: 20 minutes

360 g (12¾ oz/4 cups) desiccated
   coconut
1 teaspoon ground cinnamon
½ teaspoon ground nutmeg
a pinch of ground cloves
10 sheets filo pastry (about 150 g/5½ oz)
200 g (7 oz) unsalted butter, melted

SYRUP
400 g (14 oz/1¾ cups) caster
   (superfine) sugar
1½ tablespoons lemon juice
1½ tablespoons honey
1 tablespoon orange blossom water

COCONUT BAKLAVA

1 Preheat the oven to 180°C (350°F/
Gas 4). Lightly grease a 28 x 20 cm
(11¼ x 8 inch) rectangular shallow
tin and line the base with baking
paper. Put the coconut, cinnamon,
nutmeg and cloves in a large bowl
and stir to combine.

2 Cut the stack of filo sheets in half
widthways, so it will fit into the tin.
Brush a sheet of filo liberally with
melted butter, top with another
sheet and repeat until you have
four layers of pastry. Repeat with
the remaining filo to give five stacks
in total, each with four layers.

3 Put one stack of filo in the tin and
brush the top of the filo with
butter. Evenly spread one-quarter
of the coconut mixture over the
filo, top with another filo stack and
brush with butter. Repeat with
remaining coconut mixture and
pastry stacks, finishing with a layer
of filo. Liberally brush the top with
butter, then score into diamond
shapes using a sharp knife, making
the cuts about 1 cm (½ inch) deep
(do not cut all the way through at
this stage). Bake for 18–20 minutes,
or until golden and crisp.

4 Meanwhile, make the syrup.
Combine 400 ml (14 fl oz) water,
the sugar, lemon juice, honey
and orange blossom water in a
saucepan and stir until the sugar
dissolves. Bring to a simmer and
cook for 10 minutes, or until
slightly thickened. Cool the syrup.

5 While the baklava is still very hot,
pour over the cold syrup. Allow to
cool completely before cutting
along the scored marks into
diamond shapes to serve.

Serves 6–8

Preparation time: 25 minutes

Cooking time: 1 hour 5 minutes

120 g (4¼ oz) unsalted butter
½ teaspoon natural vanilla extract
4 pears, peeled, cored and chopped
1 teaspoon orange zest, finely grated
½ lemon, juiced
5 sheets filo pastry
120 g (4¼ oz/1½ cups) fresh
  breadcrumbs
200 g (7 oz/1½ cups) blackberries
50 g (1¾ oz/½ cup) toasted flaked
  almonds
60 g (2¼ oz/½ cup) sultanas
165 g (5¾ oz/¾ cup) caster (superfine)
  sugar
icing (confectioners') sugar, for dusting
custard or vanilla ice cream, to serve

BLACKBERRY AND PEAR STRUDEL

Thank goodness for ready-made filo pastry. Without it, few would attempt making a strudel. This version branches out from the traditional apple and raisin, or cherry and cream cheese filling by combining citrus-infused pears with blackberries, almonds and sultanas.

1 Preheat the oven to 180°C (350°F/Gas 4) and line a baking sheet with baking paper. Melt 100 g (3½ oz) of the butter with the vanilla.

2 Melt the remaining butter in a frying pan and sauté the pear over low heat for 5 minutes, or until tender. Transfer to a large bowl with the orange zest and lemon juice. Toss lightly to combine.

3 Lay a sheet of filo pastry on a flat surface. Brush the melted butter over the pastry and sprinkle lightly with breadcrumbs. Cover with another sheet of pastry and repeat the process until you have used all the pastry. Sprinkle with the remaining breadcrumbs.

4 Add the blackberries, almonds, sultanas and caster (superfine) sugar to the pear mixture and toss gently to combine. Shape the filling into a log along one long edge of the pastry, leaving a 5 cm (2 inch) border. Fold in the sides, then roll up and place, seam side down, on the prepared baking sheet. Brush with the remaining melted butter and bake for 40 minutes, or until golden brown. Dust with icing (confectioners') sugar and serve with custard or vanilla ice cream.

Makes: 30 rolls

Preparation time: 25 minutes

Cooking time: 20 minutes

125 g (4½ oz/1¼ cups) grated
    parmesan cheese
35 g (1¼ oz/⅓ cup) dry breadcrumbs
2½ tablespoons poppy seeds
2 egg yolks, lightly beaten
5 sheets filo pastry
80 g (2¾ oz) butter, melted

POPPY SEED AND PARMESAN FILO ROLLS

1 Preheat the oven to 180°C (350°F/Gas 4). Lightly grease a baking tray.

2 Combine the parmesan, breadcrumbs and poppy seeds in a bowl and season with freshly ground black pepper. Add the egg yolks, then, using a fork, work the yolks into the parmesan mixture until the mixture begins to clump together.

3 Place a sheet of filo pastry on the work surface, leaving the remaining sheets under a dampened tea towel (dish towel). Brush the pastry with some of the butter, then fold in half lengthways. Brush the pastry with the butter again, then sprinkle evenly with 45 g (1½ oz/⅓ cup slightly heaped) of parmesan mixture. Roll up the pastry as tightly as possible to form a long, thin log. Cut the log evenly into six rolls, then place the rolls, seam side down, on the baking tray. Repeat with the remaining pastry and filling mixture.

4 Brush the rolls with melted butter, then bake for 20 minutes, or until golden and crisp. Cool slightly, then serve warm or at room temperature, with drinks.

Serves 8

Preparation time: 40 minutes

Cooking time: 1 hour 10 minutes

750 g (1 lb 10 oz) orange sweet
    potato, peeled
12 small French shallots, peeled
6 baby potatoes, peeled and halved
125 ml (4 fl oz/½ cup) olive oil
1 teaspoon sweet paprika
1 teaspoon ground ginger
2 teaspoons ground cumin
¼ teaspoon ground cinnamon
100 g (3½ oz/2 cups) baby
    English spinach
60 g (2¼ oz/½ cup) sultanas
    (golden raisins)
85 g (3 oz/⅔ cup) slivered almonds,
    toasted
100 g (3½ oz/⅔ cup) pistachio
    kernels, coarsely chopped
2 large handfuls coriander (cilantro)
    leaves, coarsely chopped
2½ tablespoons golden syrup or
    maple syrup
80 g (2¾ oz/⅓ cup) plain yoghurt
400 g (14 oz) tinned chickpeas,
    drained and rinsed
3 garlic cloves, finely chopped
a pinch cayenne pepper
60 ml (2 fl oz/¼ cup) lemon juice
125 g (4½ oz) butter, melted
9 sheets filo pastry

SWEET POTATO FILO PIE

1 Preheat the oven to 200°C (400°F/
Gas 6). Cut the sweet potato into
2.5 cm (1 inch) cubes and put in a
large roasting tin, along with the
French shallots and baby potatoes.
Combine the olive oil, paprika,
ginger, cumin and cinnamon in
a small bowl and pour over the
vegetables. Toss to coat. Roast for
25 minutes, then turn the vegetables
and roast for a further 15 minutes.
Remove from the oven and reduce
the oven temperature to 180°C
(350°F/Gas 4). Put a baking tray
in the oven.

2 Add the spinach and sultanas to the
vegetables. Toss lightly, then set aside
for 5 minutes for the spinach to wilt.
Transfer to a large bowl and add the
almonds, pistachios and coriander.

3 Put 2 tablespoons of the golden
syrup, the yoghurt, chickpeas,
garlic, cayenne and lemon juice in
a food processor and blend until

smooth. Season with salt and
pepper, to taste. Add to the
vegetables and mix through.

4 Lightly dampen a tea towel and use
it to cover the sheets of filo as you
work. Brush a 28 x 21 cm (11¼ x
8¼ inch) loose-based rectangular
flan (tart) tin with butter. Brush a
sheet of filo with butter and lay
one point over one end of the tin,
so that three of the points stick out
and the overhang at the end is
about 10 cm (4 inches). Don't push
the pastry into the rippled sides of
the tin, just place it loosely on top.
Brush another sheet of filo with
butter and lay it similarly, at the
opposite end of the tin. Brush a
third sheet with butter and lay it in
the middle of the tin. Continue in
this way twice more, until all the
filo is used.

5 Pile the sweet potato mixture in
the centre of the tin. Starting in the

middle, bring the opposite sides of
the filo together, encasing the filling
tightly but with the filo points
sticking up (a little like a cloth
around a Christmas pudding, tied
at the top). Brush carefully with the
remaining butter and drizzle the
remaining golden syrup in zigzags
over the top. Place on the baking
tray and bake for 30 minutes, or
until golden. Set aside for 5 minutes
before serving.

BISCUITS AND SLICES

Makes: 16 wedges

Preparation time: 50 minutes

Cooking time: 20 minutes

225 g (8 oz) unsalted butter

115 g (4 oz/½ cup) caster (superfine) sugar, plus extra for dusting

225 g (8 oz/1¾ cups) plain (all-purpose) flour

115 g (4 oz/⅔ cup) rice flour

CLASSIC SHORTBREAD

1 Preheat the oven to 190°C (375°F/Gas 5). Lightly grease two baking trays.

2 Cream the butter and sugar in a bowl using electric beaters until pale and fluffy. Sift in the flour, rice flour and a pinch of salt and, using a wooden spoon, stir into the creamed mixture until it resembles fine breadcrumbs. Transfer to a lightly floured work surface and knead gently to form a soft dough. Cover with plastic wrap and refrigerate for 30 minutes.

3 Divide the dough in half and roll out one half on a lightly floured work surface to form a 20 cm (8 inch) round. Carefully transfer to a prepared tray. Using a sharp knife, score the surface of the dough into eight equal wedges, prick the surface lightly with a fork and, using your fingers, press the edges to form a fluted effect. Repeat this process using the remaining dough to make a second round. Lightly dust the shortbreads with the extra sugar.

4 Bake for 18–20 minutes, or until the shortbreads are light golden. Remove from the oven and while still hot, follow the score marks and cut into wedges. Cool on the baking tray for 5 minutes, then transfer to a wire rack.

5 The shortbread will keep, stored in an airtight container, for up to 1 week.

Makes: 36

Preparation time: 20 minutes

Cooking time: 1 hour

600 g (1 lb 5 oz/3⅓ cups) pitted
    whole dried dates, chopped
1 teaspoon bicarbonate of soda
    (baking soda)
125 g (4½ oz) unsalted butter, chopped
155 g (5½ oz/⅔ cup) soft brown sugar
2 eggs
125 g (4½ oz/1 cup) plain (all-purpose)
    flour
60 g (2¼ oz/½ cup) self-raising flour
½ teaspoon ground cinnamon,
    plus ½ teaspoon, extra
60 g (2¼ oz/½ cup) icing
    (confectioners') sugar

DATE AND CINNAMON SQUARES

1 Preheat the oven to 180°C (350°F/
   Gas 4). Lightly grease a 23 cm
   (9 inch) square shallow tin and
   line the base with baking paper.

2 Combine the dates and 500 ml
   (17 fl oz/2 cups) water in a medium
   saucepan, bring to the boil, then
   remove from the heat. Stir in the
   bicarbonate of soda and mix well.
   Cool to room temperature.

3 Cream the butter and sugar in a
   large bowl using electric beaters
   until pale and fluffy. Add the eggs

one at a time, beating well after
each addition. Sift the flours and
cinnamon into a bowl, then fold
into the butter mixture alternately
with the date mixture. Spread
into the prepared tin. Bake for
55–60 minutes, or until a skewer
inserted into the centre comes out
clean. Cool in the tin for 5 minutes,
then turn out onto a wire rack to
cool completely.

4 Cut into 36 pieces and place on a
   sheet of baking paper. Sift the
   combined icing sugar and extra

cinnamon over the squares and toss
to coat. Serve immediately (the
coating will be absorbed into the
cakes quite quickly if left to stand).

5 Date and cinnamon squares will
   keep (do not coat with the icing
   sugar if you intend to store them),
   stored in an airtight container, for
   up to 4 days, or up to 3 months
   in the freezer.

Makes: about 40
(depending on size of cutters)

Preparation time: 35 minutes

Cooking time: 24 minutes

350 g (12 oz) plain (all-purpose) flour
2 teaspoons baking powder
2 teaspoons ground ginger
100 g (3½ oz) chilled unsalted
   butter, diced
175 g (6 oz/¾ cup) soft brown sugar
1 egg, beaten
115 g (4 oz/⅓ cup) dark treacle
silver balls (optional)

ICING GLAZE
1 egg white
3 teaspoons lemon juice
155 g (5½ oz/1¼ cups) icing
   (confectioners') sugar

ROYAL ICING
1 egg white
200 g (7 oz) icing (confectioners')
   sugar

Pour in the egg and treacle and stir to form a soft dough.

Cut out shapes from the dough using an assortment of biscuit cutters.

GINGERBREAD

1 Preheat the oven to 190°C (375°F/Gas 5). Lightly grease two baking trays.

2 Sift the flour, baking powder, ground ginger and a pinch of salt into a bowl. Rub in the butter until the mixture resembles fine breadcrumbs, then stir in the sugar. Make a well in the centre, add the egg and treacle and, using a wooden spoon, stir until a soft dough forms. Transfer to a clean surface and knead until smooth.

3 Divide the dough in half and roll out on a lightly floured work surface until 5 mm (¼ inch) thick. Using various-shaped cutters (hearts, stars or flowers), cut into desired shapes, then transfer to the prepared trays. Bake in batches for 8 minutes, or until the biscuits are light brown. Cool on the trays for 2–3 minutes, then transfer to a wire rack to cool completely. (If using the biscuits as hanging decorations, use a skewer to make a small hole in each one while still hot.)

4 To make the glaze, whisk the egg white and lemon juice together until foamy, then whisk in the icing sugar to form a smooth, thin icing. Cover the surface with plastic wrap until needed.

5 To make the royal icing, lightly whisk the egg white until just foamy, then gradually whisk in enough icing sugar to form a soft icing. Cover the surface with plastic wrap until needed.

6 Brush a thin layer of glaze over some of the biscuits and leave to set. Using an icing bag filled with royal icing, decorate the biscuits as shown in the photograph, or as desired. Store glazed gingerbread for up to 3 days in an airtight container.

Makes: 24 squares

Preparation time: 25 minutes

Cooking time: 1 hour 10 minutes

BASE

185 g (6½ oz/1½ cups) plain (all-purpose) flour, sifted
60 g (2¼ oz/½ cup) icing (confectioners') sugar
180 g (6 oz) unsalted butter, chopped

TOPPING

6 eggs, lightly beaten
460 g (1 lb/2 cups) caster (superfine) sugar
2 teaspoons finely grated lemon zest
250 ml (9 fl oz/1 cup) lemon juice
60 g (2¼ oz/½ cup) plain (all-purpose) flour
icing (confectioners') sugar, for dusting

LEMON SQUARES

1 Preheat the oven to 170°C (325°F/ Gas 3). Lightly grease a 20 x 30 cm (8 x 12 inch) rectangular shallow tin with butter and line the base with baking paper, leaving the paper hanging over on the two long sides.

2 To make the base, mix the flour and icing sugar in a bowl. Using your fingertips, rub in the butter until the mixture resembles breadcrumbs. Press the dough evenly over the base of the tin. Bake for 25 minutes, or until golden and firm to the touch. Set aside to cool. Reduce the oven to 160°C (315°F/Gas 2–3).

3 To make the topping, whisk the eggs and sugar in a bowl for 3–4 minutes, or until pale and thick. Whisk in the lemon zest and juice, then add the flour and whisk to just combine. Pour the mixture over the base and bake for 45 minutes, or until set, covering with foil for the last 20 minutes of cooking. Cool in the tin, then carefully lift out and cut into 5 cm (2 inch) squares using a hot knife. Dust with icing sugar just before serving.

4 The lemon squares will keep, stored in an airtight container in the refrigerator, for up to 3 days.

Makes: about 45

Preparation time: 45 minutes

Cooking time: 20 minutes

250 g (9 oz) unsalted butter, softened
140 g (5 oz) icing (confectioners') sugar
1 egg yolk, lightly beaten
90 g (3¼ oz) cream cheese, softened
  and cut into chunks
1½ teaspoons natural vanilla extract
1 teaspoon finely grated lemon zest
350 g (12 oz/2¾ cups) plain
  (all-purpose) flour, sifted
¼ teaspoon baking powder
½ teaspoon bicarbonate of soda
  (baking soda)
2 tablespoons each apricot, blueberry
  and raspberry jam

THUMBPRINT BISCUITS

1 Preheat the oven to 180°C (350°F/ Gas 4) and grease three baking trays.

2 Cream the butter, icing sugar and egg yolk in a bowl using electric beaters until pale and fluffy, then beat in the cream cheese, vanilla and lemon zest until smooth. Combine the flour, baking powder, bicarbonate of soda and ¼ teaspoon salt in a large bowl and, using a wooden spoon, gradually stir into the creamed mixture until a soft dough forms. Set aside for 5–10 minutes, or until the dough firms up.

3 Break off small (15 g/½ oz) pieces of dough, shape into balls and flatten slightly to make 4 cm (1½ inch) rounds. Transfer to the prepared trays and make a small indent in the centre of each with your thumb. Spoon about ¼ teaspoon of apricot jam into one-third of the biscuits, ¼ teaspoon blueberry jam into one-third, and ¼ teaspoon of raspberry jam into the remaining one-third of the biscuits. Bake for 10–12 minutes, or until light golden. Cool for a few minutes on the trays, then transfer to a wire rack.

4 These biscuits are best eaten the same day but will keep, stored in an airtight container, for up to 2 days.

Makes: 25

Preparation time: 30 minutes
+ standing time

Cooking time: 45 minutes

200 g (7 oz) dark chocolate, chopped
175 g (6 oz) unsalted butter, chopped
2 eggs
230 g (8½ oz/1 cup) soft brown sugar
40 g (1½ oz/⅓ cup) unsweetened
  cocoa powder
125 g (4½ oz/1 cup) plain (all-purpose)
  flour
80 g (2¾ oz/½ cup) unsalted cashews,
  toasted and chopped
100 g (3½ oz) dark chocolate,
  chopped, extra

ICING
200 g (7 oz) dark chocolate, chopped
125 g (4½ oz/½ cup) sour cream
30 g (1 oz/¼ cup) icing (confectioners')
  sugar, sifted

CASHEW BROWNIES

1 Preheat the oven to 160°C (315°F/Gas 2–3). Lightly grease a 23 cm (9 inch) square shallow tin and line the base with baking paper.

2 Put the chocolate and butter in a heatproof bowl. Sit the bowl over a saucepan of simmering water, stirring frequently until the chocolate and butter have melted. Take care that the base of the bowl doesn't touch the water. Allow to cool.

3 Whisk the eggs and sugar in a large bowl for 5 minutes, or until pale and thick. Fold in the cooled chocolate mixture, then the sifted cocoa powder and flour. Fold in the cashews and extra chocolate, then pour into the tin, smoothing the top. Bake for 30–35 minutes, or until just

firm to the touch. (The brownies may have a slightly soft centre when hot but will firm when cool.) Allow to cool.

4 To make the icing, put the chocolate in a small heatproof bowl. Sit the bowl over a small saucepan of simmering water, stirring frequently until the chocolate has melted. Take care that the base of the bowl doesn't touch the water. Allow to cool slightly, then add the sour cream and icing sugar and stir to mix well. Spread evenly over the cooled brownies. Leave for a few hours or overnight to firm up, then cut into squares.

5 The brownies will keep, stored in an airtight container, for up to 5 days, or up to 3 months in the freezer.

Makes: 18 'sandwiches'

Preparation time: 40 minutes

Cooking time: 24 minutes

350 g (12 oz) unsalted butter, softened
60 g (2¼ oz/½ cup) icing
    (confectioners') sugar
grated zest from 2 mandarins
250 g (9 oz/2 cups) plain (all-purpose)
    flour
60 g (2¼ oz/½ cup) cornflour
    (cornstarch)

ICING
120 g (4¼ oz) unsalted butter, softened
250 g (9 oz/2 cups) icing
    (confectioners') sugar
2 tablespoons freshly squeezed
    mandarin juice

MANDARIN WHIRLS

1 Preheat the oven to 180°C (350°F/Gas 4). Line two baking trays with baking paper.

2 Cream the butter, icing sugar and zest in a bowl using electric beaters until pale and fluffy. Sift the flour and cornflour into the bowl, then stir with a wooden spoon until a soft dough forms.

3 Transfer the mixture to a piping bag fitted with a 4 cm (1½ inch) star nozzle and pipe thirty-six 4 cm (1½ inch) rounds, spacing them well apart, on the baking trays. Bake for 12–15 minutes, or until lightly golden on the edges. Cool on the trays for 5 minutes, then transfer to a wire rack to cool completely.

4 To make the icing, cream the butter, icing sugar and mandarin juice in a bowl using electric beaters until pale and soft. Use the icing to sandwich the whirls together.

5 Filled biscuits are best served on the day they are made. Unfilled biscuits will keep, stored in an airtight container, for up to 1 week, or frozen for up to 3 months.

Makes: 25 pieces

Preparation time: 40 minutes

Cooking time: 35 minutes

125 g (4½ oz) unsalted butter, chopped, softened
230 g (8 oz/1 cup) caster (superfine) sugar
½ teaspoon natural vanilla extract
2 eggs
250 g (9 oz/2 cups) self-raising flour
250 ml (9 fl oz/1 cup) milk
2 teaspoons instant coffee, dissolved in 2 teaspoons boiling water

ICING
375 g (13 oz/3 cups) icing (confectioners') sugar
60 g (2¼ oz/½ cup) unsweetened cocoa powder
20 g (¾ oz) unsalted butter
2 teaspoons instant coffee powder
75 g (2½ oz/1¼ cups) shredded coconut
90 g (3¼ oz/1 cup) desiccated coconut

MOCHA LAMINGTONS

1 Preheat the oven to 180°C (350°F/Gas 4). Lightly grease the base of a 23 cm (9 inch) square shallow tin and line the base with baking paper.

2 Cream the butter, sugar and vanilla in a bowl using electric beaters until pale and fluffy. Add the eggs one at a time, beating well after each addition. Sift the flour into a bowl, then stir the flour into the butter mixture alternately with the milk until combined and smooth. Spoon half the mixture into the prepared tin and spread evenly over the base. Add the dissolved coffee to the remaining mixture and stir until well combined. Carefully spread the coffee mixture over the mixture in the tin.

3 Bake for 30–35 minutes, or until a skewer inserted into the centre of the cake comes out clean. Cool in the tin for 5 minutes before turning out onto a wire rack to cool. Cut into 25 squares.

4 To make the icing, sift the icing sugar and cocoa powder into a large shallow bowl. Add the butter and coffee and gradually whisk in 150 ml (5 fl oz) boiling water until smooth. Put the shredded and desiccated coconuts in a large shallow bowl and toss to combine.

5 Using two spoons to hold the cake, dip the cake squares into the icing to cover, allowing the excess to drip off. (Add a little boiling water to the icing if it starts to thicken). Roll the cake in the coconut to cover and place on a wire rack. Repeat with the remaining cakes.

Dip the squares of cake into the chocolate icing.

Roll the iced cake in the coconut to thoroughly cover it.

Makes: 18 fingers

Preparation time: 35 minutes

Cooking time: 10 minutes

250 g (9 oz/2 cups) plain (all-purpose)
   flour
1 teaspoon baking powder
145 g (5 oz/²⁄₃ cup) caster (superfine)
   sugar
75 g (2¹⁄₂ oz) unsalted butter, melted
2 tablespoons lime juice
grated zest from 2 limes
1 teaspoon natural vanilla extract
1 egg, lightly beaten
1 egg yolk
150 g (5¹⁄₂ oz) white chocolate,
   chopped

LIME AND WHITE CHOCOLATE FINGERS

1 Preheat the oven to 170°C (325°F/Gas 3). Lightly grease and flour two baking trays.

2 Sift the flour and baking powder into a large bowl and stir in the sugar. Whisk together the butter, lime juice, zest, vanilla, egg and egg yolk until combined. Add the butter mixture to the flour mixture and stir until a firm dough forms.

3 Take tablespoonfuls of the dough and, on a lightly floured board, roll into thin logs 12 cm (4¹⁄₂ inches) long. Place on the prepared trays and bake for 10 minutes, or until firm, swapping the position of the trays halfway through cooking. Cool on the trays for 5 minutes, then remove to a wire rack to cool completely.

4 Put the chocolate in a small heatproof bowl. Sit the bowl over a small saucepan of simmering water, stirring frequently until the chocolate has melted. Take care that the base of the bowl doesn't touch the water.

5 To decorate the biscuits, place them close together on the wire rack (put a piece of paper towel under the rack to catch the drips) and, using a fork dipped into the melted chocolate, drizzle the chocolate over the biscuits. Leave to set.

6 Lime and white chocolate fingers will keep, stored in an airtight container, for up to 2 days. Undecorated biscuits will keep for up to 7 days in an airtight container, or up to 8 weeks in the freezer.

Makes: 24 squares

Preparation time: 45 minutes

Cooking time: 40 minutes

250 g (9 oz/2 cups) plain
(all-purpose) flour
1½ teaspoons ground cinnamon
60 g (2¼ oz/½ cup) icing
(confectioners') sugar
200 g (7 oz) unsalted butter, chopped

APRICOT FILLING
200 g (7 oz) chopped dried apricots
80 g (2¾ oz/⅓ cup) caster
(superfine) sugar

MERINGUE TOPPING
2 egg whites
80 g (2¾ oz/⅓ cup) caster
(superfine) sugar
115 g (4 oz/1¼ cups) desiccated
coconut

APRICOT MERINGUE SQUARES

1 Preheat the oven to 180°C (350°F/ Gas 4). Lightly grease a 20 x 30 cm (8 x 12 inch) rectangular shallow tin and line the base with baking paper, leaving the paper hanging over on the two long sides.

2 Combine the flour, cinnamon and icing sugar in a food processor and process until just combined. Add the butter and, using the pulse button, pulse until the mixture is crumbly. Add 1–1½ tablespoons

water and process until the mixture just forms a dough; do not overprocess. Using the back of a spoon, press the dough evenly into the prepared tin. Refrigerate for 20 minutes.

3 Bake the dough for 15–20 minutes, or until golden. Remove from the oven and allow to cool.

4 Meanwhile, to make the apricot filling, combine the apricots, sugar

and 250 ml (9 fl oz/1 cup) water in a small saucepan. Stir over medium heat until the sugar has dissolved, then reduce the heat and simmer for 12 minutes, or until the mixture is thick. Remove from the heat and cool, then spread over the cooled base.

5 To make the topping, whisk the egg whites in a clean, dry bowl until soft peaks form. Gradually add the sugar, whisking well after each addition. Whisk until the mixture is stiff and glossy and the sugar has dissolved. Fold in the coconut. Spread the topping evenly over the filling. Bake for 15 minutes, or until the topping is just firm to touch. Cool completely before cutting into 5 x 5 cm (2 x 2 inch) squares.

6 The apricot meringue squares will keep, stored in an airtight container, for up to 4 days.

Press the dough evenly into the tin, using the back of a spoon.

Spoon the cooled apricot mixture evenly over the cooked base.

Makes: about 40 clusters

Preparation time: 30 minutes

Cooking time: 15 minutes

200 g (7 oz) dark chocolate
60 g (2¼ oz) unsalted butter, chopped
170 g (6 oz/¾ cup) caster (superfine) sugar
1 tablespoon golden syrup or dark corn syrup
1½ teaspoons natural vanilla extract
155 g (5½ oz/1¼ cups) raisins
200 g (7 oz/1¼ cups) peanut halves, toasted and roughly chopped
40 g (1½ oz/⅓ cup) plain (all-purpose) flour
2 tablespoons unsweetened cocoa powder

CHOCOLATE, RAISIN AND PEANUT CLUSTERS

1 Preheat the oven to 170°C (325°F/Gas 3). Lightly grease two baking trays.

2 Roughly chop 80 g (2¾ oz) of the chocolate and put in a heatproof bowl along with the butter, sugar, golden syrup and vanilla. Put the bowl over a saucepan of simmering water, stirring until the chocolate and butter have melted and the mixture is smooth. Take care that the base of the bowl doesn't touch the water. Allow to cool slightly.

3 Roughly chop the remaining chocolate and combine with the raisins and peanuts in a large bowl. Sift the flour and cocoa powder over the peanut mixture and toss to combine. Add the melted chocolate mixture and, using a wooden spoon, stir until the mixture is well combined and a firm dough forms.

4 Using a tablespoon of the mixture at a time, form into rough rounds, then place on the trays, spacing the

biscuits about 4 cm (1½ inches) apart. Bake for 15 minutes, swapping the position of the trays halfway through cooking, or until the biscuits are firm and no longer glossy. Cool on the trays for 5 minutes, then carefully remove to a wire rack to cool completely.

5 The chocolate biscuits will keep, stored in an airtight container, for up to 1 week, or frozen for up to 8 weeks.

Makes: 20 fingers

Preparation time:
1 hour 15 minutes

Cooking time: 35 minutes

60 g (2¼ oz/½ cup) plain
   (all-purpose) flour
2 tablespoons self-raising flour
2 tablespoons icing (confectioners')
   sugar
60 g (2¼ oz) unsalted butter,
   chopped
1 egg yolk

TOPPING
350 g (12 oz) assorted light-coloured
   glacé fruits
(pineapple, apricots, peaches, pears)
80 ml (2½ fl oz/⅓ cup) brandy
175 g (6 oz) unsalted butter, softened
115 g (4 oz/½ cup) caster (superfine)
   sugar
2 tablespoons honey
1 egg
40 g (1½ oz/⅓ cup) plain
   (all-purpose) flour
40 g (1½ oz/⅓ cup) self-raising flour
80 g (2¾ oz/½ cup) macadamia
   nuts, toasted and chopped
icing (confectioners') sugar, for
   dusting (optional)

GLACÉ FRUIT FINGERS

1 Preheat the oven to 180°C (350°F/ Gas 4). Lightly grease a 20 x 30 cm (8 x 12 inch) rectangular shallow tin and line the base with baking paper, leaving the paper hanging over on the two long sides.

2 Process the flours and icing sugar in a food processor until just combined. Add the butter and, using the pulse button, process in short bursts until the mixture is crumbly. Add the egg yolk and about 1 tablespoon water and pulse just until a dough forms. Cover with plastic wrap and refrigerate for 30 minutes.

3 Roll out the pastry between two sheets of baking paper until large enough to cover the base of the tin. Transfer to the tin.

4 To make the topping, cut the fruit into 5 mm (¼ inch) pieces with scissors or a sharp knife. Combine the fruit and brandy in a bowl, mix well and leave, covered, for about 1 hour, or until the fruit has absorbed the brandy.

5 Cream the butter, sugar and honey in a small bowl using electric beaters until pale and fluffy. Add the egg and beat well until combined. Sift the flours together in a bowl, then stir into the creamed mixture. Stir in the glacé fruit and macadamia nuts, then spread the mixture evenly over the pastry. Bake for 30–35 minutes, or until golden brown. The topping may be slightly soft but will firm on cooling. Cool in the tin, then cut into 7.5 x 4 cm (3 x 1½ inch) pieces and dust lightly with icing sugar before serving.

6 Glacé fruit fingers will keep, stored in an airtight container, for up to 4 days, or frozen for up to 3 months.

TIP If preferred, you could use dried fruit, such as dried pears, peaches and mango, instead of glacé fruit.

Stir in the fruit and macadamia nuts.

Makes: 30 'sandwiches'

Preparation time: 45 minutes

Cooking time: 1 hour

4 egg whites
235 g (8½ oz/1 cup) caster
    (superfine) sugar
1 tablespoon rosewater
a few drops of pink food colouring
    (optional)
icing (confectioners') sugar,
    for dusting

SUGARED ROSE PETALS (OPTIONAL)
2–3 unsprayed pink or red roses
1 egg white, lightly beaten
115 g (4 oz/½ cup) caster
    (superfine) sugar

RASPBERRY CREAM
300 ml (10½ fl oz) thick
    (double/heavy) cream
1 tablespoon icing (confectioners')
    sugar, sifted
100 g (3⅓ oz) fresh raspberries,
    or frozen raspberries, thawed

Following the circles drawn on the baking paper, pipe the meringue mixture into small rounds.

Use a small paintbrush to lightly brush the egg white on both sides of the petal.

ROSEWATER MERINGUES
with raspberry cream

1 Preheat the oven to 120°C (235°F/Gas ½). Line two baking trays with baking paper and mark thirty 3 cm (1¼ inch) rounds on each sheet of paper.

2 Whisk the egg whites in a clean, dry bowl until stiff peaks form. Add the sugar gradually, whisking well after each addition. Whisk until the mixture is stiff and glossy and the sugar has dissolved. Add the rosewater and food colouring, if using, to tint the meringue pale pink.

3 Transfer the mixture, in batches if necessary, to a piping bag fitted with a 1 cm (½ inch) plain nozzle. Following the marked rounds as a guide, pipe sixty 3 cm (1¼ inch) rounds, each about 2 cm (¾ inch) high, onto the paper. Bake for 1 hour, then turn off the oven and leave the meringues to cool in the oven with the door slightly ajar.

4 To make sugared rose petals, if using, remove the petals from the roses. Working on one petal at a time, use a small paintbrush to lightly brush the egg white over both sides of the petal. Toss lightly in the sugar and set aside to dry. Repeat with the remaining petals. If not using immediately, store in an airtight container.

5 To make the raspberry cream, beat the cream and icing sugar until thick, then fold in the raspberries. Spread the raspberry cream over the bases of half the meringues and then join together with the remaining meringues to make a 'sandwich'. Decorate with the sugared rose petals, if using, and dust lightly with icing sugar. Serve immediately. Unfilled meringues will keep, stored in an airtight container in a cool place, for up to 2 weeks.

Makes: 25 slices

Preparation time: 30 minutes

Cooking time: 55 minutes

55 g (2 oz/½ cup) ground almonds
170 g (6 oz/⅔ cup) plain yoghurt
230 g (8 oz/1 cup) caster (superfine) sugar
125 g (4½ oz) unsalted butter, melted
½ teaspoon natural vanilla extract
2 eggs, lightly beaten
185 g (6½ oz/1½ cups) semolina
1 teaspoon baking powder
2 tablespoons whole unsalted pistachio nuts, for decoration

SYRUP
170 g (6 oz/¾ cup) caster (superfine) sugar
1 teaspoon finely grated lemon zest
1 tablespoon lemon juice

SEMOLINA SYRUP SLICE

1 Preheat the oven to 180°C (350°F/ Gas 4). Lightly grease a 23 cm (9 inch) square shallow tin and line the base with baking paper.

2 To make the syrup, combine the sugar, lemon zest and lemon juice in a saucepan with 125 ml (4 fl oz/ ½ cup) water. Stir over low heat until the sugar has dissolved. Increase the heat, bring the mixture to the boil and simmer for 10 minutes without stirring. Allow to cool, then strain.

3 Put the ground almonds in a small frying pan and stir over medium heat for 3–5 minutes, or until lightly browned, then remove from the heat and cool.

4 Combine the yoghurt and sugar in a bowl, stir until well combined, then stir in the butter, vanilla and eggs. Combine the semolina and baking powder in a bowl, stir to mix well, then stir into the yoghurt mixture. Stir in the almonds. Spread the mixture over the base

of the tin, smoothing the surface, then arrange the pistachios evenly over the top. Bake for 35 minutes, or until the top is lightly browned and a skewer inserted into the centre comes out clean. Pour the cold syrup over the hot slice. Leave to cool completely in the tin before cutting into squares.

5 The slice will keep, stored in an airtight container, for up to 3 days.

Makes: 32 star shapes

Preparation time: 50 minutes

Cooking time: 18 minutes

200 g (7 oz/1²⁄₃ cups) plain
(all-purpose) flour
40 g (1¹⁄₂ oz/¹⁄₃ cup) unsweetened
cocoa powder
1¹⁄₂ teaspoons ground cinnamon
250 g (9 oz) unsalted butter
60 g (2¹⁄₄ oz/¹⁄₂ cup) icing
(confectioners') sugar
caster (superfine) sugar, for sprinkling

CINNAMON CHOCOLATE SHORTBREAD

1 Preheat the oven to 160°C
(315°F/Gas 2–3). Line two
baking trays with baking paper.
Sift together the flour, cocoa and
cinnamon. Using electric beaters,
beat the butter and icing sugar
until light and creamy. Using a
large metal spoon, fold in the sifted
flour mixture. Turn the dough out
onto a lightly floured surface and
knead gently until smooth.

2 Roll out the dough between
two sheets of baking paper until
1 cm (¹⁄₂ inch) thick. Using a 7 cm
(2³⁄₄ inch) star cutter, cut out the
biscuits. Place on the prepared
trays, leaving room for spreading.
Prick the dough with a fork,
sprinkle the top with the caster
sugar and refrigerate for 30 minutes.

3 Bake for 15–18 minutes, swapping
trays halfway through cooking.
Allow to cool on the trays.

Makes: 20 fingers

Preparation time: 45 minutes
+ soaking time

Cooking time: 55 minutes

250 g (9 oz) dried pears
1 tablespoon caster (superfine) sugar
275 g (9¾ oz) unsalted butter, chopped
140 g (5 oz/¾ cup) lightly packed soft
    brown sugar
80 g (2¾ oz/⅓ cup) caster (superfine)
    sugar
3 eggs
280 g (10 oz/2¼ cups) plain
    (all-purpose) flour
1 teaspoon baking powder
1 teaspoon ground cardamom
icing (confectioners') sugar, for dusting

CARDAMOM PEAR SHORTCAKE

1 Preheat the oven to 180°C (350°F/Gas 4). Lightly grease a 20 x 30 cm (8 x 12 inch) rectangular shallow tin with butter and line with baking paper, leaving the paper hanging over on the two long sides.

2 Put the dried pears in a bowl, cover with boiling water and soak for several hours, or until the pears have softened a little and the water has cooled. Drain off the water, reserving 125 ml (4 fl oz/½ cup). Put the pears and sugar in a saucepan with the reserved soaking water. Stir to dissolve the sugar, then return to the boil and cook, covered, for 5 minutes, or until the pears are soft.

3 Cream the butter and sugars in a bowl using electric beaters until pale and fluffy. Add the eggs one at a time,

beating well after each addition. Sift over the flour, baking powder and cardamom, then, using a large metal spoon, fold the flour mixture into the butter mixture until well combined. Spread half the mixture evenly over the base of the prepared tin. Scatter the pears over, then dot the remaining mixture over the pears to cover.

4 Bake for 40–45 minutes, or until golden and a skewer inserted into the centre of the cake comes out clean. Leave to cool in the tin, then carefully lift out, dust with icing sugar and cut into 10 x 3 cm (4 x 1¼ inch) fingers.

5 The cardamom pear shortcake will keep, stored in an airtight container in a cool place, for up to 3 days.

Makes: about 40 biscuits

Preparation time: 30 minutes

Cooking time: 45 minutes
+ cooling time

250 g (9 oz/2½ cups) walnut halves,
    lightly toasted
310 g (11 oz/2½ cups) plain (all-purpose)
    flour, plus extra for rolling
1 teaspoon baking powder
½ teaspoon bicarbonate of soda
    (baking soda)
170 g (6 oz/¾ cup) caster (superfine)
    sugar
3 eggs, lightly beaten
grated zest from 3 oranges
2 teaspoons natural vanilla extract

WALNUT AND ORANGE BISCOTTI

1   Preheat the oven to 170°C (325°F/Gas 3). Lightly grease
    a baking tray.

2   Roughly chop the walnuts and set aside. Sift the flour,
    baking powder and bicarbonate of soda into a large
    bowl, then stir in the sugar. Combine the eggs, orange
    zest and vanilla in a bowl and stir with a fork to mix
    well. Pour the egg mixture into the flour mixture and
    stir until nearly combined, then, using your hands,
    knead briefly to form a firm dough. Put the dough on
    a lightly floured work surface and knead the walnuts
    into the dough.

3   Divide the dough into three even-sized pieces. Working
    with one piece of dough at a time, roll each piece to

form a 29 cm (11½ inch) log. Gently pat the surface to
flatten the log to a 4 cm (1½ inch) width, then place on
the prepared tray and bake for 30 minutes, or until light
golden and firm. Remove from the oven and allow to
cool for 15 minutes.

4   Reduce the oven to 150°C (300°F/Gas 2). When the
    logs are cool enough to handle, remove to a board
    and, using a sharp, serrated knife, cut the logs on the
    diagonal into 1 cm (½ inch) thick slices. Arrange in
    a single layer on the two baking trays and bake for
    15 minutes, swapping the position of the trays halfway
    through cooking, or until the biscotti are dry. Cool on
    a wire rack. Biscotti will keep, stored in an airtight
    container, for up to 3 weeks.

Makes: about 25 slices

Preparation time: 1 hour 10 minutes

Cooking time: 45 minutes

300 g (10½ oz) rhubarb, trimmed and cut into 5 mm (¼ inch) slices
115 g (4 oz/½ cup) caster (superfine) sugar
185 g (6½ oz) unsalted butter, chopped
230 g (8 oz/1 cup) caster (superfine) sugar
½ teaspoon natural vanilla extract
3 eggs
90 g (3¼ oz/¾ cup) plain (all-purpose) flour
¾ teaspoon baking powder
1 tablespoon sugar
icing (confectioners') sugar, for dusting

RHUBARB SLICE

1 Combine the rhubarb and sugar in a bowl and set aside, stirring occasionally, for 1 hour, or until the rhubarb has released its juices and the sugar has dissolved. Strain well, discarding the liquid.

2 Preheat the oven to 180°C (350°F/Gas 4). Lightly grease a 20 x 30 cm (8 x 12 inch) rectangular shallow tin with butter. Line the base with baking paper, leaving the paper hanging over on the two long sides.

3 Cream the butter, sugar and vanilla in a bowl using electric beaters until pale and fluffy. Add the eggs one at a time, beating well after each addition. Sift the flour and baking powder over the mixture, then stir to combine. Spread the mixture evenly over the base of the prepared tin, then put the rhubarb over the top in a single layer. Sprinkle with the sugar. Bake for 40–45 minutes, or until golden. Leave to cool slightly in the tin, then carefully lift out and cut into squares. Dust with icing sugar and serve warm as a dessert with cream, or at room temperature as a snack. The rhubarb slice is best eaten on the day it is made.

Makes: about 50 biscuits

Preparation time: 4 hour 30 minutes

Cooking time: 30 minutes

125 g (4½ oz/1 cup) icing
   (confectioners') sugar, sifted
175 g (6 oz) unsalted butter, softened
2 egg yolks
2 teaspoons lemon juice
185 g (6½ oz/1½ cups) plain
   (all-purpose) flour, sifted
110 g (3¾ oz/1 cup) ground hazelnuts
150 g (5½ oz/1½ cups) sweetened
   dried cranberries
80 g (2¾ oz/½ cup) poppy seeds

CRANBERRY AND HAZELNUT REFRIGERATOR BISCUITS

1 Cream the icing sugar and butter in a bowl until pale and fluffy. Add the egg yolks and lemon juice and beat to combine well. Add the flour and ground hazelnuts and stir to combine well, then stir in the cranberries. Divide the mixture in half.

2 Scatter half the poppy seeds over a 30 cm (12 inch) long piece of foil. Place one half of the mixture on the work surface and form into a 21 cm (8 inch) long sausage shape.

Transfer the dough to the foil, firmly rolling the dough in the poppy seeds to coat, then roll tightly in the foil to form a neat cylinder, twisting the ends tight. Repeat with the remaining poppy seeds and dough and another piece of foil. Refrigerate the dough for a minimum of 4 hours, but it can be left for up to 5 days.

3 When you are ready to bake the biscuits, preheat the oven to 170°C (325°F/Gas 3). Lightly grease two

baking trays. Remove the foil and, using a large serrated knife, cut the dough into 8 mm (⅜ inch) thick slices. Place the rounds on the baking trays and bake for 12–15 minutes, or until firm and lightly coloured. Cool on the trays for 5 minutes, then transfer to a wire rack.

4 An uncooked log of dough can be frozen, ready to be thawed, sliced and baked, when needed. Cooked, the biscuits will keep, stored in an airtight container, for up to 1 week.

Makes: 20 slices

Preparation time: 25 minutes

Cooking time: 55 minutes

BASE
200 g (7 oz) unsalted butter, chopped
310 g (11 oz/2½ cups) plain
    (all-purpose) flour
115 g (4 oz/½ cup) caster (superfine)
    sugar
2 egg yolks, lightly beaten

FILLING
2 x 395 g (14 oz) tins sweetened
    condensed milk
100 g (3½ oz) unsalted butter, chopped
115 g (4 oz/⅓ cup) honey

HONEY CARAMEL SLICE

1 Preheat the oven to 180°C (350°F/Gas 4). Lightly grease a 20 x 30 cm (8 x 12 inch) rectangular shallow tin with butter and line the base with baking paper, leaving the paper hanging over on the two long sides.

2 To make the base, combine all the ingredients, except the egg yolks, in a food processor and process until the mixture resembles fine breadcrumbs. Add the yolks and 1–2 tablespoons chilled water and process just until a dough forms, adding a little more water if necessary; do not overprocess. Using lightly floured hands, press half the dough over the base of the tin. Bake for 12–15 minutes, or until golden and firm to the touch. Wrap the remaining dough in plastic wrap and refrigerate until firm.

3 To make the filling, put the condensed milk and butter in a heavy-based saucepan and stir over low heat until the butter has melted. Increase the heat to medium and cook for 5–8 minutes, stirring continuously, or until the mixture has thickened. Remove from the heat and stir in the honey. Allow to cool, then pour the filling over the base and spread evenly to cover.

4 Using a grater, grate the cold dough over the caramel filling to cover, then bake for 20–30 minutes, or until golden. Cool in the tray, then carefully lift out and cut into 10 x 3 cm (4 x 1¼ inch) fingers. The honey caramel slice will keep, stored in an airtight container, for up to 3 days.

Makes: about 64 biscuits

Preparation time: 35 minutes

Cooking time: 30 minutes

4 egg whites, lightly beaten
450 g (1 lb/2 cups) caster (superfine)
   sugar
1½ tablespoons liquid glucose
1½ teaspoons natural vanilla extract
180 g (6 oz/2 cups) desiccated coconut
125 g (4½ oz/1 cup) plain (all-purpose)
   flour

COCONUT MACAROONS

1 Combine the egg whites, sugar and liquid glucose in a large heatproof bowl and whisk to combine. Place the bowl over a saucepan of simmering water and whisk until the mixture is just warm. Remove from the heat and add the vanilla, coconut and flour and stir to combine well. Cover the bowl with plastic wrap and refrigerate the mixture until firm.

2 Meanwhile, preheat the oven to 150°C (300°F/Gas 2). Line two baking trays with baking paper. Take a heaped teaspoonful of the mixture and, using wet hands, form the mixture into balls. Flatten the balls slightly and place them on the trays, spacing them apart. Bake for 15 minutes, or until the macaroons are light golden, swapping the position of the trays halfway through cooking. Cool for 5 minutes on the tray, then transfer to a wire rack to cool completely.

3 Macaroons will keep, stored in an airtight container, for up to 1 week, or frozen for up to 8 weeks.

TIP Use large baking trays, if you have them, as you will need to give the macaroons room to spread. Alternatively, cook them in two batches.

Makes: 10 slices

Preparation time: 20 minutes

Cooking time: 35 minutes

250 g (9 oz) wheatmeal biscuits
  (cookies), such as Granita
½ teaspoon ground cinnamon,
  plus 1 teaspoon extra
½ teaspoon ground nutmeg
100 g (3½ oz) unsalted butter, melted
500 g (1 lb 2 oz) cream cheese,
  at room temperature
4 tablespoons honey
3 eggs, at room temperature
85 g (3 oz/⅔ cup) sultanas
  (golden raisins)
1 teaspoon ground cinnamon, extra

SPICED CHEESECAKE SLICE

1 Brush a 27 x 17 cm (10¾ x 6½ inch) rectangular shallow tin with melted butter and line the base and two long sides with baking paper. Put the biscuits in a food processor with the cinnamon and nutmeg and process into crumbs. Add the butter and process until well combined. Press firmly into the prepared tin and refrigerate until firm. Preheat the oven to 170°C (325°F/Gas 3).

2 Using electric beaters, beat the cream cheese and honey together until the mixture is creamy. Add the eggs one at a time, beating well after each addition. Stir through the sultanas. Pour the mixture over the base. Sprinkle over the extra cinnamon, and swirl gently with a thick bamboo skewer to create a swirled effect on the top. Bake for 30–35 minutes, or until just set. Cool in the tin, then cut into pieces to serve.

Makes: 30 biscuits

Preparation time: 20 minutes

Cooking time: 1 hour

2 eggs, at room temperature
250 g (9 oz/heaped 1 cup) caster
   (superfine) sugar
280 g (10 oz/2¼ cups) plain
   (all-purpose) flour
½ teaspoon baking powder
2 teaspoons ground cinnamon
125 g (4½ oz/1¼ cups) pecans

CINNAMON PECAN BISCOTTI

1 Preheat the oven to 170°C (325°F/Gas 3). Line a baking tray with baking paper. Using electric beaters, beat the eggs and sugar for 2 minutes, or until pale and thick. Add the sifted flour, baking powder, cinnamon and pecans. Use a flat-bladed knife to mix to a soft dough. Turn out onto a lightly floured surface and knead until the mixture comes together.

2 Divide the mixture into two equal portions. Shape each portion into logs about 25 cm (10 inches) long and 8 cm (3¼ inches) wide. Place the logs onto the prepared tray, leaving room for spreading, and bake for 35–40 minutes, or until lightly coloured. Set aside to cool completely.

3 Using a serrated knife, cut the logs into 1 cm (½ inch) thick slices and place in a single layer, cut side down, on the tray. Bake for 15–20 minutes, or until crisp and lightly golden in colour, turning halfway through cooking. Allow to cool completely on the tray.

Makes: 12 slices

Preparation time: 50 minutes

Cooking time: 1 hour 15 minutes

30 g (1 oz) rice flour
40 g (1½ oz/⅓⅓ cup) cornflour
(cornstarch)
60 g (2¼ oz/½ cup) ground almonds
2 tablespoons icing (confectioners')
sugar
60 g (2¼ oz) unsalted butter,
chopped

FILLING
1 small orange
1 egg, separated
55 g (2 oz/¼ cup) caster (superfine)
sugar
80 g (2¾ oz/¾ cup) ground almonds
1 tablespoon caster (superfine) sugar,
extra

LEMON ICING
90 g (3¼ oz/¾ cup) icing
(confectioners') sugar
1 teaspoon unsalted butter
1–1½ tablespoons lemon juice

ORANGE AND ALMOND SLICE

1 Preheat the oven to 180°C (350°F/ Gas 4). Lightly grease the base and sides of a 35 x 11 cm (14 x 4¼ inch) loose-based rectangular fluted shallow tart tin.

2 Combine the rice flour, cornflour, almonds and icing sugar in a food processor and process briefly to just combine. Add the butter and, using the pulse button, process in short bursts just until a dough forms. Press the dough into the base of the tin, then refrigerate for 30 minutes.

3 Meanwhile, to make the filling, put the orange in a small saucepan with enough water to cover. Bring to the boil, then reduce the heat, cover and simmer for 30 minutes, or until soft. Drain and cool. Cut the orange in half widthways,

remove any seeds, and process in a food processor until smooth.

4 Whisk the egg yolk and sugar in a bowl for 5 minutes, or until pale and thick, then fold in the orange purée and almonds. Using clean beaters, whisk the egg white in a clean, dry bowl until stiff peaks form. Add the extra sugar, beating until well combined, then fold into the orange mixture. Gently spread the filling over the base. Bake for 40 minutes, or until lightly browned. Cool in the tin, then remove.

To make the lemon icing, combine the sifted icing sugar and butter in a heatproof bowl with enough juice to form a thick paste. Sit the bowl over a saucepan of simmering water, stirring until the icing is smooth and runny, then remove

from the heat. Working quickly, spread the icing evenly over the filling, then leave to set. Cut into 2.5 cm (1 inch) thick slices. The slice will keep, stored in an airtight container, for up to 4 days.

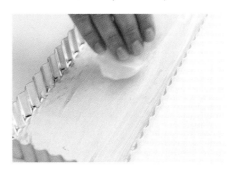

Grease the base and sides of a rectangular fluted tart tin.

Makes: 20–24

Preparation time: 55 minutes

Cooking time: 20 minutes

250 g (9 oz/2 cups) plain (all-purpose)
  flour
30 g (1 oz/¼ cup) unsweetened
  cocoa powder
200 g (7 oz) unsalted butter, chilled
  and diced
100 g (3½ oz) icing (confectioners')
  sugar
2 egg yolks, lightly beaten
1 teaspoon natural vanilla extract

FILLING
100 g (3½ oz/⅔ cup) chopped
  dark chocolate
1 tablespoon golden syrup or dark
  corn syrup
25 g (1 oz) unsalted butter, softened

CHOCOLATE FUDGE SANDWICHES

1 Preheat the oven to 200°C
  (400°F/Gas 6). Lightly grease
  two baking trays.

2 Sift the flour and cocoa powder
  into a bowl and rub in the butter
  until the mixture resembles fine
  breadcrumbs. Sift in the icing sugar
  and stir to combine. Using a
  wooden spoon, gradually stir in the
  egg yolks and vanilla until a soft
  dough forms.

3 Transfer the dough to a lightly
  floured work surface and shape
  into a 4 x 6 x 26 cm (1½ x 2½ x

10½ inch) block. Wrap in plastic
wrap and chill for 30 minutes,
or until firm. Cut the dough into
40–48 slices, about 5 mm (¼ inch)
wide. Place the slices, spacing
them well apart, on the baking
trays. Bake for 10 minutes, or
until firm. Cool on the trays for
5 minutes, then transfer to a wire
rack to cool completely.

4 To make the filling, put the
chocolate in a small heatproof
bowl. Sit the bowl over a small
saucepan of simmering water,
stirring frequently until the

chocolate has melted. Take care
that the base of the bowl doesn't
touch the water. Remove from the
heat, stir in the golden syrup and
butter and continue stirring until
the mixture is smooth. Allow to
cool a little, then put in the
refrigerator and chill for 10 minutes,
or until the mixture is thick enough
to spread. Use the chocolate filling
to sandwich the biscuits together.

5 Filled biscuits are best eaten on
the day they are made. Unfilled
biscuits will keep, stored in an
airtight container, for up to 3 days.

Makes: 16 slices

Preparation time: 25 minutes

Cooking time: 25 minutes

125 g (4½ oz) unsalted butter,
  softened, chopped
115 g (4 oz/½ cup) caster (superfine)
  sugar
1 teaspoon natural vanilla extract
165 g (5¾ oz/1⅓ cups) plain
  (all-purpose) flour
2 teaspoons ground ginger
1 teaspoon baking powder

GINGER ICING (FROSTING)
50 g (1¾ oz) unsalted butter
1½ tablespoons golden or dark
  corn syrup
2 teaspoons ground ginger
90 g (3¼ oz/¾ cup) icing
  (confectioners') sugar

3 tablespoons chopped crystallized
  ginger

GINGER CRUNCH SLICE

1 Preheat the oven to 180°C
  (350°F/Gas 4). Line the base and
  two long sides of a 27 x 18 cm
  (10¾ x 7 inch) shallow tin with
  baking paper.

2 Put the chopped butter, sugar and
  vanilla in a bowl and beat with
  electric beaters until creamy. Sift
  together the combined plain flour,
  ginger and baking powder. Use a

metal spoon to stir in the flour
mixture in two batches until well
incorporated.

3 Use your fingers to press firmly and
  evenly into the prepared tin. Bake
  for 20 minutes, or until pale golden
  and firm to touch.

4 Meanwhile, to make the ginger
  icing, put the butter, golden syrup,

ginger, and icing sugar in a small
saucepan. Stir over low heat until
smooth. Pour and spread the icing
evenly over the slice while the slice
is hot. Mark into 16 slices and
scatter over the crystallized ginger.
Set aside to cool, then cut, using
marks as a guide.

TIP This slice will keep refrigerated in
an airtight container for up to 8 days.

Makes: 24 biscuits

Preparation time: 25 minutes

Cooking time: 20 minutes

200 g (7 oz) unsalted butter
150 g (5½ oz/⅔ cup) caster (superfine)
  sugar
3 tablespoons honey
250 g (9 oz/2 cups) plain (all-purpose)
  flour
1 teaspoon baking powder
80 g (2¾ oz/¾ cup) ground almonds
2 teaspoons ground cardamom
icing (confectioners') sugar, for dusting

HONEY AND CARDAMOM BISCUITS

1 Preheat the oven to 170°C (325°F/ Gas 3). In a small saucepan, melt the butter, sugar and honey over medium heat, stirring until the sugar dissolves.

2 In a large bowl, sift the flour and baking powder. Stir in the ground almonds and cardamom. Make a well in the centre and add the butter mixture. Stir until just combined.

3 Place tablespoons of the mixture onto baking trays lined with baking paper. Flatten slightly with the base of a glass and bake for 15–18 minutes, or until lightly golden. Rest on trays for 5 minutes before transferring to a wire rack to cool completely. Dust lightly with icing sugar.

HONEY AND ALMOND SLICE

Makes: about 30 slices

Preparation time: 25 minutes

Cooking time: 45 minutes

BASE
215 g (7½ oz/1¾ cups) plain (all-purpose) flour
150 g (5½ oz) unsalted butter, chopped
90 g (3¼ oz/¾ cup) icing (confectioners') sugar
1 egg, lightly beaten

FILLING
125 g (4½ oz) unsalted butter
125 g (4½ oz) caster (superfine) sugar
2 eggs
30 g (1 oz/¼ cup) plain (all-purpose) flour
155 g (5½ oz/1½ cups) ground almonds

TOPPING
90 g (3¼ oz) unsalted butter, chopped
80 g (2¾ oz/⅓ cup) caster (superfine) sugar
1½ tablespoons honey
125 g (4½ oz/1 cup) slivered almonds

1 Preheat the oven to 180°C (350°F/Gas 4). Lightly grease a 20 x 30 cm (8 x 12 inch) rectangular tin and line the base with baking paper, leaving the paper hanging over on the two long sides.

2 To make the base, combine the flour, butter and icing sugar in a food processor and process until the mixture resembles fine breadcrumbs. Add the egg and process until a dough forms; do not overprocess. Using lightly floured hands, press the dough evenly over the base of the tin. Bake for 10 minutes, or until light golden. Cool slightly before adding the filling.

3 Meanwhile, to make the filling, cream the butter and sugar in a bowl using electric beaters until pale and fluffy. Add the eggs one at a time, beating well after each addition. Fold in the flour and ground almonds, then spread the mixture over the partly cooked base. Bake for 16–18 minutes, or until golden and firm to the touch. Set aside to cool.

4 To make the topping, put the butter, sugar, honey and almonds in a saucepan and stir over low heat until the butter melts and the sugar dissolves. Increase the heat, then boil the mixture for 3 minutes, or until it starts to come away from the side of the saucepan. Working quickly and using an oiled metal spatula or palette knife, spread the mixture over the filling. Bake for a further 10 minutes, or until golden brown. Cool in the tin, then lift out and cut into squares. Honey and almond slice will keep, stored in an airtight container, for up to 5 days.

Working quickly, spread the almond mixture over the top of the filling.

Makes: about 32 letters

Preparation time: 1 hour

Cooking time: 10 minutes

125 g (4½ oz) unsalted butter, softened
115 g (4 oz) caster (superfine) sugar
1 egg, lightly beaten
½ teaspoon natural vanilla extract
225 g (8 oz) plain (all-purpose) flour
30 g (1 oz/¼ cup) unsweetened
  cocoa powder
½ teaspoon baking powder
2 teaspoons ground cinnamon
1 egg white
1 tablespoon caster (superfine) sugar,
  extra
1 teaspoon ground cinnamon

CHOCOLATE AND CINNAMON ALPHABET BISCUITS

1 Preheat the oven to 190°C (375°F/Gas 5). Lightly grease two baking trays.

2 Cream the butter and sugar in a bowl using electric beaters until pale and fluffy, then beat in the egg and vanilla. Sift in the flour, cocoa powder, baking powder and cinnamon and, using a wooden spoon, stir into the creamed mixture until a soft dough forms.

Cover the dough with plastic wrap and refrigerate for 30 minutes.

3 Roll out the dough between two sheets of baking paper to 5 mm (¼ inch) thick, then cut out the letters using alphabet cutters.

4 To make a glaze for the biscuits, whisk the egg white with a fork until frothy, then set aside.

Combine the extra sugar and ground cinnamon in a small bowl.

5 Brush the tops of the biscuits with the glaze, scatter over the cinnamon sugar and bake for 10 minutes, or until browned. Cool on the trays for 2 minutes, then transfer to a wire rack to cool completely. The biscuits will keep, stored in airtight container, for up to 1 week.

Makes: 24 slices

Preparation time: 25 minutes

Cooking time: 35 minutes

20 g (3¼oz/⅓ cup) shredded
    coconut
90 g (¾oz/¾ cup) self-raising flour
50 g (½ cup) plain (all-purpose) flour
140 g (5 oz/¾ cup) soft brown sugar
2 tablespoons sunflower seeds
2 tablespoons sesame seeds
70 g (2½ oz/½ cup) chopped
    macadamia nuts
60 g (2¼ oz/⅓ cup) chopped dates
1 tablespoon chopped glacé ginger
45 g (1½ oz/½ cup) desiccated
    coconut
230 g (8 oz) tin crushed pineapple,
    drained
100 g (3½ oz) unsalted butter,
    melted
2 eggs, lightly beaten

ICING

250 g (9 oz/2 cups) icing
    (confectioners') sugar
30 g (1 oz) unsalted butter, melted
1½ tablespoons lemon juice

COCONUT AND PINEAPPLE SLICE

1 Preheat the oven to 170°C (325°F/Gas 3). Spread the coconut evenly on
   a baking tray and toast for 5–8 minutes. Grease a 20 x 30 cm (8 x 12 inch)
   shallow baking tin and line with enough baking paper to overlap on the
   longer sides, this will make the slice easier to remove once baked.

2 Sift the self-raising and plain flours into a large bowl. Add the brown sugar,
   seeds, macadamia nuts, dates, ginger and desiccated coconut. Stir in the
   pineapple, melted butter and beaten egg, and mix well.

3 Spoon the mixture into the prepared tin. Bake for 25–30 minutes, or until
   golden brown. Cool in the tin, remove and cover with the icing.

4 To make the icing, combine the icing sugar, melted butter and lemon juice
   in a small bowl. Stir in 1–2 teaspoons of boiling water to reach a smooth
   consistency. Spread evenly over the slice. Sprinkle the top with the toasted
   shredded coconut and when set, slice and serve.

NOTE: Use other nuts or seeds, such as pumpkin seeds or almonds, if desired.

PINEAPPLE

*A native of tropical South America, the
pineapple is actually several individual
fruit joined together: each of these fruit
are the result of numerous unfertilized
flowers fused together. To most of us,
however, it is a deliciously juicy and
sweet fruit, the very emblem of warm
weather. Like most fruit, pineapple is
best eaten fresh, but it is also used in
dishes such as ice creams, sorbets, cakes
and as a controversial topping for pizza.*

Makes: 24 biscuits

Preparation time: 2 hours 30 minutes

Cooking time: 12 minutes

80 g (2¾ oz) butter, softened
60 g (2¼ oz) cream cheese, chopped
115 g (4 oz/½ cup) caster (superfine)
   sugar
1 teaspoon natural vanilla extract
2 egg yolks
1½ teaspoons caraway seeds
150 g (5½ oz/1¼ cups) plain
   (all-purpose) flour
plum jam
icing (confectioners') sugar, for dusting

PLUM AND CARAWAY BISCUITS

1 Cream the butter, cream cheese and sugar in a bowl using electric beaters until pale and fluffy. Add the vanilla and 1 egg yolk and beat to combine well. Add the caraway seeds and flour and stir until a dough forms. Turn the dough out onto a lightly floured work surface, form into a flat rectangle, then cover with plastic wrap and refrigerate for 2 hours, or until firm.

2 Preheat the oven to 180°C (350°F/Gas 4). Lightly grease two baking trays. Combine the remaining egg yolk with 2 teaspoons water and stir to combine well.

3 Cut the dough in half, then roll out each half on a lightly floured work surface to form an 18 x 24 cm (7 x 9½ inch) rectangle. Using a lightly floured sharp knife, cut the dough

into 6 cm (2½ inch) squares. Place a scant teaspoon of jam diagonally across the centre of each square, then brush all four corners of the square with the egg mixture. Take one corner and fold it into the centre. Take the opposite corner and fold it into the centre, overlapping the first corner slightly, to partially enclose the jam.

4 Brush the tops of the biscuits with the egg mixture, then place them, seam side up, on the baking trays. Bake for 10–12 minutes, or until light golden, swapping the position of the trays halfway through cooking. Cool on the trays for 5 minutes, then transfer to a wire rack to cool completely. Dust with icing sugar before serving. The biscuits will keep, stored in an airtight container, for up to 1 week.

Makes: 15 slices

Preparation time: 20 minutes

Cooking time: 35 minutes

125 g (4½ oz) unsalted butter, softened
55 g (2 oz/¼ cup) soft brown sugar
1 teaspoon ground cinnamon
185 g (6½ oz/1½ cups) plain
   (all-purpose) flour
375 g (2⅓ cups) dried figs
1 cinnamon stick
125 g (4½ oz/½ cup) caster (superfine)
   sugar

FIG AND CINNAMON SLICE

1 Preheat the oven to 180°C (350°F/Gas 4). Lightly grease an 18 x 27 cm (7 x 10¾ inch) baking tin and line with baking paper, hanging over the two long sides.

2 Beat the butter, brown sugar and cinnamon until light and fluffy, then fold in the flour with a large metal spoon. Press the mixture evenly into the tin and bake for 25 minutes. Cool slightly.

3 Place the dried figs, cinnamon stick, sugar and 375 ml (13 fl oz/1½ cups) boiling water in a saucepan, mix together and bring to the boil. Reduce the heat and simmer for 20 minutes, or until the figs have softened and the water has reduced by one third. Remove the cinnamon stick and place the mixture in a food processor. Process in short bursts until smooth.

4 Pour onto the cooked base and bake for 10 minutes, or until set. Cool in the tin, then lift out and cut into squares.

CINNAMON

It seems every spice worth the name is difficult to harvest and has been prized and bitterly fought over in equal measure. Cinnamon is no exception. Its use dates back to ancient Egyptian times, where it was used as an embalming agent, and more recently battles have been fought for its control in its native Sri Lanka. As to harvesting, the inner bark is prised away from the tree Cinnamomum zeylanicum, *cleaned, dried and sold as quills or sticks. Cassia bark is often sold as cinnamon, though it does not have the same fine qualities. Cinnamon is also available ground.*

Makes: 12 pieces

Preparation time: 30 minutes

Cooking time: 20 minutes

55 g (2 oz) unsalted butter
45 g (1¾ oz/¼ cup) soft brown sugar
2 teaspoons honey
25 g (1 oz/¼ cup) flaked almonds,
  roughly chopped
2 tablespoons chopped dried apricots
2 tablespoons chopped glacé cherries
2 tablespoons mixed peel (mixed
  candied citrus peel)
40 g (1½ oz/⅓ cup) plain (all-purpose)
  flour, sifted
120 g (4¼ oz/dark chocolate

FLORENTINES

1 Preheat the oven to 180°C (350°F/Gas 4). Melt the butter, brown sugar and honey in a pan until the butter is melted and all the ingredients are combined. Remove from the heat and add the almonds, apricots, glacé cherries, mixed peel and the flour. Mix well.

2 Grease and line two baking trays with baking paper. Place level tablespoons of the mixture well apart on the trays. Reshape and flatten the biscuits into 5 cm (2 inch) rounds before cooking.

3 Bake for 10 minutes, or until lightly browned. Cool on the tray, then allow to cool completely on a wire rack.

4 To melt the chocolate, break it up into small pieces and put it in a heatproof bowl. Bring a pan of water to a simmer, remove from the heat and place the bowl over the pan. Stir the chocolate until melted. Spread the melted chocolate on the bottom of each florentine and, using a fork, make a wavy pattern on the chocolate before it sets. Let the chocolate set before serving.

Makes: 9 pieces

Preparation time: 25 minutes

Cooking time: 10 minutes

500 g (1lb 2 oz) ready-made puff pastry
250 g (9 oz/1 cup) caster (superfine)
 sugar
90 g (3¼ oz/¾ cup) cornflour
 (cornstarch)
60 g (2¼ oz/½ cup) custard powder
1 litre (35 fl oz/4 cups) cream
60 g (2¼ oz) unsalted butter, cubed
2 teaspoons natural vanilla extract
3 egg yolks

ICING
185 g (6½ oz/1½ cups) icing
 (confectioners') sugar
60 g (2¼ oz/¼cup) passionfruit pulp
15 g (½ oz) unsalted butter, melted

VANILLA SLICE

1 Preheat the oven to 210°C (415°F/Gas 6–7). Lightly grease two baking trays with oil. Line the base and sides of a shallow 23 cm (9 inch) square cake tin with foil, leaving the foil hanging over two opposite sides.

2 Divide the pastry in half, roll each piece to 25 cm (10 inch) square 3 mm (⅛ inch) thick and put on a baking tray. Prick all over with a fork and bake for 8 minutes, or until golden. Trim each pastry sheet to a 23 cm (9 inch) square. Put one sheet top-side-down in the cake tin.

3 Combine the sugar, cornflour and custard powder in a saucepan. Add the cream, stirring constantly over medium heat for 2 minutes, or until it boils and thickens. Add the butter and vanilla and stir until smooth. Remove from the heat and whisk in the egg yolks until combined. Spread the custard over the pastry in the tin, then cover with the other pastry sheet, top-side-down. Cool completely.

4 To make the icing, combine the icing sugar, passionfruit pulp and butter in a bowl, and stir until smooth.

5 Lift the slice out of the tin using the foil as handles. Ice the top and leave to set before cutting with a serrated knife.

Vanilla comes from the bean of a climbing orchid vine native to Central America. The best-quality beans have a warmly sweet, caramel vanilla aroma and flavour.

Makes: 25 biscuits

Preparation time: 25 minutes

Cooking time: 18 minutes

100 g (3½ oz) unsalted butter
125 g (4½ oz/⅔ cup) soft brown sugar
1 teaspoon natural vanilla extract
2 eggs, at room temperature
250 g (9 oz/2 cups) plain (all-purpose)
  flour
1½ teaspoons baking powder
2 teaspoons ground ginger
100 g (3½ oz/⅔ cup) pistachio nuts,
  roughly chopped
white chocolate, for drizzling (optional)

GINGER AND PISTACHIO BISCUITS

1 Preheat the oven to 170°C (325°F/Gas 3). Line two baking trays with baking paper. Using electric beaters, beat together the butter, sugar and vanilla until light and creamy. Add the eggs, one at a time, and beat until well combined.

2 Fold through the combined sifted flour, baking powder and ginger. Stir through the pistachio nuts. Using lightly floured hands, roll tablespoons of the mixture into balls, place on the prepared trays, allowing room for spreading. Flatten the biscuits slightly with a lightly floured fork.

3 Bake for 15–18 minutes, or until crisp and golden, swapping the trays halfway through cooking. Allow to cool on the trays for 5 minutes before transferring to a wire rack to cool. Drizzle the biscuits with white chocolate, if desired

Makes: 30 pieces

Preparation time: 30 minutes

Cooking time: 1 hour 25 minutes

280 g (10 oz/2¼ cups) plain
    (all-purpose) flour
3 tablespoons ground almonds
500 g (1 lb 2 oz/2 cups) caster
    (superfine) sugar
250 g (9 oz) unsalted butter, chilled
½ teaspoon ground nutmeg
½ teaspoon baking powder
4 eggs
1 teaspoon natural vanilla extract
1 tablespoon lemon juice
300 g (10½ oz/2½ cups) fresh or
    thawed frozen raspberries
90 g (3¼ oz/1 cup) desiccated coconut
icing (confectioners') sugar, to dust

RASPBERRY AND COCONUT SLICE

COCONUT
The coconut tree and its fruit have been appreciated for centuries. Its uses range from supplying material for thatching and weaving to providing a nutritious and refreshing drink — complete with its own cup. When not quite ripe, coconut flesh is soft and jelly-like and the juice sweet and watery. As the coconut ripens, the flesh hardens and the amount of juice decreases. This juice is quite different from coconut milk and cream, which are produced by soaking grated coconut flesh in boiling water and squeezing out the resulting liquid. Other products include copra, which is dried coconut flesh; coconut oil, which is made from copra; desiccated coconut; and coconut liqueur.

1 Preheat the oven to 180°C (350°F/Gas 4). Lightly grease a 20 x 30 cm (8 x 12 inch) shallow tin and line with baking paper, hanging over the two long sides.

2 Sift 220 g (7¾ oz/1¾ cups) of the flour into a bowl. Add the ground almonds and 125 g (4½ oz/½ cup) of the caster sugar and stir to combine. Rub the butter into the flour with your fingertips until it resembles fine breadcrumbs. Press the mixture into the tin and bake for 20–25 minutes, or until golden. Reduce the oven to 150°C (300°F/Gas 2).

3 Sift the nutmeg, baking powder and the remaining flour onto a piece of baking paper. Beat the eggs, vanilla and remaining sugar with electric beaters for 4 minutes, or until light and fluffy. Fold in the flour with a large metal spoon. Stir in the lemon juice, raspberries and coconut and pour over the base.

4 Bake for 1 hour, or until golden and firm. Chill in the tin, then cut into pieces. Dust with icing sugar.

Makes: about 60 cookies

Preparation time: 3 hours 25 minutes

Cooking time: 40 minutes

125 g (4½ oz) unsalted butter, cubed
    and softened
370 g (13 oz/2 cups) soft brown sugar
1 teaspoon natural vanilla extract
2 eggs
60 g (2¼ oz) dark chocolate, melted
80 ml (2½ fl oz/⅓ cup) milk
340 g (11¾ oz/2¾ cups) plain (all-
    purpose) flour
2 tablespoons unsweetened cocoa
    powder
2 teaspoons baking powder
¼ teaspoon ground allspice
85 g (⅔ cup) chopped pecan nuts
icing (confectioners') sugar, to coat

*Not to be confused with mixed spice,
allspice is native to the West Indies and
tastes like a combination of nutmeg,
cinnamon, cloves and black pepper.*

CRACKLE COOKIES

1 Lightly grease two baking trays. Beat the butter, sugar and vanilla until light and creamy. Beat in the eggs, one at a time. Stir the chocolate and milk into the butter mixture.

2 Sift the flour, cocoa, baking powder, allspice and a pinch of salt into the butter mixture and mix well. Stir the pecans through. Refrigerate for at least 3 hours, or overnight.

3 Preheat the oven to 180°C (350°F/Gas 4). Roll tablespoons of the mixture into balls and roll each in the icing sugar to coat.

4 Place well apart on the trays. Bake for 20–25 minutes, or until lightly browned. Leave for 3–4 minutes, then cool on a wire rack.

Makes: 24 slices

Preparation time: 3 hours 20 minutes

Cooking time: 30 minutes

175 g (6 oz) unsalted butter, softened
70 g (2½ oz/⅓ cup) caster (superfine)
    sugar
1 egg yolk
250 g (9 oz/2 cups) plain (all-purpose)
    flour, sifted
300 g (10½ oz/1⅓ cups) mascarpone
60 g (2¼ oz/½ cup) icing
    (confectioners') sugar, sifted
1 tablespoon lemon juice
300 g (10½ oz/2 cups) strawberries,
    cut into quarters
50 g (1¾ oz) dark chocolate

STRAWBERRY AND MASCARPONE SLICE

1 Preheat the oven to 180°C (350°F/Gas 4). Lightly grease a 20 x 30 cm (8 x 12 inch) shallow baking tin and line with baking paper, leaving it hanging over the two long sides.

2 Beat the butter and sugar with electric beaters until light and fluffy. Add the egg yolk and beat well. Fold in the sifted flour until well combined. Press firmly into the prepared baking tin and prick all over with a fork. Bake for 25 minutes, or until light brown. Cool completely.

3 Beat the mascarpone, icing sugar and juice with a wooden spoon until smooth. Stir in the strawberries. Spoon over the base and refrigerate for 3 hours, or until firm.

4 Chop the chocolate into small even-sized pieces and place in a heatproof bowl. Bring a saucepan of water to the boil, then remove from the heat. Sit the bowl over the pan — ensure the bowl doesn't touch the water. Stand, stirring occasionally, until the chocolate has melted. Drizzle over the slice, then cut into pieces.

MASCARPONE

A cream cheese originally from Lombardy. Made with cream rather than milk, it is very high in fat. Mascarpone is generally used in desserts such as tiramisù or instead of cream in sauces. Widely available, it is usually sold in tubs.

Makes: about 22 stars

Preparation time: 20 minutes

Cooking time: 20 minutes

125 g (4½ oz) unsalted butter, cubed
    and softened
125 g (4½ oz/½ cup) caster (superfine)
    sugar
2 egg yolks
2 teaspoons finely grated lemon zest
155 g (5½ oz/1¼ cups) plain
    (all-purpose) flour
110 g (3¾ oz/¾ cup) coarse cornmeal
icing (confectioners') sugar, to dust

LEMON STARS

1 Preheat the oven to 160°C (315°F/Gas 2–3). Line a baking tray with baking paper. Beat the butter and sugar until creamy. Mix in the egg yolks, lemon zest, flour and cornmeal until they form a ball of soft dough. Roll out on a lightly floured surface to 1 cm (½ inch) thick.

2 Cut out stars from the dough using a 3 cm (1¼ inch) star-shaped cutter. Place on the tray and bake for 15–20 minutes, or until lightly golden. Cool on a wire rack and dust with the icing sugar.

Makes: 15 slices

Preparation time: 55 minutes

Cooking time: 45 minutes

125 g (4½ oz/1 cup) plain (all-purpose) flour
30 g (1 oz/¼ cup) icing (confectioners') sugar
170 g (5¾ oz) unsalted butter, chilled and chopped
1 egg yolk
125 g (4½ oz/½ cup) caster (superfine) sugar
4 eggs
125 g (4½ oz/1¼ cups) ground almonds
2 drops almond extract
160 g (5½ oz/½ cup) raspberry jam
25 g (1 oz/¼ cup) flaked almonds

BAKEWELL SLICE

1 Preheat the oven to 180°C (350°F/ Gas 4). Lightly grease a 20 x 30 cm (8 x 12 inch) baking tin and line with baking paper, hanging over the two long sides.

2 Sift the flour and 1 tablespoon of the icing sugar into a bowl, add 50 g (1¾ oz) of the butter and rub it in until the mixture resembles breadcrumbs. Add the egg yolk and 2 tablespoons cold water and mix with a flat-bladed knife until the

mixture comes together in beads. Gather into a ball, cover with plastic wrap and refrigerate for 30 minutes. Roll out between two sheets of baking paper, remove the paper and put in the tin, pressing into the edges. Bake for 10 minutes. Cool.

3 Beat the remaining butter and the caster sugar with electric beaters until creamy. Add the eggs and fold in the ground almonds and almond extract.

4 Spread the jam over the pastry base and pour over the filling. Sprinkle with almonds and bake for 30–35 minutes, or until firm. Allow to cool.

5 Sift the remaining icing sugar into a bowl and mix in 2–3 teaspoons warm water to form a free-flowing paste. Drizzle over the slice in a zigzag pattern and leave to set. Trim the edges and cut into squares.

Makes: 16 cookies

Preparation time: 20 minutes

Cooking time: 15 minutes

125 g (4½ oz) unsalted butter
185 g (6½ oz/1 cup) soft brown sugar
1 teaspoon natural vanilla extract
1 egg, lightly beaten
1 tablespoon milk
215 g (7½ oz/1¾ cups) plain (all-
   purpose) flour
1 teaspoon baking powder
250 g (9 oz/1½ cups) dark chocolate
   bits (chocolate chips)

CHOC CHIP COOKIES

1   Preheat the oven to 180°C (350°F/Gas 4). Line a large baking tray with baking paper.

2   Cream the butter and sugar with electric beaters in a large bowl. Mix in the vanilla extract and gradually add the egg, beating well. Stir in the milk. Sift the flour and baking powder into a large bowl, then fold into the butter and egg mixture. Stir in the dark chocolate bits.

3   Drop level tablespoons of the cookie mixture onto the baking tray, leaving about 4 cm (1½ inch) between each cookie, then lightly press with a floured fork. Bake for 15 minutes, or until lightly golden. Cool on a wire rack.

Makes: 24 slices

Preparation time: 1 hour

Cooking time: 50 minutes

100 g (3½ oz/¾ cup) slivered almonds
125 g (4½ oz/1 cup) plain (all-purpose)
    flour
1 teaspoon baking powder
100 g (3½ oz) unsalted butter, chopped
125 g (4½ oz/½ cup) caster
    (superfine) sugar
1 egg yolk
25 g (1 oz/¼ cup) desiccated coconut
750 g (1 lb 10 oz/3 cups) cream cheese,
    softened
2 eggs
185 ml (6 fl oz/¾ cup) coconut milk
3 teaspoons natural vanilla extract
½ teaspoon lemon juice
185 g (6½ oz/¾ cup) caster (superfine)
    sugar, extra

TOPPING
90 g (3¼ oz/¾ cup) icing
    (confectioners') sugar
40 g (1½ oz) unsalted butter, softened
1 tablespoon cornflour (cornstarch)
2 tablespoons strained passionfruit juice
65 g (2¼ oz/¾ cup) flaked almonds,
    toasted

PASSIONFRUIT AND COCONUT CHEESE SLICE

1 Finely chop the almonds in a food processor. Sift the flour and baking powder into a bowl. Rub the butter into the flour until it resembles breadcrumbs. Stir in the almonds and sugar. Make a well in the centre and add the egg yolk. Mix with a flat-bladed knife until the mixture comes together in beads. Remove to a lightly floured work surface and shape into a ball. Flatten slightly, cover in plastic wrap and refrigerate for 30 minutes.

2 Preheat the oven to 170°C (325°F/Gas 3). Grease a 30 x 20 x 5 cm (12 x 8 x 2 inch) tin and line with baking paper, hanging over the two long sides. Roll the dough out to fit the tin and press in evenly. Sprinkle over the coconut and lightly press it in. Bake for 10 minutes and cool for 10 minutes. Combine the cream cheese and eggs in the food processor. Add coconut milk, vanilla, lemon juice and the extra sugar, and blend until smooth. Pour over the base. Bake for 40 minutes. Cool in the tin.

3 To make the topping, mix the icing sugar and butter with a wooden spoon until smooth. Stir in the cornflour, then the passionfruit juice. Mix until smooth, then spread over the slice. Scatter over the toasted almonds. Leave to set, then cut into 5 cm (2 inch) squares.

Makes: 20–22 biscuits

Preparation time: 25 minutes

Cooking time: 15 minutes

125 g (4½ oz) unsalted butter, softened
80 g (2¾ oz/⅓ cup) caster (superfine)
  sugar
1 teaspoon orange flower water
finely grated zest from 1 orange
2 eggs, lightly beaten
165 g (5¾ oz/1⅓ cups) plain
  (all-purpose) flour
80 g (2¾ oz/½ cup) polenta

ORANGE POLENTA BISCUITS

1 Preheat the oven to 200°C (400°F/ Gas 6). Line two baking trays with baking paper.

2 Combine the butter, sugar, orange flower water and orange zest in a food processor and process until light and creamy. Add the eggs and process until smooth. Add the flour and polenta and pulse until a sticky dough forms.

3 Transfer the mixture to a piping bag fitted with a 2 cm (¾ inch) star nozzle. Pipe the mixture onto the prepared baking trays to form 7 cm (2¾ inch) crescents. Bake for 15 minutes, or until the biscuits are golden around the edges. Cool on the trays for 5 minutes, then transfer to a wire rack to cool completely.

TIP Orange polenta biscuits will keep, stored in an airtight container, for up to 3 days.

Makes: 20 pieces

Preparation time: 25 minutes

Cooking time: 45 minutes

40 g (1½ oz/⅓ cup) plain (all-purpose) flour
1 tablespoon unsweetened cocoa powder
1 teaspoon ground ginger
½ teaspoon ground cardamom
1 teaspoon ground cinnamon
125 g (4½ oz/¾ cup) dried figs, chopped
50 g (1¾ oz/¼ cup) glacé ginger, chopped
50 g (1¾ oz/¼ cup) glacé pineapple, chopped
50 g (1¾ oz/¼ cup) glacé apricots, chopped
50 g (1¾ oz/¼ cup) chopped mixed peel (mixed candied citrus peel)
175 g (6 oz/1 cup) blanched almonds, toasted
90 g (3¼ oz/⅓ cup) caster (superfine) sugar
90 g (3¼ oz/¼ cup) honey

GINGER PANFORTE SLICE

1 Preheat the oven to 160°C (315°F/Gas 2–3). Lightly grease a 7 x 25 cm (2¾ x 10 inch) shallow baking tin and line with baking paper, hanging over at the two short ends.

2 Sift the flour, cocoa, ginger and spices into a large bowl. Add the fruit and almonds.

3 Heat the caster sugar, honey and 2 teaspoons water in a small saucepan over low heat, stirring until melted and it just comes to the boil. Pour onto the dry ingredients and mix well. Press the mixture into the tin and bake for 35–40 minutes, or until just firm. Cool in the tin, then chill until firm. Cut into thin slices.

Panforte is a medieval Italian recipe from the twelfth or thirteenth century, a speciality of Siena where nearly every shop seems to feature it. This rich cake is sold in huge wheels of both blonde and dark panforte (the latter made by adding cocoa) and will keep for about two weeks.

Makes: 24

Preparation time: 2 hours 30 minutes

Cooking time: 15 minutes

CREAM CHEESE PASTRY

90 g (3¼ oz/⅓ cup) cream cheese, softened
60 g (2¼ oz/¼ cup) caster (superfine) sugar
1 egg yolk
3 tablespoons milk
185 g (6½ oz/1½ cups) plain (all-purpose) flour
1 teaspoon baking powder
1 egg white, to glaze

DRIED FRUIT FILLING

60 g (2¼ oz/⅓ cup) chopped dried figs
95 g (3¼ oz/½ cup) chopped dried apricots
60 g (2¼ oz/½ cup) raisins, chopped
60 g (2¼ oz) dark chocolate, chopped
½ teaspoon grated lemon zest
80 g (2¾ oz/¼ cup) clear honey
large pinch ground allspice
large pinch ground cinnamon

DRIED FRUIT AND CHOCOLATE PILLOWS

1 To make the cream cheese pastry, beat the cheese and sugar until fluffy. Beat in the egg yolk and milk, then sift in the flour, a pinch of salt and the baking powder and form into a smooth dough. Cover with plastic wrap and refrigerate for 2 hours.

2 To make the dried fruit filling, put all the ingredients in a food processor and process in short bursts until finely chopped.

3 Preheat the oven to 180°C (350°F/Gas 4). Divide the fruit filling into three portions and roll into 32 cm (13 inch) long ropes. Divide the pastry into three and,

on a lightly floured surface, roll out to 10 x 32 cm (4 x 13 inch) rectangles.

4 Brush one length of a rectangle with water. Lay a portion of filling on the strip of pastry near the dry side. Roll the pastry over and press to seal, then cut into eight diagonal pieces and lay, seam-side-down, on an ungreased baking tray. Repeat with the remaining pastry and filling.

5 Mix the egg white with 1 tablespoon of cold water and glaze the biscuits, then bake for 13–15 minutes, or until golden. Leave for 2–3 minutes, then cool on a wire rack.

Makes: 24 pieces

Preparation time: 30 minutes

Cooking time: 40 minutes

60 g (2¼ oz) unsalted butter
1½ tablespoons golden syrup
150 ml (5 fl oz/⅔ cup) alcoholic
    apple cider
250 g (9 oz/2 cups) self-raising flour
⅛ teaspoon ground ginger
50 g (1¾ oz/¼ cup) soft brown sugar
70 g (2½ oz/⅓ cup) pitted dates,
    chopped
150 g (5½ oz/1½ cups) walnuts,
    chopped
1 egg
1 large granny smith apple
2½ tablespoons caster (superfine) sugar
60 g (2¼ oz/½ cup) plain
    (all-purpose) flour

CIDER CRUMBLE SLICE

1 Preheat the oven to 170°C (325°F/ Gas 3). Lightly grease a 20 x 30 cm (8 x 12 inch) baking tin and line with baking paper, hanging over on the two long sides.

2 Melt 20 g (¾ oz) of the butter and the golden syrup in a saucepan. Remove from the heat and stir

in the cider. Sift the flour and ginger into a bowl. Stir in the brown sugar, dates and half the nuts. Beat in the golden syrup mixture and egg until smooth. Spoon into the tin.

3 Peel, core and thinly slice the apple, then cut into 1.5 cm (⅝ inch) pieces. Melt the

remaining butter in a small saucepan, add the caster sugar, flour, apple and remaining nuts and stir well. Spread over the cake mixture. Bake for 30 minutes, or until golden and a skewer comes out clean. Cool in the tin, remove and cut into squares.

Makes: 30–32 oatcakes

Preparation time: 20 minutes

Cooking time: 20 minutes

400 g (14 oz/3¼ cups) fine oatmeal
100 g (3½ oz/⅔ cup) oat bran
1 teaspoon bicarbonate of soda
   (baking soda)
60 g (2¼ oz) butter, melted

OATCAKES

1 Preheat the oven to 200°C (400°F/Gas 6). Lightly grease two baking trays.

2 Combine the oatmeal, oat bran, bicarbonate of soda and 1 teaspoon salt in a bowl. Make a well in the centre and, using a wooden spoon, stir in the melted butter and 250 ml (9 fl oz/1 cup) water to form a firm, slightly sticky dough.

3 Transfer the dough to a lightly floured work surface and knead until smooth. Roll out on a floured surface to a

2 mm (¹⁄₁₆ inch) round and, using a 7 cm (2¾ inch) pastry cutter, cut out rounds from the dough (rerolling the pastry scraps to press out a total of 30–32 rounds).

4 Transfer to the baking trays and bake for 18–20 minutes, or until the edges are lightly browned. Cool on trays for 5 minutes, then transfer to a wire rack to cool. Serve with cheeses, such as a blue cheese or aged cheddar.

5 Oatcakes will keep, stored in an airtight container, for up to 1 week.

Makes: 48 wafers

Preparation time: 55 minutes

Cooking time: 12 minutes

250 g (9 oz/2 cups) plain
(all-purpose) flour
1 teaspoon baking powder
60 g (2¼ oz) vegetable shortening,
chilled
1 tablespoon cumin seeds, toasted

CUMIN SEED WAFERS

1 Preheat the oven to 180°C (350°F/Gas 4). Lightly grease two baking trays.

2 Sift the flour, baking powder and 1 teaspoon salt into a bowl. Rub in the vegetable shortening until the mixture resembles fine breadcrumbs. Stir in the cumin seeds. Make a well in the centre of the mixture and gradually add 125 ml (4 fl oz/½ cup) water, stirring with a wooden spoon until a dough forms. Knead the dough gently on a lightly floured work surface until

just smooth. Cover with plastic wrap and refrigerate for 30 minutes.

3 Divide the dough into quarters and roll out each quarter on a floured work surface until 1 mm (1/16 inch) thick, then trim the sides to form a 20 x 30 cm (8 x 12 inch) rectangle. Cut in half down the length, then cut across the width to form 5 cm (2 inch) wide fingers. You should end up with 12 fingers from each quarter of dough. Place on the baking trays and bake in batches

for 10–12 minutes, or until light golden. Transfer to a wire rack to cool.

4 These wafers will keep, stored in an airtight container, for up to 1 week.

TIP Take care when dry-roasting cumin seeds, as they can burn quite quickly. Place the seeds in a dry, heavy-based frying pan over low heat and heat just until fragrant.

CAKES AND PUDDINGS

Serves 6

Preparation time: 40 minutes

Cooking time: 20 minutes

30 g (1 oz) butter, melted
60 g (2¼ oz/½ cup) plain (all-purpose)
   flour
60 g (2¼ oz/½ cup) cornflour
   (cornstarch) (cornstarch) (cornstarch)
2 teaspoons cream of tartar
1 teaspoon bicarbonate of soda
   (baking soda)
4 eggs
170 g (6 oz/¾ cup) caster (superfine)
   sugar
2 tablespoons hot milk
300 ml (10½ fl oz) whipping cream
1 tablespoon icing (confectioners')
   sugar, plus extra for dusting
2 tablespoons strawberry jam
500 g (1 lb 2 oz/3⅓ cups) strawberries,
   hulled and sliced in half

EASY SPONGE CAKE
with strawberries and cream

1 Preheat the oven to 180°C (350°F/Gas 4). Grease two 20 cm (8 inch) round cake tins with the melted butter and line the bases with baking paper. Dust the sides of the tins with a little flour, shaking out any excess.

2 Sift the flour, cornflour (cornstarch), cream of tartar and bicarbonate of soda into a bowl, then repeat the sifting twice more.

3 Whisk the eggs and sugar in a large bowl for 5 minutes, or until pale and thick. Using a large metal spoon, carefully fold in the sifted flour mixture and the hot milk until they are just incorporated; take care not to overmix. Divide the mixture evenly between the two tins, then bake for 18–20 minutes, or until the cakes are

golden and have shrunk slightly from the side of the tins. Leave in the tins for 5 minutes, then turn out onto a wire rack to cool.

4 Combine the cream and icing sugar in a bowl, then whip until soft peaks form. Place one sponge cake on a serving plate and spread with jam. Top with half the cream and half of the sliced strawberries. Cover with the second sponge cake. Spread the remaining cream over the top and top with the remaining strawberries. Dust with icing sugar and serve immediately.

5 Sponge cake is best eaten on the day it is made. Unfilled sponges will freeze well for up to 1 month, wrapped loosely in plastic wrap.

Serves 10–12

Preparation time: 20 minutes

Cooking time: 1 hour 30 minutes

185 g (6½ oz) unsalted butter,
  chopped
250 g (9 oz/1½ cups) dark chocolate
  bits (chocolate chips)
215 g (7½ oz/1¾ cups) self-raising flour
40 g (1½ oz/⅓ cup) unwseetened
  cocoa powder
375 g (13 oz/1½ cups) caster
  (superfine) sugar
3 eggs, lightly beaten

CHOCOLATE TOPPING
20 g (¾ oz) unsalted butter, chopped
125 g (4½ oz) dark chocolate, chopped

RICH DARK CHOCOLATE CAKE

1 Preheat the oven to 160°C (315°F/Gas 2–3). Grease a 22 cm (8½ inch) springform tin and line the base with baking paper. Place the butter and chocolate bits in a small heatproof bowl and melt, stirring frequently, over a saucepan of simmering water. Make sure the base of the bowl doesn't touch the water.

2 Sift the flour and cocoa into a large bowl. Combine the melted butter and chocolate mixture, sugar and egg, then add 250 ml (9 fl oz/1 cup) water and mix well. Add to the flour and cocoa and stir until well combined.

3 Pour the mixture into the prepared tin and bake for 1 hour 30 minutes, or until a skewer comes out clean when inserted into the centre of the cake. Leave in the tin for 15 minutes before turning out onto a wire rack to cool.

4 To make the chocolate topping, place the butter and chocolate pieces in a small heatproof bowl and melt, stirring frequently, over a saucepan of simmering water — ensure the base of the bowl doesn't touch the water. Spread the topping over the cooled cake in a swirl pattern.

Serves 6

Preparation time: 25 minutes

Cooking time: 1 hour

1 vanilla bean or 1 teaspoon natural
  vanilla extract
185 g (6½ oz) unsalted butter, chopped
230 g (8 oz/1 cup) caster (superfine)
  sugar
3 eggs
280 g (10 oz/2¼ cups) self-raising flour
185 ml (6 fl oz/¾ cup) milk
2 tablespoons unsweetened
  cocoa powder
1½ tablespoons warm milk, extra

MARBLE CAKE

1 Preheat the oven to 200°C (400°F/
Gas 6). Lightly grease a 25 x 11 x
7.5 cm (10 x 4¼ x 3 inch) loaf tin
and line the base with baking paper.

2 If using the vanilla bean, split it
down the middle and scrape out
the seeds. Put the seeds (or vanilla
extract) in a bowl with the butter
and sugar and, using electric
beaters, cream the mixture until
pale and fluffy. Add the eggs one
at a time, beating well after each
addition. Sift the flour, then fold
it into the creamed mixture

alternately with the milk until
combined. Divide the mixture in
half and put the second half into
another bowl.

3 Combine the cocoa powder and
warm milk in a small bowl and stir
until smooth, then add to one half
of the cake mixture, stirring to
combine well. Spoon the two
mixtures into the prepared tin in
alternate spoonfuls. Using a metal
skewer, cut through the mixture
four times to create a marble
effect. Bake for 50–60 minutes, or

until a skewer inserted into the
centre of the cake comes out
clean. Leave in the tin for 5
minutes before turning out onto a
wire rack to cool.

4 This cake will keep, stored in an
airtight container, for 3–4 days.
It is also suitable to freeze.

TIP Cooling the cake on a wire rack
ensures the base of the cake dries out
and the cake does not steam in its
own heat.

Makes: 6 cakes

Preparation time: 20 minutes

Cooking time: 20 minutes

180 g (6 oz) unsalted butter, chopped
230 g (8½ oz/1 cup) caster (superfine)
   sugar
4 eggs
125 g (4½ oz/1 cup) self-raising flour
35 g (1¼ oz/⅓ cup) ground almonds
80 ml (2½ fl oz/⅓ cup) milk
thick (double/heavy) cream, to serve

RED WINE SYRUP
350 g (12 oz/1½ cups) caster
   (superfine) sugar
300 ml (10½ fl oz) red wine
170 ml (5½ fl oz/⅔ cup) blackcurrant
   juice

ALMOND CAKES with red wine syrup

1 Preheat the oven to 200°C (400°F/Gas 6). Lightly grease six 250 ml (9 fl oz/1 cup) capacity kugelhopf tins and dust with flour, shaking out any excess.

2 Cream the butter and sugar in a bowl using electric beaters until pale and fluffy. Add the eggs one at a time, beating well after each addition. Sift the flour over the mixture and gently stir it in, then add the almonds and milk and stir until just combined. Spoon into the prepared tins and bake for 15–20 minutes, or until a skewer inserted into the centre of a cake comes out

clean. Remove from the oven and cool in the tin for 5 minutes, then turn out onto a wire rack.

3 To make the red wine syrup, put all the ingredients in a small saucepan and stir over a low heat until the sugar has dissolved. Increase the heat to medium and simmer for 10 minutes, or until the liquid is thick and syrupy.

4 Serve the almond cakes with the warm syrup poured over them and with cream to the side.

Serves 6–8

Preparation time: 45 minutes

Cooking time: 25 minutes

60 g (2¼ oz) dark chocolate, chopped
4 eggs
115 g (4 oz/½ cup) caster (superfine) sugar
100 g (3⅓ oz) tinned sweetened chestnut purée
60 g (2¼ oz/½ cup) self-raising flour, sifted
2 tablespoons hot water
unsweetened cocoa powder, for dusting

CHESTNUT CREAM
150 g (5½ oz) tinned sweetened chestnut purée
300 ml (10½ fl oz) thick (double/heavy) cream
1 tablespoon dark rum

CHOCOLATE CHESTNUT ROULADE

1 Preheat the oven to 180°C (350°F/ Gas 4). Lightly grease a 25 x 30 cm (10 x 12 inch) shallow Swiss roll tin (jelly roll tin) and line the base with baking paper.

2 Put the chocolate in a heatproof bowl. Sit the bowl over a saucepan of simmering water, stirring frequently until the chocolate has melted. Take care that the base of the bowl doesn't touch the water. Allow to cool.

3 Whisk the eggs and sugar in a large bowl for 5 minutes, or until pale and very thick. Beat in the chestnut purée and chocolate, then fold in the flour and water. Gently spread the mixture into the prepared tin and bake for 20 minutes, or until just cooked and springy to the touch (do not overcook or the cake will crack when it is rolled).

4 Put a tea towel (dish towel) on the work surface, cover with a sheet of baking paper and sprinkle the paper lightly with cocoa powder. Turn the cake out onto the paper, then carefully remove the baking paper from the base of the cake. Trim the edges to neaten. Using the tea towel as a guide, carefully roll the cake up from the long side, rolling the paper inside the roll. Put the rolled cake on a wire rack and leave to cool for 10 minutes, then carefully unroll the cake and cool completely.

5 To make the chestnut cream, combine the purée, cream and rum in a small bowl, then beat until just thick. Spread the cake with the chestnut cream, then carefully reroll, using the paper to guide you. Place the roulade seam side down and dust the top lightly with cocoa powder.

6 This roulade is best eaten on the day it is made.

Starting from the long side, carefully roll up the cake, enclosing the baking paper inside the roll.

Spread the cream over the cooled cake, then roll it up again, using the paper to guide you.

Makes: 2 cakes, each serving 8

Preparation time: 30 minutes

Cooking time: 1 hour

180 g (6 oz) unsalted butter, softened
90 g (3¼ oz/¼ cup) honey
230 g (8 oz/1 cup) caster (superfine) sugar
1½ teaspoons natural vanilla extract
3 eggs
360 g (12¾ oz/1½ cups) mashed ripe banana — about 4 bananas
185 g (6½ oz/¾ cup) plain yoghurt
½ teaspoon bicarbonate of soda (baking soda)
375 g (13 oz/3 cups) self-raising flour, sifted

HONEY ICING
125 g (4½ oz) unsalted butter
3 tablespoons honey
125 g (4½ oz/1 cup) icing (confectioners') sugar
1 tablespoon milk

YOGHURT BANANA CAKES with honey icing

1 Preheat the oven to 180°C (350°F/ Gas 4). Lightly grease two 15 cm (6 inch) round cake tins and line the bases with baking paper.

2 Cream the butter, honey, sugar and vanilla in a bowl using electric beaters until pale and fluffy. Add the eggs one at a time, beating well after each addition, then beat in the banana.

3 Combine the yoghurt and bicarbonate of soda in a small bowl. Fold the flour alternately with the yoghurt into the banana mixture. Divide the mixture evenly between the tins, smoothing the tops. Bake for 50–60 minutes, or until a skewer inserted into the centre of a cake comes out clean. Cool in the tins for 5 minutes, then turn out onto a wire rack.

4 To make the honey icing, cream the butter and honey in a small bowl using electric beaters until pale and fluffy. Gradually add the icing sugar alternately with the milk, beating well until the mixture is very pale. When the cakes are cold, divide the honey icing between the tops, spreading the icing to form rough peaks.

5 These cakes will keep, stored in an airtight container, for up to 4 days. Un-iced cakes can be frozen for up to 3 months.

Serves 6–8

Preparation time: 25 minutes

Cooking time: 1 hour

150 g (5½ oz) butter
230 g (8½ oz/1 cup) soft brown sugar
115 g (4 oz/½ cup) caster (superfine)
    sugar
5 eggs
185 ml (6 fl oz/¾ cup) sour cream
¾ teaspoon almond extract
1 teaspoon natural vanilla extract
155 g (5½ oz/1¼ cups) plain
    (all-purpose) flour
1½ teaspoons baking powder
150 g (5½ oz/1 cup) polenta (cornmeal)
thick (double/heavy) cream, to serve

BLACKBERRY COMPOTE
80 g (2¾ oz/⅓ cup) caster (superfine)
    sugar
2 teaspoons lemon juice
500 g (1 lb 2 oz) blackberries

POLENTA POUNDCAKE
with blackberry compote

1 Preheat the oven to 180°C (350°F/Gas 4). Grease a 24 x 14 cm (9½ x 5½ inch) loaf tin with butter.

2 Cream the butter, brown sugar and sugar in a large bowl using electric beaters for 2 minutes, or until pale and fluffy. Add the eggs one at a time, beating well after each addition. Reduce the speed to low and mix in the sour cream and almond and vanilla extracts.

3 Sift together the flour, baking powder and a pinch of salt. Add the flour mixture and polenta to the butter mixture and fold in. Pour into the prepared tin. Bake for 50 minutes, or until a skewer inserted into the centre of the cake comes out clean. Leave to cool in the tin for 5 minutes, then unmould the cake by running a knife around the inside edge to loosen. Turn out onto a wire rack to cool.

4 While the cake is cooking, make the blackberry compote. Combine the sugar, lemon juice and 2 tablespoons water in a saucepan, then stir over medium heat for 3 minutes, or until the sugar dissolves. Add the berries and stir to coat, then bring the mixture to a simmer. Cook over medium–low heat for 5 minutes, stirring occasionally, or until the berries are soft but still holding their shape. Cool to room temperature. Serve at room temperature or chilled.

5 Cut the cake into thick slices and serve toasted with the compote and cream.

Serves 6

Preparation time: 30 minutes

Cooking time: 25 minutes

1½ tablespoons instant coffee granules
90 g (3¼ oz/⅓ cup) sour cream
125 g (4½ oz) unsalted butter
165 g (5¾ oz/¾ cup) soft brown sugar
2 eggs
155 g (5½ oz/1¼ cups) self-raising
    flour, sifted

COFFEE SYRUP
2 teaspoons instant coffee granules
165 g (5¾ oz/¾ cup) soft brown sugar

COFFEE SYRUP CAKES

1 Preheat the oven to 180°C (350°F/ Gas 4). Lightly grease six mini 250 ml (9 fl oz/1 cup) rectangular tins, then lightly dust with flour, shaking out any excess.

2 Dissolve the coffee in 2 tablespoons boiling water in a bowl. Allow to cool, then add the sour cream and stir to combine well.

3 Cream the butter and sugar in a bowl using electric beaters until pale and fluffy. Add the eggs one at a time, beating well after each addition. Fold in the flour alternately with the sour cream mixture, then divide the mixture between the prepared tins and smooth the tops. Bake for about 25 minutes, or until a skewer inserted into the centre of a cake comes out clean.

4 To make the coffee syrup, combine the coffee, sugar and 170 ml (5½ fl oz/⅔ cup) water in a small saucepan and stir over medium heat until the sugar has dissolved. Bring to the boil, then remove from the heat. Spoon the hot coffee syrup over the hot cakes in the tin and allow to cool before turning out onto a wire rack.

5 Coffee cakes will keep, stored in an airtight container, for 3–4 days, or up to 3 months in the freezer.

Serves 6–8

Preparation time: 30 minutes

Cooking time: 1 hour

150 g (5½ oz) dark chocolate, chopped
125 g (4½ oz) unsalted butter, chopped
150 g (5½ oz/⅔ cup) caster (superfine) sugar
5 eggs, separated
200 g (7 oz/1¾ cups) ground hazelnuts
½ teaspoon baking powder
40 g (1½ oz/⅓ cup) unsweetened cocoa powder
1 teaspoon ground cinnamon
icing (confectioners') sugar, for dusting

VANILLA CREAM
1 vanilla bean or 1 teaspoon natural vanilla extract
300 ml (10½ fl oz) whipping cream
1 tablespoon caster (superfine) sugar

FLOURLESS CHOCOLATE CAKE

1 Preheat the oven to 170°C (325°F/ Gas 3). Lightly grease a 20 cm (8 inch) round cake tin and line the base with baking paper. Put the chocolate in a heatproof bowl. Sit the bowl over a saucepan of simmering water, stirring frequently until the chocolate has melted. Take care that the base of the bowl doesn't touch the water. Set aside and allow to cool.

2 Cream the butter and sugar in a bowl using electric beaters until pale and fluffy. Add the egg yolks one at a time, beating well after each addition. Fold in the cooled, melted chocolate. Sift the hazelnuts, baking powder, cocoa powder and cinnamon into a bowl, then fold into the butter mixture.

3 Whisk the egg whites in a clean, dry bowl until stiff peaks form. Using a large metal spoon, fold the egg whites into the chocolate mixture, working in two batches. Gently spread the mixture into the tin and bake for about 1 hour, or until a skewer inserted into the centre of the cake comes out clean. Cool the cake in the tin.

4 Meanwhile, make the vanilla cream. If using the vanilla bean, split it down the middle and scrape out the seeds. Beat the cream, vanilla seeds (or vanilla extract) and sugar in small bowl using electric beaters until soft peaks form. Serve the cake dusted with icing sugar and with the vanilla cream.

5 This cake will keep, stored in an airtight container, for 3–4 days. It is also suitable to freeze.

Serves 10–12

Preparation time: 15 minutes

Cooking time: 1 hour

1 kg (2 lb 4 oz/4 cups) fresh ricotta
   cheese (see tip)
175 g (6 oz/½ cup) honey
1½ teaspoons natural vanilla extract
60 ml (2 fl oz/¼ cup) lemon juice
finely grated zest from 2 lemons
½ teaspoon ground cinnamon
4 eggs, lightly beaten
35 g (1¼ oz/¼ cup) plain
   (all-purpose) flour
poached nectarines or peaches, to serve
   (optional)

LEMON AND HONEY RICOTTA CAKE

1 Preheat the oven to 170°C (325°F/ Gas 3). Lightly grease and flour an 18 cm (7 inch) round spring-form cake tin.

2 Drain the ricotta if necessary, then process in a food processor until smooth. Add the honey, vanilla, lemon juice, zest, cinnamon and eggs and process until well combined. Add the flour and pulse until just combined and the mixture is smooth.

3 Spoon the mixture into the prepared tin and bake for 1 hour, or until light golden and still slightly soft in the middle. Turn the oven off, open the door slightly and cool the cake in the oven. Put in the refrigerator to chill, then remove the cake from the tin. Serve at room temperature with poached fruit such as peaches or nectarines, if desired.

TIP Buy fresh ricotta cheese sold in a large block at the delicatessen. It has a much better texture than the ricotta cheese sold in tubs.

Serves 12–14

Preparation time: 20 minutes

Cooking time: 2 hours 15 minutes

310 g (11 oz/2½ cups) sultanas
   (golden raisins)
250 g (9 oz/2 cups) raisins
225 g (8 oz/1½ cups) currants
185 ml (6 fl oz/¾ cup) vegetable oil
125 ml (4 fl oz/½ cup) dark rum
125 ml (4 fl oz/½ cup) orange juice
230 g (8½ oz/1 cup) soft brown sugar
2 tablespoons treacle or golden syrup
½ teaspoon bicarbonate of soda
   (baking soda)
1 tablespoon grated orange zest
4 eggs, lightly beaten
185 g (6½ oz/1½ cups) plain
   (all-purpose) flour
60 g (2¼ oz/½ cup) self-raising flour
1 tablespoon mixed (pumpkin pie)
   spice
40 g (1½ oz/¼ cup) blanched whole
   almonds
80 g (2¾ oz/¼ cup) apricot jam,
   to glaze

BUTTERLESS RUM FRUIT CAKE

1 Preheat the oven to 150°C (300°F/ Gas 2). Lightly grease a 20 cm (8 inch) round cake tin. Cut a double layer of baking paper into a strip long enough to fit around the outside of the tin and tall enough to come 5 cm (2 inches) above the edge of the tin. Fold down a cuff about 2 cm (¾ inch) deep along the length of the strip, along the folded edge. Make cuts along the cuff, cutting up to the fold line, about 1 cm (½ inch) apart. Fit the strip around the inside of the tin, with the cuts on the base, pressing the cuts out at right angles so they sit flat around the base. Place the cake tin on a doubled piece of baking paper and draw around the edge. Cut out and sit the paper circles in the base of the tin.

2 Combine the dried fruit, oil, rum, orange juice, sugar and treacle in a large saucepan and stir over medium heat until the sugar has dissolved. Bring to the boil, reduce the heat and simmer, covered, over low heat for 10 minutes. Remove from the heat and stir in the bicarbonate of soda, then cool to room temperature. Stir in the zest, eggs, sifted flours and mixed spice.

3 Spread the mixture into the prepared tin and smooth the surface, then arrange the almonds over the top of the cake. Bake for 2 hours 15 minutes, or until a skewer inserted into the centre of the cake comes out clean (the skewer may be slightly sticky if inserted into fruit). Allow to cool in the tin.

4 Heat the jam in a saucepan over low heat for 3–4 minutes, or until runny. Brush the top of the cake with the jam.

5 When storing the cake, cover the top with baking paper and then foil to keep it moist. This fruit cake will keep, stored in an airtight container, in a cool place for up to 1 month, or up to 3 months in the freezer.

Place the circles of baking paper in the base of the tin.

Serves 8–10

Preparation time: 20 minutes

Cooking time: 1 hour

8 egg whites
200 g (7 oz) caster (superfine) sugar
250 g (9 oz) good-quality white
  chocolate, chopped
195 g (7 oz/1¼ cups) whole blanched
  almonds, toasted, then chopped
200 g (7 oz/1½ cups) sweetened dried
  cranberries
40 g (1½ oz/⅓ cup) self-raising flour

WHITE CHOCOLATE, ALMOND AND CRANBERRY TORTE

1 Preheat the oven to 180°C (350°F/ Gas 4). Lightly grease a 24 cm (9½ inch) round spring-form cake tin and line the base with baking paper. Dust the side of the tin with a little flour, shaking out any excess.

2 Whisk the egg whites in a clean, dry bowl until stiff peaks form. Gradually add the sugar, whisking well after each addition. Whisk until the mixture is stiff and glossy and the sugar has dissolved. Put the chocolate, almonds and cranberries into a bowl, add the flour and toss to combine. Gently fold the chocolate mixture into the egg whites. Spread the mixture into the prepared tin and gently tap the base.

3 Bake for 1 hour, covering the cake with foil halfway through cooking if it begins to brown too quickly. Turn off the oven and leave to cool completely in the oven. Run a knife around the edge of the tin to loosen the torte, then remove it from the tin.

4 The torte will keep, stored in an airtight container in a cool place, for up to 1 week. It is not suitable to freeze.

TIP Sweetened dried cranberries are sometimes labelled as craisins.

Serves 18–20

Preparation time: 25 minutes

Cooking time: 1 hour 10 minutes

440 g (15½ oz/1¼ cups) honey
60 ml (2 fl oz/¼ cup) red wine
235 g (8½ oz/1½ cups) blanched
    almonds, toasted and chopped
450 g (1 lb) glacé fruit (choose a
    mixture of citron, orange, pears,
    peaches and red glacé cherries),
    chopped into large chunks
410 g (14½ oz/3⅓ cups) plain
    (all-purpose) flour
115 g (4 oz/½ cup) caster (superfine)
    sugar
60 g (2¼ oz/½ cup) unsweetened
    cocoa powder
80 g (2¾ oz) dark chocolate,
    finely chopped
¼ teaspoon bicarbonate of soda
    (baking soda)
½ teaspoon ground cinnamon
½ teaspoon ground nutmeg
a large pinch of ground cloves
1 teaspoon finely grated orange zest
1 teaspoon finely grated lemon zest

TOPPING
200 g (7 oz) glacé orange slices
30 g (1 oz) red glacé cherries
115 g (4 oz/⅓ cup) warm honey

*Decorate the top of the cake with
orange slices and cherries.*

ITALIAN CHRISTMAS CAKE

1 Preheat the oven to 170°C (325°F/Gas 3). Lightly grease a 23 cm (9 inch)
round spring-form cake tin and line the base with baking paper. Dust the
side of the tin with a little flour, shaking off any excess.

2 Combine the honey and red wine in a small saucepan and heat, stirring
often, over low–medium heat for 2 minutes, or until the honey has just
melted and the mixture is smooth.

3 Combine the almonds, glacé fruit, flour, sugar, cocoa powder, chocolate,
bicarbonate of soda, spices and citrus zest in a large bowl and stir to
combine well. Pour in the honey mixture, then, using a wooden spoon,
stir until a firm dough forms; it may be necessary to use your hands.

4 Transfer the mixture into the prepared tin and smooth the top. Bake for
60 minutes, or until a skewer inserted into the centre of the cake comes out
a little sticky. Using the skewer, pierce the cake all over, decorate with the
orange slices and cherries and then spoon over the warm honey. Return the
cake to the oven and bake for a further 10 minutes. Allow to cool.

5 Remove the cake from the tin, leave to cool completely, then wrap in plastic
wrap and store for 1–2 days before using. Slice thinly to serve. This cake will
keep, stored in an airtight container, for up to 1 month.

TIP Glacé orange slices are available from some delicatessens and health
food stores.

Serves 6–8

Preparation time: 25 minutes

Cooking time: 45 minutes

150 g (5½ oz/1 cup) polenta
60 g (2¼ oz) unsalted butter, chopped
115 g (4 oz/½ cup) caster (superfine) sugar
150 g (5½ oz) pitted dates, chopped
95 g (3¼ oz/½ cup) chopped dried apricots
a pinch of nutmeg
1½ teaspoons finely grated lemon zest
2 eggs, lightly beaten
125 g (4½ oz/1 cup) plain (all-purpose) flour, sifted
55 g (2 oz/⅓ cup) pine nuts
icing (confectioners') sugar, for dusting

POLENTA FRUIT CAKE

1 Preheat the oven to 180°C (350°F/ Gas 4). Grease a 21 x 11 cm (8¼ x 4¼ inch) loaf tin and line the base with baking paper.

2 Bring 500 ml (17 fl oz/2 cups) water to the boil in a large saucepan. Gradually add the polenta and a pinch of salt, stirring constantly. Reduce the heat to medium, add the butter and continue to stir for 1–2 minutes,

or until the mixture thickens and comes away from the side of the pan. Remove from the heat, allow to cool slightly, then add all the remaining ingredients, except the pine nuts.

3 Spoon the mixture into the prepared tin, smoothing the surface with the back of a wet spoon. Sprinkle the pine nuts over the top and press gently onto the top of the

cake. Bake for 40–45 minutes, or until firm and a skewer inserted into the centre of the cake comes out clean. Leave in the tin for 10 minutes, then turn out onto a wire rack to cool. Dust with icing sugar and serve.

4 Polenta fruit cake will keep, stored in an airtight container, for up to 3 days.

Serves 12

Preparation time: 25 minutes

Cooking time: 45 minutes

3 eggs
185 g (6½ oz/1 cup) soft brown sugar
40 g (1½ oz) unsalted butter, melted
170 ml (5½ fl oz/⅔ cup) ready-made
   apple sauce
60 ml (2 fl oz/¼ cup) low-fat milk
85 g (3 oz/⅔ cup) unsweetened cocoa
   powder
185 g (6½ oz/1½ cups) self-raising flour

CHOCOLATE ICING
125 g (4½ oz/1 cup) icing
   (confectioners') sugar, sifted
2 tablespoons unsweetened cocoa
   powder
1–2 tablespoons low-fat milk

LOW-FAT CHOCOLATE CAKE

1 Preheat the oven to 180°C (350°F/Gas 4). Brush a 20 cm (8 inch) kugelhopf tin with melted butter, dust lightly with flour and shake out any excess.

2 Whisk the eggs and sugar in a bowl for 5 minutes, or until pale and thick. Combine the butter, apple sauce and milk in a small bowl, stirring to mix well, then fold into the egg mixture. Sift the cocoa powder and flour together into a bowl, then fold into the egg mixture.

3 Pour the mixture into the tin and bake for 35–40 minutes, or until a skewer inserted into the centre

of the cake comes out clean. Leave the cake to cool in the tin for 5 minutes, then turn out onto a wire rack to cool completely.

4 To make the chocolate icing, combine the icing sugar and cocoa powder in a bowl, then stir in enough milk to form a thick paste. Stand the bowl over a saucepan of simmering water, stirring until the icing is smooth, then remove from the heat. Spread the icing over the cake and leave to set.

5 This chocolate cake is best eaten on the day it is made.

Makes: 18 friands

Preparation time: 20 minutes

Cooking time: 30 minutes

250 g (9 oz) unsalted butter, softened
350 g (12 oz/1½ cups) caster
  (superfine) sugar
8 eggs
1 teaspoon finely grated orange zest
80 g (2¾ oz/¾ cup) ground almonds
300 g (10½ oz/1¾ cups) rice flour,
  sifted
60 ml (2 fl oz/¼ cup) madeira
80 g (2¾ oz/½ cup) chopped blanched
  almonds
icing (confectioners') sugar, for dusting
whipped cream and berries, to serve

RICE FLOUR AND MADEIRA FRIANDS

1 Preheat the oven to 170°C (325°F/ Gas 3). Grease eighteen 125 ml (4 fl oz/½ cup) friand tins.

2 Cream the butter and sugar in a bowl using electric beaters until pale and fluffy. Add the eggs one at a time, beating well after each addition, then add the orange zest and continue to beat for 5 minutes. Combine the ground almonds and

rice flour and fold into the butter mixture, in three stages, alternately with the madeira, until just combined.

3 Spoon the mixture into the prepared tins and sprinkle over the almonds. Bake for 25–30 minutes, or until golden and a skewer inserted into the centre of a friand comes out clean. Leave in the tins

for 5 minutes, then turn out onto a wire rack to cool. Dust with icing sugar and serve with whipped cream and berries.

4 The friands will keep, stored in an airtight container, for up to 4 days, or frozen for up to 3 months.

TIP If madeira is unavailable, substitute sweet sherry.

Makes: 12 cupcakes

Preparation time: 20 minutes

Cooking time: 23 minutes

150 g (5½ oz) unsalted butter,
   cut into cubes
115 g (4 oz/½ cup) caster (superfine)
   sugar
2 teaspoons natural vanilla extract
2 eggs
185 g (6½ oz/1½ cups) plain
   (all-purpose) flour
1 teaspoon baking powder
45 g (1½ oz/½ cup) desiccated
   coconut
125 ml (4 fl oz/½ cup) milk

VANILLA ICING (FROSTING)
60 g (2¼ oz/1 cup) flaked coconut
20 g (¾ oz) unsalted butter,
   cut into cubes
2 teaspoons natural vanilla extract
185 g (6½ oz/1½ cups) icing
   (confectioners') sugar, sifted

VANILLA COCONUT CUPCAKES

1 Preheat the oven to 180°C
(350°F/Gas 4). Line twelve 125 ml
(4 fl oz/ ½ cup) muffin holes with
paper cases.

2 Put the butter, sugar and vanilla
extract in a bowl and beat with
electric beaters for 2–3 minutes,
or until thick and creamy. Add the
eggs, one at a time, and beat in
each until well combined.

3 Sift together the flour and baking
powder. Use a metal spoon to stir

the sifted flour and baking powder
in two lots. Stir in the desiccated
coconut and the milk.

4 Put spoonfuls evenly into the paper
cases. Bake for 18–20 minutes, or
until firm and golden brown. Cool
on a wire rack.

5 For the vanilla icing, spread the
flaked coconut on a tray and lightly
toast for 2–3 minutes in the oven.
Put the butter in a small bowl and
pour over 2 teaspoons

of hot water to soften the butter.
Add the vanilla extract. Put the
icing sugar in a bowl, add the
butter mixture and mix together
until smooth, adding a little more
water if necessary to make a
spreading consistency.

6 Use a small spatula to spread the
cooled cakes with the icing and dip
each into the coconut flakes. Set
aside to firm the icing.

Serves 8–10

Preparation time: 25 minutes

Cooking time: 1 hour 5 minutes

250 ml (9 fl oz/1 cup) Guinness
350 g (12 oz/1 cup) molasses
2 teaspoons baking powder
3 eggs
230 g (8½ oz/1 cup) soft brown sugar
200 ml (7 fl oz) vegetable oil
250 g (9 oz/2 cups) self-raising flour
2½ tablespoons ground ginger
2 teaspoons ground cinnamon
100 g (3½ oz/⅓ cup) marmalade
80 g (2¾ oz) candied orange peel
    quarters, julienned (optional)

GUINNESS SPICE CAKE

1 Preheat the oven to 180°C (350°F/ Gas 4). Grease a 2.5 litre (87 fl oz/ 10 cup) kugelhopf tin and lightly dust with flour, shaking out any excess.

2 Combine the Guinness and molasses in a large saucepan and bring to the boil. Remove from the heat, add the baking powder and allow the foam to subside.

3 Whisk the eggs and sugar in a large bowl for 1–2 minutes, or until pale and slightly thickened. Add the oil and whisk to combine, then add to the beer mixture. Sift the flour and spices into a large bowl. Gradually whisk in the beer mixture until combined. Pour into the prepared tin and bake for 1 hour, or until firm to the touch and a skewer inserted into the centre of the cake comes out clean. Cool in the tin for 20 minutes, then turn out onto a wire rack.

4 Heat the marmalade in a saucepan over low heat for 3–4 minutes, or until runny. Strain, then brush the top of the cake with some of the marmalade. Arrange the candied orange peel strips, if using, on top and brush with the remaining marmalade.

5 This cake will keep, stored in an airtight container, for up to 7 days, or frozen for up to 3 months.

TIP Candied orange peel is available in thick pieces (about the size of a quarter of an orange) from specialist food stores and delicatessens.

Makes: 1 loaf

Preparation time: 20 minutes

Cooking time: 1 hour 20 minutes

375 g (13 oz) mixed dried fruit
160 g (5¾ oz/1 cup) chopped pitted
   dried dates
75 g (2½ oz/⅓ cup) glacé ginger,
   chopped
60 g (2¼ oz) unsalted butter, chopped
185 g (6½ oz/1 cup) soft brown sugar
1 tablespoon golden or dark corn syrup
1 teaspoon natural vanilla extract
2 eggs, lightly beaten
185 g (6½ oz/1½ cups) plain
   (all-purpose) flour
1 teaspoon baking powder
2 teaspoons ground ginger
1 teaspoon ground nutmeg
20 blanched almonds

GINGER FRUIT LOAF

1 Put the mixed fruit, dates, glacé ginger, butter, brown sugar, golden syrup, vanilla extract and 310 ml (10¾ fl oz/1¼ cups) water in a saucepan. Bring slowly to the boil, then simmer over low heat for 5 minutes. Set aside to cool.

2 Preheat the oven to 160°C (315°F/ Gas 2–3). Grease the base and sides of a 25 x 11 cm (10 x 4¼ inch) loaf (bar) tin and line the base with baking paper.

3 Stir the beaten eggs into the cooled fruit mixture. Sift together the flour, baking powder and spices. Stir the flour mixture into the fruit mixture and mix until smooth.

4 Spoon into the prepared tin and smooth the surface. Arrange the almonds over the surface. Bake for 1 hour 20 minutes, or until a skewer inserted in the centre comes out clean. Cover with foil if the surface and almonds are

browning too much. Leave to cool in the tin for 10 minutes, then turn out onto a wire rack to cool. Serve cut into thick slices.

TIP Store in an airtight container for up to 2 weeks. This loaf is also suitable to freeze.

Makes: 10

Preparation time: 15 minutes

Cooking time: 20 minutes

165 g (5¾ oz/1⅓ cups) icing (confectioners') sugar, plus extra for dusting
40 g (1½ oz/⅓ cup) plain (all-purpose) flour
125 g (4½ oz/1 cup) ground pistachio nuts
160 g (5¾ oz) unsalted butter, melted
5 egg whites, lightly beaten
½ teaspoon natural vanilla extract
55 g (2 oz/¼ cup) caster (superfine) sugar
35 g (1¼ oz/¼ cup) chopped pistachio nuts

PISTACHIO FRIANDS

1 Preheat the oven to 190°C (375°F/ Gas 5). Lightly grease ten 125 ml (4 fl oz/½ cup) friand tins.

2 Sift the icing sugar and flour into a bowl. Add the ground pistachios, butter, egg whites and vanilla and stir with a metal spoon until just combined.

3 Spoon the mixture into the prepared tins, place on a baking tray and bake for 15–20 minutes,

or until a skewer inserted into the centre of a friand comes out clean. Leave in the tins for 5 minutes, then turn out onto a wire rack to cool.

4 Meanwhile, put the sugar and 60 ml (2 fl oz/¼ cup) water in a small saucepan and stir over low heat until the sugar has dissolved. Increase the heat, then boil for 4 minutes, or until thick and syrupy. Remove from the heat and stir in the chopped pistachios,

then, working quickly, spoon the mixture over the tops of the friands. Dust with icing sugar and serve.

5 Friands will keep, stored in an airtight container, for up to 4 days, or frozen for up to 3 months.

TIP Friand tins can be purchased from kitchenware shops. Alternatively, you can bake the friands in a 12-hole standard muffin tin.

Serves 8–10

Preparation time: 30 minutes

Cooking time: 55 minutes

150 g (5½ oz/1 cup) finely grated carrots
165 g (5¾ oz/1½ cups) ground
    hazelnuts
70 g (2½ oz/¾ cup) dry breadcrumbs
a pinch of ground nutmeg
6 eggs, separated
230 g (8½ oz/1 cup) caster (superfine)
    sugar
2 tablespoons sweet sherry

ORANGE GLAZE
155 g (5½ oz/1¼ cups) icing
    (confectioners') sugar, sifted
10 g (¼ oz) unsalted butter, softened
2–3 tablespoons orange juice

CARROT AND HAZELNUT CAKE

1 Preheat the oven to 180°C (350°F/ Gas 4). Lightly grease a 24 cm (9½ inch) round spring-form cake tin and line the base with baking paper. Dust the side of the tin with a little flour, shaking out any excess.

2 Put the carrots and hazelnuts in a bowl and mix until combined. Add the breadcrumbs and nutmeg and mix until combined, then set aside.

3 Whisk the egg yolks and sugar in a large bowl for 5 minutes, or until

pale and thick. Stir in the sherry, then fold into the carrot mixture.

4 Whisk the egg whites in a clean, dry bowl until soft peaks form. Gently fold the egg whites, a third at a time, into the carrot mixture. Spoon into the prepared tin and bake for 50 minutes, or until firm to the touch and a skewer inserted into the centre of the cake comes out clean. Leave to cool for 10 minutes, then remove from the tin and transfer to a wire rack to cool completely.

5 To make the orange glaze, combine the icing sugar and butter in a heatproof bowl, then add just enough orange juice to make a soft, slightly runny glaze. Place the bowl over a saucepan of simmering water and stir for 1–2 minutes, or until the mixture is smooth and glossy. Pour the icing over the top of the cake and smooth over with a flat-bladed knife or palette knife. Allow to set, then serve.

Makes: 12

Preparation time: 20 minutes

Cooking time: 30 minutes

30 g (1 oz/¼ cup) self-raising flour
40 g (1½ oz/⅓ cup) semolina
230 g (8 oz/1 cup) caster (superfine)
  sugar
25 g (1 oz/¼ cup) ground almonds
½ teaspoon finely grated lemon zest
4 egg whites, lightly beaten
125 g (4½ oz) unsalted butter, melted
80 g (2¾ oz/½ cup) blueberries
45 g (1½ oz/½ cup) flaked almonds
icing (confectioners') sugar, for dusting

BLUEBERRY SEMOLINA CAKES

1 Preheat the oven to 170°C (325°F/ Gas 3). Line a 12-hole standard muffin tin with paper cases.

2 Sift the flour and semolina into a large bowl and add the sugar, ground almonds and lemon zest and stir to combine. Add the egg whites and, using electric beaters, beat until the ingredients are combined. Pour in the melted butter and continue to beat until smooth and well combined. Add the blueberries and fold in to just combine, then spoon the batter into the paper cases.

3 Sprinkle the flaked almonds over the cakes and bake for 30 minutes, or until a skewer inserted into the centre of a cake comes out clean. Turn out onto a wire rack to cool. Dust with icing sugar to serve.

4 The blueberry cakes are best served on the day they are made.

Serves 6–8

Preparation time: 20 minutes

Cooking time: 45 minutes

3 eggs
170 g (6 oz/¾ cup) caster (superfine)
    sugar
2 teaspoons finely grated orange zest
2 teaspoons finely grated lemon zest
2 teaspoons finely grated lime zest
60 ml (2 fl oz/¼ cup) extra virgin
    olive oil
60 ml (2 fl oz/¼ cup) olive oil
185 g (6½ oz/1½ cups) self-raising
    flour, sifted
125 ml (4 fl oz/½ cup) dessert wine
icing (confectioners') sugar, for dusting

OLIVE OIL AND SWEET WINE CAKE

1 Preheat the oven to 180°C (350°F/ Gas 4). Grease a deep 20 cm (8 inch) round cake tin and line the base with baking paper. Dust the side of the tin with a little flour, shaking out any excess.

2 Whisk the eggs and sugar in a large bowl for 3–5 minutes, or until pale and thick. Add the orange, lemon and lime zests and both the oils and beat until combined. Fold in the flour alternately with the wine until combined.

3 Pour into the prepared tin and bake for 40–45 minutes, or until a skewer inserted into the centre of the cake comes out clean. Leave to cool in the tin for 10 minutes, then turn out onto a wire rack. Dust with icing sugar to serve.

4 This cake will keep, stored in an airtight container, for 4 days, or frozen for up to 3 months.

Makes: 12

Preparation time: 50 minutes

Cooking time: 30 minutes

100 g (3½ oz) unsalted butter, softened
125 g (4½ oz/⅔ cup) soft brown sugar
115 g (4 oz/⅓ cup) treacle or dark corn syrup
2 eggs
125 g (4½ oz/1 cup) self-raising flour
85 g (3 oz/⅔ cup) plain (all-purpose) flour
2 teaspoons ground cinnamon
1 tablespoon ground ginger
60 ml (2 fl oz/¼ cup) buttermilk

GINGER GANACHE
100 g (3½ oz) good-quality dark chocolate, chopped
60 ml (2 fl oz/¼ cup) pouring cream
1 tablespoon finely chopped glacé ginger

GINGER CAKES
with chocolate centres

1 Preheat the oven to 180°C (350°F/ Gas 4). Line a 12-hole standard muffin tin with paper cases.

2 To make the ginger ganache, put the chocolate in a small heatproof bowl. Heat the cream until almost

Divide three-quarters of the mixture between the cases. Top with a ganache ball and cover with the remaining mixture

boiling, then pour over the chocolate and stir until it has melted and the mixture is smooth. Stir in the glacé ginger. Cool to room temperature, then chill in the refrigerator until firm. Divide the mixture into 12 equal portions and roll each into a ball. Freeze until required.

3 Cream the butter, sugar and treacle in a small bowl using electric beaters until pale and fluffy. Add the eggs one at a time, beating well after each addition. Transfer to a large bowl. Sift the flours and spices into a bowl, then fold into the butter mixture alternately with the buttermilk.

4 Divide three-quarters of the mixture between the paper cases. Top each with a ball of frozen

ginger ganache, then spread the remaining mixture over the top of the ganache to cover. Bake for 25–30 minutes, or until deep golden (the cakes cannot be tested with a skewer as the centres will be molten). Leave to cool for 5 minutes, then remove from the muffin holes. Remove the paper cases and serve warm.

5 These ginger cakes will keep, stored in an airtight container, for up to 4 days, or up to 3 months in the freezer. Reheat to serve.

TIP Treacle is a blend of concentrated refinery syrups and extract molasses. It is used in baking to give a distinctive colour and flavour. Golden syrup can be substituted but has a milder flavour.

Serves 6–8

Preparation time: 20 minutes

Cooking time: 1 hour 10 minutes

245 g (9 oz/2½ cups) walnuts
500 g (17½ oz) courgettes (zucchini)
250 ml (9 fl oz/1 cup) canola oil
330 g (11¾ oz/1½ cups) raw sugar
3 eggs
310 g (11 oz/2½ cups) self-raising flour, sifted
1½ teaspoons ground cinnamon
1 teaspoon ground nutmeg

COURGETTES

Courgettes (zucchini) are baby marrows. They are one of the most versatile of vegetables, being delicious raw, cooked, stuffed, baked, fried, stewed or in fritters. There are myriad ways, from ratatouille to freshly baked zucchini bread, to make the most of this cheap and abundant ingredient. There are pale green, dark green and yellow varieties. Baby zucchini lend themselves perfectly to fresh, raw and lightly cooked dishes, while their larger, older siblings are definitely the go for heartier, slow-cooked dishes. When shopping look for firm, unblemished zucchini. Eat as soon as possible after purchase, as refrigeration makes the texture deteriorate. There is no need to peel them; in fact, most of the flavour is in the skin

COURGETTE AND WALNUT CAKE

1 Preheat the oven to 170°C (325°F/Gas 3). Grease a 22 x 12 cm (8½ x 4½ inch) loaf tin and line the base and two long sides with a sheet of baking paper.

2 Roughly chop 185 g (6½ oz/1¾ cups) of the walnuts. Grate the courgettes, then put the zucchini in a large bowl with the oil, sugar, eggs and chopped walnuts and mix well. Stir in the flour, cinnamon and nutmeg.

3 Spoon the mixture into the tin and arrange the remaining walnuts on top. Bake for 1 hour 10 minutes, or until a skewer comes out clean when inserted into the centre of the cake. Leave in the tin for 20 minutes before turning out onto a wire rack to cool. Cut into slices and serve.

STORAGE: Wrap in foil when cooled. The cake will keep for 4–5 days.

Makes: 12

Preparation time: 20 minutes

Cooking time: 20 minutes

280 g (10 oz/2¼ cups) self-raising flour
170 g (6 oz/¾ cup) caster (superfine)
  sugar
250 ml (9 fl oz/1 cup) milk
2 eggs, lightly beaten
½ teaspoon natural vanilla extract
75 g (2½ oz) unsalted butter, melted
80 g (2¾ oz/¼ cup) strawberry jam
12 small strawberries, hulled
icing (confectioners') sugar, for dusting

LITTLE JAM-FILLED CAKES

1 Preheat the oven to 200°C (400°F/Gas 6). Grease a 12-hole standard muffin tin.

2 Sift the flour into a bowl, add the sugar and stir to combine. Make a well in the centre. Put the milk, eggs, vanilla and butter in a bowl, whisking to combine. Pour into the well and, using a metal spoon, gradually fold the milk mixture into the flour mixture until just combined. Divide three-quarters of the cake batter between the muffin holes. Top each with 1 teaspoon of the jam and cover with the remaining cake batter. Gently press a strawberry into the centre.

3 Bake for 20 minutes, or until light golden. Cool in the tin for 5 minutes, then turn out onto a wire rack to cool completely. Dust with icing sugar to serve.

4 The cakes are best served on the day they are made.

Makes: 12

Preparation time: 25 minutes

Cooking time: 35 minutes

60 g (2¼ oz) unsalted butter, softened
115 g (4 oz/½ cup) caster (superfine)
    sugar
1 teaspoon finely grated lemon zest
1 egg
1 egg yolk
60 g (2¼ oz/½ cup) plain (all-purpose)
    flour
1 tablespoon self-raising flour
2 tablespoons sour cream

CHEESECAKE TOPPING
250 g (9 oz) cream cheese, softened
115 g (4 oz/½ cup) caster (superfine)
    sugar
2 eggs
160 g (5¾ oz/⅔ cup) sour cream
1 vanilla bean or 1 teaspoon natural
    vanilla extract
2 tablespoons pine nuts

VANILLA AND CREAM CHEESE CAKES

1 Preheat the oven to 180°C (350°F/Gas 4). Lightly grease twelve 125 ml (4 fl oz/½ cup) friand tins and line the bases with baking paper. Dust the sides of the tins with a little flour, shaking off any excess.

2 Cream the butter, sugar and zest in a bowl using electric beaters until pale and fluffy. Add the egg, then the egg yolk, beating well after each addition. Sift the flours into a bowl, then gently stir into the butter mixture alternately with the sour cream.

3 Divide the mixture between the friand tins. Bake for 15 minutes, or until a skewer inserted into the centre of a cake comes out clean. Remove from the oven and allow to cool. Reduce the oven to 160°C (315°F/Gas 2–3).

4 To make the cheesecake topping, beat the cream cheese and sugar in a small bowl until pale and fluffy. Add the eggs one at a time, beating well after each addition, then beat in the sour cream. If using the vanilla bean, split it down the middle and scrape out the seeds. Add the seeds (or vanilla extract) to the cheese mixture, mixing well. Spoon the topping evenly over the cooled cakes and sprinkle with the pine nuts.

5 Return to the oven and bake for 15 minutes, or until the topping is just set. Remove from the oven, leave to cool slightly, then run a knife around the edge of the cakes to loosen them. Turn out onto a wire rack and allow to cool.

6 The cakes will keep, stored in an airtight container in the refrigerator, for 3 days.

Serves 6–8

Preparation time: 25 minutes

Cooking time: 1 hour 15 minutes

200 g (7 oz/1⅓ cups) good-quality
   dark chocolate, chopped
200 g (7 oz/1½ cups) blanched
   hazelnuts
200 g (7 oz) unsalted butter, softened
175 g (6 oz/¾ cup) raw caster
   (superfine) sugar
4 eggs, at room temperature,
   separated
3 teaspoons espresso instant coffee
   granules
1 orange, zest finely grated
100 g (3½ oz/heaped ¾ cup)
   cornflour (cornstarch) (cornstarch)
icing (confectioners') sugar, for dusting
thick (double/heavy) cream, to serve

BLOOD ORANGE SYRUP
250 ml (9 fl oz/1 cup) blood orange
   juice, strained
55 g (2 oz/¼ cup) caster (superfine)
   sugar
1 teaspoon orange liqueur, such as
   Cointreau, optional

CHOCOLATE, HAZELNUT AND ORANGE DESSERT CAKE
with blood orange sauce

This is a lovely moist cake, nicely complemented by the citrus sauce. Blood oranges have only a short season, so grab them when you can. They are rich, sweet and aromatic, with bold red pigmentation in the flesh and skin. You will need four to five blood oranges for the syrup.

1 Preheat the oven to 170°C (325°F/ Gas 3) and grease a 20 cm (8 inch) spring-form cake tin.

2 Put the chocolate in a heatproof bowl and place the bowl over a saucepan of simmering water, making sure the base of the bowl doesn't touch the water. Heat until melted.

3 Put the hazelnuts in a food processor and process until finely chopped. Cream the butter and caster (superfine) sugar in a large bowl with electric beaters until pale and fluffy. Add the egg yolks, one at a time, beating well after each

addition. Gently stir in the melted chocolate, coffee granules and orange zest. Mix in the cornflour (cornstarch) and chopped hazelnuts.

4 Whisk the egg whites until soft peaks form. Using a large metal spoon, fold a scoop of egg whites into the chocolate mixture. Gently fold in the remaining egg whites. Spoon the mixture into the prepared tin and level the surface. Bake for 30 minutes, then cover loosely with foil and bake for another 40–45 minutes, or until a skewer inserted into the centre of the cake comes out clean. Don't be

too concerned if the surface cracks.

5 Meanwhile, to make the blood orange syrup, pour the strained orange juice into a small saucepan and add the sugar. Stir over low heat until the sugar has dissolved. Bring to the boil, then reduce the heat and simmer for 10–12 minutes, or until reduced by half. Stir in the liqueur, if using, and set aside to cool slightly.

To serve, cut the warm cake into slices. Lightly dust with icing sugar, spoon over a little of the warm orange syrup and serve with thick cream.

Serves 12

Preparation time: 25 minutes

Cooking time: 40 minutes

ALMOND PEAR TOPPING
50 g (1¾ oz) unsalted butter, melted
2 tablespoons soft brown sugar
1 teaspoon ground nutmeg
425 g (15 oz) tin pear halves, drained
   and halved
75 g (2½ oz/½ cup) finely chopped
   blanched almonds, lightly toasted

CAKE BATTER
125 g (4½ oz) unsalted butter
115 g (4 oz/½ cup) caster (superfine)
   sugar
1 teaspoon natural vanilla extract
2 eggs
55 g (2 oz/½ cup) ground almonds
250 g (9 oz/2 cups) self-raising flour
1 teaspoon ground nutmeg
125 ml (4 fl oz/½ cup) milk
cream (whipping), to serve

*Arrange the pears over the base of the
tin, and scatter with almonds.*

*Spoon the batter over the pears and
smooth the surface.*

PEAR AND ALMOND CAKE

1 Preheat the oven to 180°C (350°F/Gas 4). Lightly grease and line the base
   of a 23 cm (9 inch) tin with baking paper. In a bowl, combine the melted
   butter, brown sugar and nutmeg. Evenly pour over the base of the tin.
   Arrange the pear quarters over and scatter the almonds over the pear slices.

2 Put the butter, caster (superfine) sugar and vanilla into a mixing bowl and
   beat with electric beaters for 2–3 minutes, or until creamy. Add the eggs,
   one at a time, beating well between each addition.

3 Stir in the ground almonds. Fold in the sifted flour and nutmeg in two to
   three batches, alternating with the milk. Carefully spoon the batter into the
   tin on top of the pears and smooth the surface.

4 Bake for 40 minutes, or until a skewer inserted in the centre comes out
   clean. Cool in the tin for 20 minutes, then remove and cool on a wire rack,
   pear side up. Carefully peel away the baking paper. Cut into wedges and
   serve warm with cream.

TIP This cake will keep in an airtight container for up to 5 days. It is also
suitable to freeze.

Serves 8

Preparation time: 20 minutes

Cooking time: 50 minutes

165 g (5¾ oz/1⅓ cups) plain
   (all-purpose) flour
85 g (3 oz/⅔ cup) unsweetened cocoa
   powder
1 teaspoon bicarbonate of soda
   (baking soda)
250 g (9 oz/1 cup) sugar
250 ml (9 fl oz/1 cup) buttermilk
2 eggs, lightly beaten
125 g (4½ oz) unsalted butter, softened
125 ml (4 fl oz/½ cup) whipping cream
icing (confectioners') sugar, to dust
fresh berries, to garnish

DEVIL'S FOOD CAKE

1 Preheat the oven to 180°C (350°F/Gas 4). Grease a deep 20 cm (8 inch) round cake tin and line the base with baking paper. Sift the flour, cocoa and bicarbonate of soda into a large bowl.

2 Add the sugar to the sifted dry ingredients. Combine the buttermilk, eggs and butter, then pour onto the dry ingredients. Beat with electric beaters on low speed for 3 minutes, or until just combined. Increase the speed to high and beat for 3 minutes, or until the mixture is free of lumps and increased in volume. Spoon the mixture into the prepared tin and smooth the surface.

3 Bake for 40–50 minutes, or until a skewer comes out clean when inserted into the centre of the cake. Leave in the tin for 15 minutes before turning out onto a wire rack to cool completely. Cut the cake in half horizontally and fill with whipped cream. Dust with icing sugar and garnish with fresh berries.

STORAGE: Unfilled, the cake will keep for 3 days in an airtight container or up to 3 months in the freezer. The filled cake is best assembled and eaten on the day of baking.

Serves 6–8

Preparation time: 20 minutes

Cooking time: 45 minutes

125 g (4½ oz) unsalted butter, softened,
  cut into cubes
125 g (4½ oz/½ cup) caster (superfine)
  sugar
2 eggs
1 teaspoon natural vanilla extract
250 g (9 oz/2 cups) self-raising flour
2 teaspoons ground cardamom
125 ml (4 fl oz/½ cup) milk
150 g (5½ oz) raspberries, fresh or frozen
whipped cream, to serve

HONEY SYRUP
175 g (6 oz/½ cup) honey
2 tablespoons caster (superfine) sugar
¼ teaspoon natural vanilla extract

RASPBERRY AND CARDAMOM CAKE
with honey syrup

1 Preheat the oven to 180°C (350°F/ Gas 4). Grease a 20 cm (8 inch) round cake tin and line the base with baking paper.

2 Using an electric mixer, beat the butter until soft. Add the caster (superfine) sugar gradually and beat until the mixture is pale and creamy. Add the eggs and vanilla, and beat until the mixture is well combined.

3 Sift the flour and cardamom together. Using a large metal spoon, fold the flour into the creamed mixture alternately with the milk, starting with the flour and ending with flour. Do not overmix.

4 Lightly fold the raspberries into the mixture. Pour the batter into the prepared tin and gently smooth the surface. Bake for 40–45 minutes, or until a skewer inserted into the centre comes out clean. Remove the cake from the oven and insert a thin metal skewer all over the cake.

5 To make the honey syrup, put 125 ml (4 fl oz/½ cup) of water, and the honey and sugar in a small saucepan and stir over low heat until the sugar has dissolved. Remove the pan from the heat and add the vanilla extract. Pour half of the honey syrup over the cake. Allow the cake to stand for 10 minutes. Turn the cake out.

Serve warm with whipped cream and the remaining honey syrup.

Pour half of the honey syrup over the cake and stand for 10 minutes.

Serves 6–8

Preparation time: 10 minutes

Cooking time: 55 minutes

3 ripe bananas, mashed (about 1 cup)
185 g (6½ oz/¾ cup) caster (superfine)
    sugar
185 g (6½ oz/1½ cups) self-raising flour
2 eggs, lightly beaten
3 tablespoons olive oil
60 ml (2 fl oz/¼ cup) milk
100 g (3½ oz) dark chocolate, grated
90 g (3¼ oz/¾ cup) walnuts, chopped

CHOCOLATE BANANA CAKE

1 Preheat the oven to 180°C (350°F/Gas 4). Grease a 20 x 10 cm (8 x 4 inch) loaf tin and line the base with baking paper.

2 Mix the mashed banana and sugar in a large bowl until just combined. Add the sifted flour, eggs, oil and milk. Stir the mixture gently for 30 seconds with a wooden spoon. Fold in the chocolate and walnuts.

3 Pour the mixture into the tin and bake for 55 minutes, or until a skewer comes out clean when inserted into the centre of the cake. Leave to cool in the tin for 5 minutes before turning onto a wire rack. If desired, serve warm with cream.

NOTE: In warm weather, chocolate can be grated more easily if it is left to harden in the freezer for a few minutes before grating.

Serves 8–10

Preparation time: 30 minutes
+ overnight refrigeration time

Cooking time: 45 minutes

CAKE
200 g (7 oz) unsalted butter, softened
150 g (5½ oz/⅔ cup) caster
    (superfine) sugar
6 eggs, at room temperature,
    separated
125 g (4½ oz/1¼ cups) ground
    almonds
150 g (5½ oz/1 cup) dark chocolate,
    chopped, melted

GANACHE
150 ml (5 fl oz) cream (whipping)
225 g (8 oz/1½ cups) dark
    chocolate, chopped
2 teaspoons instant coffee granules

CHOCOLATE GANACHE LOG

A ganache is basically a foolishly rich icing (frosting) made of chocolate and cream. The two are heated until the chocolate has melted, then the mixture is cooled and spread over a cake. This dessert is nothing if not indulgent, and deserves to be approached with gusto.

1 To make the cake, preheat the oven to 180°C (350°F/ Gas 4). Grease and line a 25 x 30 cm (10 x 12 inch) Swiss roll tin (jelly roll tin).

2 Beat the butter and sugar with electric beaters until light and fluffy. Add the egg yolks, one at a time, beating well after each addition. Stir in the ground almonds and melted chocolate. Beat the egg whites in a separate clean, dry bowl until stiff peaks form, then gently fold into the chocolate mixture.

Stir the ground almonds and chocolate into the cake mixture.

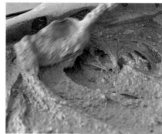

Spread the batter evenly into the prepared tin.

3 Spread the mixture into the prepared tin and bake for 15 minutes. Reduce the oven to 160°C (315°F/Gas 2–3) and bake for another 30–35 minutes, or until a skewer comes out clean when inserted into the centre of the cake. Turn the cake onto a wire rack to cool.

4 To make the ganache, put the cream and chopped chocolate in a heatproof bowl over a small saucepan of barely simmering water, making sure the base of the bowl doesn't touch the water. Stir occasionally until the mixture is melted and combined. Stir in the coffee until it has dissolved. Remove from the heat and set aside to cool for 2 hours, or until thickened to a spreading consistency.

5 Cut the cake lengthways into three even pieces. Place a piece of cake on a serving plate and spread with a layer of ganache. Top with another layer of cake and another layer of ganache, followed by the remaining cake. Refrigerate for 30 minutes to set slightly. Cover the top and sides of the log with the remaining ganache and refrigerate for 3 hours, or preferably overnight.

Serves 6–8

Preparation time: 15 minutes
+ overnight refrigeration time

Cooking time: 25 minutes

3 eggs, at room temperature
80 g (2¾ oz/⅓ cup) caster (superfine)
   sugar
80 g (2¾ oz/½ cup) white chocolate,
   chopped, melted
60 g (2¼ oz/½ cup) plain (all-purpose)
   flour, sifted
white chocolate curls, to serve

TOPPING
150 ml (5 fl oz) thickened (whipping)
   cream
250 g (9 oz/1⅔ cups) white chocolate,
   chopped
125 g (4½ oz/scant ⅔ cup)
   mascarpone cheese

WHITE CHOCOLATE TORTE

What an ingredient list — eggs, sugar, chocolate, flour, cream, more chocolate and mascarpone cheese! This cake is a very simple one to prepare, but rich. Serve a slice with strong coffee and some fresh winter fruit.

1 Preheat the oven to 180°C (350°F/ Gas 4) and grease a 20 cm (8 inch) spring-form cake tin.

2 Beat the eggs and sugar with electric beaters until thick and pale. Fold in the melted white chocolate and sifted flour. Pour into the prepared tin and bake for 20 minutes, or until a skewer inserted into the centre of the cake comes out clean. Set aside in the tin to cool completely.

3 To make the topping, put the cream and white chocolate in a saucepan. Stir constantly over low heat for 5–6 minutes, or until the chocolate has melted and the mixture is smooth. Remove from the heat and set aside to cool slightly. Stir the mascarpone into the chocolate mixture.

4 Remove the cake from the tin and use a spatula to spread the topping over the top and side. Refrigerate overnight, or until the topping is firm. Serve topped with the chocolate curls.

Makes: 4

Preparation time: 1 hour

Cooking time: 30 minutes

1 orange
100 g (3½ oz/1 cup) ground
   almonds
80 g (2¾ oz/⅓ cup) caster
   (superfine) sugar
1 tablespoon poppy seeds
1 teaspoon baking powder
2 eggs, lightly beaten
cream or ice cream, to serve

ORANGE SAUCE
thin strips of zest from 1 orange
4 tablespoons fresh orange juice
55 g (2 oz/¼ cup) caster (superfine)
   sugar
2 tablespoons chunky orange
   marmalade

ORANGE AND ALMOND POPPY SEED CAKES
with orange syrup sauce

1 Put the orange in a saucepan with enough water to cover. Bring to the boil, then reduce the heat and simmer for about 45 minutes, ensuring the orange stays covered with water. Drain, refresh under cold water, then leave to cool. Cut into quarters and remove the pips. Put the skin and flesh in a food processor and process until smooth.

2 Preheat the oven to 180°C (350°F/Gas 4). Grease and line the bases of four giant muffin holes with baking paper. Put an ovenproof dish in the oven and half-fill with hot water.

3 In a large bowl combine the ground almonds, sugar, poppy seeds and baking powder, then stir in the egg and orange purée. Pour into the prepared muffin holes and smooth the surfaces. Cover with a sheet of well-greased baking paper.

4 Put the muffin tin in the ovenproof dish and bake for 30 minutes, or until the cakes are firm to the touch and come away from the sides a little. Remove from the oven and leave for 5 minutes before turning out of the tin. Peel away the paper.

5 Meanwhile, to make the orange sauce, put the orange zest, juice and sugar in a saucepan over low heat and stir until the sugar has dissolved. Stir in the marmalade, increase the heat and boil for 5 minutes, or until thick and syrupy.

6 Serve the cakes face down, topped with the orange sauce and a little cream or ice cream. These are delicious warm or at room temperature.

Put the orange skin and flesh in a food processor and process until smooth.

Stir in the marmalade and boil until the sauce is thick and syrupy.

Serves 6–8

Preparation time: 1 hour 25 minutes

Cooking time: 1 hour 20 minutes

60 g (2¼ oz/½ cup) plain (all-purpose) flour
30 g (1 oz/¼ cup) self-raising flour
50 g (1¾ oz) unsalted butter
2 tablespoons caster (superfine) sugar
grated zest from 1 lemon
2 tablespoons lemon juice

FILLING
600 g (1 lb 5 oz) cream cheese, softened
170 g (6 oz/¾ cup) caster (superfine) sugar
30 g (1 oz/¼ cup) plain (all-purpose) flour
125 ml (4 fl oz/½ cup) strained passionfruit juice
4 eggs
170 ml (5½ fl oz/⅔ cup) pouring cream

BAKED PASSIONFRUIT CHEESECAKE

1 Combine the flours, butter, sugar and lemon zest in a food processor. Add the lemon juice and, using the pulse button, process until a dough forms. Cover with plastic wrap and refrigerate for 1 hour.

2 Meanwhile, preheat the oven to 180°C (350°F/Gas 4). Grease a 22 cm (8½ inch) round spring-form cake tin.

3 Roll out the pastry to 5 mm (¼ inch) thick. Roll the pastry around the pin, lift and ease it into the tin, pressing to fit, then trim the edges. Refrigerate for 10 minutes. Bake for 15–20 minutes, or until golden. Remove from the oven and cool. Reduce the oven to 150°C (300°F/Gas 2).

4 To make the filling, beat the cream cheese and sugar using electric beaters until smooth. Add the flour and passionfruit juice and beat until combined. Add the eggs one at a time, beating well after each addition. Stir in the cream, then pour the mixture over the cooled base. Bake for 1 hour, or until the centre is just firm to the touch (move the cheesecake to the lowest shelf of the oven for the last 10 minutes of cooking and cover with foil to prevent overbrowning). Cool the cheesecake in the tin before removing and serving in slices.

TIP You will need about 6 passionfruit to obtain 125 ml (4 fl oz/½ cup) passionfruit juice. Tinned passionfruit pulp is not an adequate substitute.

Serves 6

Preparation time: 20 minutes

Cooking time: 35 minutes

1 large ruby grapefruit

40 g (1½ oz/⅓ cup) stem ginger in
    syrup, drained and finely chopped,
    plus 3 teaspoons syrup

1½ tablespoons golden syrup or dark
    corn syrup

125 g (4½ oz) unsalted butter, softened

115 g (4 oz/½ cup) caster (superfine)
    sugar

2 eggs, at room temperature

185 g (6½ oz/1½ cups) self-raising flour

1 teaspoon ground ginger

4 tablespoons milk

MASCARPONE CREAM

125 g (4½ oz/heaped ½ cup)
    mascarpone cheese

125 ml (4 fl oz/½ cup) cream
    (whipping)

1 tablespoon icing (confectioners')
    sugar, sifted

GINGER AND GRAPEFRUIT PUDDINGS
with mascarpone cream

1 Preheat the oven to 170°C (325°F/ Gas 3). Grease six 170 ml (5½ fl oz /⅔ cup) pudding basins (moulds) or ramekins.

2 Finely grate 2 teaspoons of zest from the grapefruit. Slice the grapefruit around its circumference, one-third of the way down. Peel the larger piece, removing any white pith, and cut the flesh into six 1 cm (½ inch) slices. Squeeze 3 teaspoons of juice from the remaining grapefruit. Combine the juice, ginger syrup and

golden syrup in a bowl. Spoon the mixture into the basins and top with a slice of grapefruit.

3 Beat the butter and sugar with electric beaters until pale and smooth. Beat in the eggs, one at a time. Sift in the flour and ground ginger, add the milk, grapefruit zest and chopped ginger and mix well. Divide the mixture among the basins. Cover each basin with foil and put them in a deep roasting tin. Pour in enough boiling water

to come halfway up the side of the basins. Cover the roasting tin with foil, sealing the edges well. Bake the puddings for 30–35 minutes, or until set.

4 To make the mascarpone cream, combine the ingredients in a bowl until smooth.

5 To serve, gently invert the puddings onto serving plates and serve warm with a good dollop of mascarpone cream.

Serves 8

Preparation time: 25 minutes

Cooking time: 35 minutes

200 g (7 oz) good-quality dark
    chocolate, roughly chopped
125 g (4½ oz) unsalted butter
4 eggs
2 egg yolks
115 g (4 oz/½ cup) caster (superfine)
    sugar
50 g (1¾ oz) plain (all-purpose) flour,
    sifted
2 teaspoons ground star anise
50 g (1¾ oz) ground almonds

COFFEE CARAMEL CREAM
125 ml (4 fl oz/½ cup) thick
    (double/heavy) cream
3 tablespoons soft brown sugar
2 tablespoons brewed espresso
    coffee, cooled

CHOCOLATE STAR ANISE CAKE
with coffee caramel cream

1 Preheat the oven to 190°C (375°F/Gas 5). Grease and line a 23 cm (9 inch) spring form cake tin.

2 Put the chocolate and butter in a bowl set over a saucepan of gently simmering water, but do not allow the base of the bowl to come into contact with the water. Heat gently until the mixture is melted.

3 Put the eggs, egg yolks and sugar into a bowl and beat with a electric beaters for 5 minutes until thickened. Fold in the flour, ground star anise and ground almonds and then fold in the melted chocolate mixture until

evenly combined (the mixture should be runny at this stage).

4 Pour the mixture into the prepared tin and bake for 30–35 minutes, or until a skewer inserted in the middle comes out clean. Cool in the tin for 5 minutes and then remove and cool on a wire rack.

5 To make the coffee caramel cream, whip the cream, sugar and coffee together until soft peaks form and the colour is a soft caramel. Serve the cold cake cut into wedges with a spoonful of the coffee caramel cream.

Makes: 8

Preparation time: 15 minutes

Cooking time: 35 minutes

185 g (6½ oz) unsalted butter, chopped
95 g (3¼ oz/½ cup) soft brown sugar
115 g (4 oz/½ cup) caster (superfine) sugar
3 eggs
1 teaspoon finely grated orange zest
310 g (11 oz/2½ cups) self-raising flour, sifted
1 teaspoon ground cardamom
185 ml (6 fl oz/¾ cup) milk
4 tinned plums, drained and patted dry, cut in half
1 tablespoon raw (demerara) sugar
thick (double/heavy) cream, to serve

CARDAMOM, ORANGE AND PLUM DESSERT CAKES

1 Preheat the oven to 180°C (350°F/ Gas 4). Lightly grease eight 250 ml (9 fl oz/1 cup) ceramic ramekins and dust with flour, shaking out any excess flour.

2 Cream the butter and sugars in a bowl using electric beaters until pale and fluffy. Add the eggs, one at a time and beating well after each addition, then stir in the orange zest. Fold the flour and cardamom into the butter mixture alternately with the milk until combined and smooth.

3 Divide the mixture between the ramekins and place a plum half, cut side down, on top of the batter. Sprinkle with raw sugar, place the ramekins on a baking tray and bake for 30–35 minutes, or until golden and firm to the touch. Serve warm or at room temperature with thick cream.

Serves 4–6

Preparation time: 35 minutes

Cooking time: 30 minutes

30 g (1 oz) butter, softened
8 slices white bread
2 tablespoons caster (superfine) sugar
2 teaspoons mixed spice
90 g (3¼ oz/½ cup) pitted dried dates, chopped
3 eggs
2 tablespoons caster (superfine) sugar, extra
1 teaspoon grated lemon zest
250 ml (9 fl oz/1 cup) cream (whipping), plus extra to serve
250 ml (9 fl oz/1 cup) milk
80 g (2¾ oz/¼ cup) apricot jam

BREAD AND BUTTER PUDDING

1 Lightly grease a shallow baking dish. Lightly butter the bread and cut each slice into four triangles, leaving the crusts on. Combine the caster (superfine) sugar and mixed spice in a small bowl.

2 Arrange half the bread triangles over the dish, sprinkling with all the chopped dates and half the combined sugar and mixed spice. Arrange the remaining bread over the top and sprinkle over the remaining sugar mixture.

3 Preheat the oven to 180°C (350°F/ Gas 4). Put a baking tin in the oven and half-fill it with hot water.

4 In a large bowl, whisk together the eggs, extra sugar and lemon zest. Put the cream and milk in a small saucepan and bring slowly to the boil. Immediately whisk into the egg mixture, then pour over the bread slices. Set aside for 20 minutes to allow the bread to absorb the liquid.

5 Cover the pudding loosely with foil. Bake in the water bath for 15 minutes. Remove the foil and bake for a further 15 minutes, or until golden brown.

Warm the jam in a microwave or in a small saucepan. Use a pastry brush to coat the top of the pudding with the jam. Return to the oven for 5 minutes. Serve with cream.

Serves 6

Preparation time: 15 minutes

Cooking time: 40 minutes

185 g (6½ oz/1 cup) pitted dates,
    roughly chopped
1 teaspoon bicarbonate of soda
    (baking soda)
70 g (2½ oz) unsalted butter, softened
150 g (5½ oz/⅔ cup) soft brown sugar
1 teaspoon natural vanilla extract
2 eggs
150 g (5½ oz/1¼ cups) self-raising
    flour, sifted
100 g (3½ oz/1 cup) walnut halves,
    roughly chopped

CARAMEL SAUCE
155 g (5½ oz/⅔ cup) soft brown sugar
60 g (2¼ oz) unsalted butter
250 ml (9 fl oz/1 cup) cream (whipping)

STICKY DATE PUDDINGS

1 Preheat the oven to 180°C (350°F/
Gas 4). Brush six 250 ml (9 fl oz/
1 cup) ramekins with melted butter
and line the bases with rounds
of baking paper. Put the dates,
bicarbonate of soda and 250 ml
(9 fl oz/1 cup) of water in a saucepan, bring to the boil, then remove
from the heat and leave to cool
(the mixture will become foamy).

2 Using electric beaters, beat the
butter, sugar and vanilla until light
and creamy. Add 1 egg, beat well

then fold in 1 tablespoon of the
flour. Add the other egg and repeat
the process. Fold in the remaining
flour, walnuts and date mixture,
and mix well. Spoon the mixture
into the ramekins.

3 Arrange the ramekins in a large
roasting tin, then pour enough hot
water into the tin to come halfway
up the sides of the ramekins.
Cover with foil and bake for
about 35–40 minutes, or until
slightly risen and firm to the touch.

4 To make the caramel sauce,
combine the brown sugar, butter
and cream in a saucepan over low
heat and simmer for 5 minutes,
or until the sugar has dissolved.

5 Loosen the side of each pudding
with a small knife, turn out onto
serving plates and remove the
baking paper. Pour the sauce
over the top and serve.

Serves 6–8

Preparation time: 30 minutes

Cooking time: 55 minutes

50 g (1¾ oz/½ cup) pecans
300 g (10½ oz) dried pears
150 g (5½ oz) unsalted butter
175 g (6 oz/¾ cup) caster (superfine)
    sugar
1 teaspoon natural vanilla extract
3 eggs
185 g (6½ oz/1½ cups) plain
    (all-purpose) flour
2 teaspoons baking powder
½ teaspoon ground cinnamon
½ teaspoon ground ginger
2 tablespoons milk
whipped cream, to serve

BROWN SUGAR SYRUP
150 g (5½ oz/⅔ cup) soft brown
    sugar
1 teaspoon ground cinnamon
4 tablespoons brandy
60 g (2¼ oz) unsalted butter,
    softened

PEAR AND PECAN DESSERT CAKE

1 Preheat the oven to 180°C (350°F/ Gas 4). Grease and line a 24 cm (9½ inch) round cake tin, then arrange the pecans in the base of the tin.

2 Cover the dried pears with warm water and leave for about 10–15 minutes, or until softened. Pat dry with paper towels.

3 Using electric beaters, beat the butter and sugar until light and fluffy. Add the vanilla and the eggs one at a time, beating well after each addition. Sift the flour, baking powder, cinnamon and ginger into a bowl, add to the cake mixture and beat slowly to combine. Add the milk and beat for a further minute.

4 To make the brown sugar syrup, combine the sugar, cinnamon, brandy and butter in a small saucepan over medium heat and cook for 3 minutes, or until the sugar has dissolved.

5 Pour the warm syrup over the nuts in the cake tin. Arrange the pears over the nuts. Spoon the cake mixture over the pears and smooth the surface with a spatula. Cover the cake tin with a large square of foil, then place the cake tin a large roasting tin. Pour in enough hot water to come halfway up the side of the cake tin, then bake for 40 minutes. Remove the foil and bake for a further 15 minutes, or until golden and cooked through when tested with a skewer.

Pour in enough hot water to come halfway up the side of the cake tin.

Leave the cake in the tin for 5 minutes, then carefully invert onto a plate and serve warm with whipped cream.

Serves 6–8

Preparation time: 20 minutes

Cooking time: 50 minutes

150 g (5½ oz/1¼ cups) toasted
   slivered almonds
750 g (1 lb 10 oz) neufchatel cheese
2 tablespoons plain (all-purpose)
   flour
300 g (10½ oz/1⅓ cups) caster
   (superfine) sugar
2 teaspoons natural vanilla extract
1½ teaspoons finely grated lemon
   zest
4 eggs
125 g (4½ oz/1 cup) redcurrants),
   plus extra to serve
2 teaspoons crème de cassis or
   cherry brandy
1 tablespoon icing (confectioners')
   sugar

TOPPING
300 g (10½ oz/1¼ cups) sour cream
2 tablespoons caster (superfine) sugar
1 teaspoon natural vanilla extract

CRUSTLESS REDCURRANT CHEESECAKE

1 Preheat the oven to 170°C (325°F/Gas 3). Grease a 22 cm (8½ inch) spring-form cake tin. Put the almonds in a large processor fitted with the metal blade and whizz in 2-second bursts for 12 seconds, or until they resemble fine breadcrumbs. Do not grind the almonds to a powder. Transfer the almonds to the prepared tin and roll the tin around to coat with the almonds. Spread the excess almonds over the base of the tin.

2 Put the neufchatel cheese, flour, caster (superfine) sugar, vanilla and lemon zest in the cleaned processor and whizz for 12–15 seconds, or until smooth. Add the eggs and whizz for 10 seconds, or until well combined, scraping down the side of the bowl as needed. Transfer the mixture to a bowl.

3 Without cleaning the processor bowl, add the redcurrants, crème de cassis or cherry brandy and icing sugar and whizz for 10–12 seconds, or until smooth. Add 250 ml (9 fl oz/1 cup) of the cheese mixture and briefly whizz to combine.

4 Gently pour the remaining cheese mixture into the tin, being careful not to disturb the almond crumbs. Bake for 20 minutes. Gently spoon the redcurrant mixture over the surface and bake for a further 30 minutes, or until the surface is just set. Remove from the oven and set aside to cool for 15 minutes.

Put the chopped almonds in the tin and roll the tin around to coat the base and side with the almonds.

5 To make the topping, mix the sour cream, sugar and vanilla in a small bowl until smooth. Spread over the cheesecake and return to the oven for 10 minutes. Set aside to cool in the tin, then turn out and chill before serving. Serve topped with extra redcurrants.

Serves 8

Preparation time: 20 minutes

Cooking time: 45 minutes

4 eggs, separated
175 g (6 oz/¾ cup) caster (superfine)
    sugar
1 teaspoon natural vanilla extract
90 g (3¼ oz/¾ cup) cornflour
    (cornstarch) (cornstarch)
3 tablespoons plain (all-purpose) flour
1½ teaspoons baking powder
boiling water, for steaming
2 tablespoons icing (confectioners')
    sugar, for dusting

PASSIONFRUIT CREAM
310 ml (10¾ fl oz/1¼ cups) cream
    (whipping), whipped
3 tablespoons icing (confectioners')
    sugar, sifted
2 tablespoons passionfruit pulp
    (about 2 passionfruit)

PASSIONFRUIT CREAM SPONGE ROLL

1 Preheat the oven to 180°C (350°F/Gas 4) and line a 29 x 24 x 3 cm (11½ x 9½ x 1¼ inch) Swiss roll tin (jelly roll tin) with baking paper.

2 Using electric beaters, beat the egg whites and a pinch of salt until soft peaks form. Gradually beat in the sugar until the mixture is thick and glossy. Add the egg yolks and vanilla extract, and beat until well combined.

3 In a separate bowl, mix together the cornflour (cornstarch), plain (all-purpose) flour and baking powder. Sift the flours twice, then carefully fold into the egg mixture. Don't over-stir as the cake will lose its light texture.

4 Pour the mixture into the prepared tin and smooth with a spatula. Cover with foil, then place the tin in a large

deep roasting tin and pour in enough boiling water to come halfway up the sides of the Swiss roll tin. Bake for 35–45 minutes, or until golden and springy to the touch. Cool in the tin for 1 minute, then run a knife around the edges of the tin to loosen the sponge cake. Place a large piece of baking paper on a clean surface. Invert the cake onto the baking paper then gently peel away the baking paper from the bottom of the cake. Using the baking paper as a guide, gently roll the cake into a log, starting from the long side. This needs to be done while the cake is still hot to prevent cracking. Leave to cool for 20 minutes.

5 Meanwhile, to make the passionfruit cream, whip the cream and icing sugar until stiff, then fold in the passion-fruit pulp. Gently unroll the cake and spread with the passionfruit cream. Re-roll, then dust with icing sugar

Serves 8

Preparation time: 20 minutes

Cooking time: 40 minutes

150 g (5½ oz) unsalted butter
175 g (6 oz/¾ cup) caster (superfine)
  sugar
100 g (3½ oz) dark chocolate, melted
  and cooled (see tip)
2 eggs
60 g (2¼ oz/½ cup) plain (all-purpose)
  flour
90 g (3¼ oz/¾ cup) self-raising flour
30 g (1 oz/¼ cup) unsweetened
  cocoa powder
1 teaspoon bicarbonate of soda
  (baking soda)
125 ml (4 fl oz/½ cup) milk
whipped cream, to serve

SAUCE
50 g (1¾ oz) unsalted butter, chopped
125 g (4½ oz) dark chocolate, chopped
125 ml (4 fl oz/½ cup) cream (whipping)
1 teaspoon natural vanilla extract

CHOCOLATE FUDGE PUDDINGS

1 Preheat the oven to 180°C (350°F/ Gas 4). Lightly grease eight 250 ml (9 fl oz/1 cup) ramekins or ovenproof tea cups.

Half-fill the ramekins or tea cups with the chocolate mixture.

2 Using electric beaters, beat the butter and sugar until light and creamy. Add the melted chocolate, beating well. Add the eggs one at a time, beating well after each addition.

3 Sift together the flours, cocoa and bicarbonate of soda, then gently fold into the chocolate mixture. Add the milk and fold through. Half-fill the ramekins, then cover with pieces of greased foil and place in a large, deep roasting tin. Pour in enough hot water to come halfway up the sides of the ramekins. Bake for 35–40 minutes, or until a skewer

inserted into the centre of each pudding comes out clean.

4 To make the sauce, combine the butter, chocolate, cream and vanilla in a saucepan and stir over low heat until the butter and chocolate have completely melted. Pour over the puddings and serve with whipped cream.

TIP To melt chocolate, cut it into cubes and place in a heatproof bowl. Sit the bowl over a saucepan of simmering water, making sure the water does not touch the base, and stir with a metal spoon until melted.

Serves 8

Preparation time: 15 minutes

Cooking time: 35 minutes

125 g (4½ oz) unsalted butter, softened
125 g (4½ oz/heaped ½ cup) caster
  (superfine) sugar
2 eggs, at room temperature
125 g (4½ oz/1 cup) self-raising flour
2 tablespoons milk
250 g (9 oz/2¼ cups) blackberries

CREME ANGLAISE
325 ml (11 fl oz) milk
4 egg yolks, at room temperature
80 g (2¾ oz/⅓ cup) caster (superfine)
  sugar

BLACKBERRY PUDDINGS with crème anglaise

1 Preheat the oven to 180°C (350°F/Gas 4) and grease eight 125 ml (4 fl oz/½ cup) dariole moulds.

2 Using electric beaters, cream the butter and sugar together until light and fluffy. Add the eggs, one at time, beating well after each addition. Sift the flour and gently fold in with enough milk to form a dropping consistency.

3 Cover the base of each mould with a layer of blackberries. Spoon enough of the pudding mixture over the berries so that the moulds are three-quarters full. Cover the moulds with foil, sealing tightly. Place the puddings in a roasting tin and pour in enough hot water to come halfway up the sides of the moulds. Bake for about 30–35 minutes, or until the puddings spring back when lightly touched.

4 Meanwhile, to make the crème anglaise, heat the milk to just below boiling point, then set aside. Beat the egg yolks and sugar with electric beaters until thick and pale. Slowly whisk in the hot milk and pour the mixture into a saucepan. Cook over low heat, stirring constantly, for 5–7 minutes, or until the custard is thick enough to coat the back of a spoon. Remove from the heat.

5 To serve, unmould the puddings onto plates and drizzle with the crème anglaise.

Serves 8–10

Preparation time: 15 minutes

Cooking time: 40 minutes

115 g (4 oz/½ cup) caster (superfine)
    sugar
310 g (11 oz/2½ cups) fine semolina
150 g (5½ oz/1½ cups) ground almonds
3 teaspoons baking powder
½ teaspoon bicarbonate of soda
    (baking soda)
1 lemon, zested and juiced
125 ml (4 fl oz/½ cup) olive oil
2 eggs, at room temperature, beaten
185 g (6½ oz/¾ cup) Greek-style
    yoghurt
125 ml (4 fl oz/½ cup) milk
60 g (2¼ oz/½ cup) chopped walnuts
7 fresh or semi-dried figs, chopped, plus
    4 sliced

HONEY YOGHURT
250 g (9 oz/1 cup) Greek-style yoghurt
90 g (3¼ oz/¼ cup) honey
2 teaspoons natural vanilla extract

LEMON, FIG AND WALNUT CAKE
with honey yoghurt

This delightful cake features almost all of the classic elements of Mediterranean food: figs, walnuts, lemon, wheat and olive oil. The only element missing, of course, is the vine, which can be easily introduced with a little glass of something appropriate.

1 Preheat the oven to 180°C (350°F/Gas 4) and grease and line a 23 cm (9 inch) square cake tin.

2 Combine the sugar, semolina, ground almonds, baking powder and bicarbonate of soda in a large bowl. In a separate bowl, combine the lemon zest, lemon juice, olive oil, eggs, yoghurt and milk, then stir the lemon mixture into the semolina mixture. Fold in the walnuts and chopped figs. Pour the mixture into the tin, smooth the top and decorate with the extra sliced figs. Bake for 40 minutes, or until a skewer comes out clean when inserted into the cake.

3 Meanwhile, to make the honey yoghurt, put the yoghurt, honey and vanilla in a small bowl and stir to combine. Keep refrigerated until needed.

4 Serve the cake warm accompanied by the honey yoghurt.

First published by Bay Books, an imprint of Murdoch Books Pty Limited.

Murdoch Books Australia
Pier 8/9, 23 Hickson Road
Millers Point
NSW 2000
Phone: +61 (0) 2 8220 2000
Fax: +61 (0) 2 8220 2558

Concept: James Mills-Hicks
Design: Peta Nugent
Cover design: David Fairs
Production: Nikla Martin

This edition published 2008 for Index Books Ltd

© Text, design, photography and illustrations Murdoch Books Limited 2008.

ISBN 978 1 74196 333 5

Printed by i-Book Printing Ltd. PRINTED IN CHINA.

IMPORTANT: Those who might be at risk from the effects of salmonella poisoning (the elderly, pregnant women, young children and those suffering from immune deficiency diseases) should consult their doctor with any concerns about eating raw eggs.

CONVERSION GUIDE: You may find cooking times vary depending on the oven you are using. For fan-forced ovens, as a general rule, set the oven temperature to 20º (35ºF) lower than indicated in the recipe.